Professional Examination

CW01667651

Paper F8 (INT)

Audit and Assurance

EXAM KIT

ACCA
Approved Publisher

KAPLAN
PUBLISHING

British Library Cataloguing-in-Publication Data

A catalogue record for this book is available from the British Library.

Published by:
Kaplan Publishing UK
Unit 2, The Business Centre
Molly Millars Lane
Wokingham
Berkshire
RG41 2QZ

ISBN 978 1 84710 286 7

© FTC Kaplan Limited, August 2007

Printed and bound in Great Britain by William Clowes Ltd, Beccles, Suffolk

Acknowledgements

The past ACCA exam questions are the copyright of the Association of Chartered Certified Accountants. The original answers to the questions from June 1994 onwards were produced by the examiners themselves and have been adapted by Kaplan Publishing.

We are grateful to the Chartered Institute of Management Accountants and the Institute of Chartered Accountants in England and Wales for permission to reproduce past exam questions. The answers have been prepared by Kaplan Publishing.

All rights reserved. No part of this publication may be reproduced, stored in a retrieval system, or transmitted, in any form or by any means, electronic, mechanical, photocopying, recording or otherwise, without the prior written permission of Kaplan Publishing.

CONTENTS

INDEX TO QUESTIONS AND ANSWERS

SYLLABUS AND EXAM FORMAT

Format of the exam

	Number of marks
Five compulsory questions:	
Question 1 (scenario-based question)	30
Question 2 (knowledge-based question)	10
Questions 3, 4 and 5 (20 marks each)	60
	100
Total time allowed: 3 hours	

This syllabus and study guide is designed to help with planning study and to provide detailed information on what could be assessed in any examination session.

The structure of the syllabus and study guide

Relational diagram of paper with other papers

This diagram shows direct and indirect links between this paper and other papers preceding or following it. Some papers are directly underpinned by other papers such as Advanced Performance Management by Performance Management. These links are shown as solid line arrows. Other papers only have indirect relationships with each other such as links existing between the accounting and auditing papers. The links between these are shown as dotted line arrows. This diagram indicates where you are expected to have underpinning knowledge and where it would be useful to review previous learning before undertaking study.

Overall aim of the syllabus

This explains briefly the overall objective of the paper and indicates in the broadest sense the capabilities to be developed within the paper.

Main capabilities

This paper's aim is broken down into several main capabilities that divide the syllabus and study guide into discrete sections.

Relational diagram of the main capabilities

This diagram illustrates the flows and links between the main capabilities (sections) of the syllabus and should be used as an aid to planning teaching and learning in a structured way.

Syllabus rationale

This is a narrative explaining how the syllabus is structured and how the main capabilities are linked. The rationale also explains in further detail what the examination intends to assess and why.

Detailed syllabus

This shows the breakdown of the main capabilities (sections) of the syllabus into subject areas. This is the blueprint for the detailed study guide.

Approach to examining the syllabus

This section briefly explains the structure of the examination and how it is assessed.

Study guide

This is the main document that students, tuition providers and publishers should use as the basis of their studies, instruction and materials. Examinations will be based on the detail of the study guide that comprehensively identifies what could be assessed in any examination session. The study guide is a precise reflection and breakdown of the syllabus. It is divided into sections based on the main capabilities identified in the syllabus. These sections are divided into subject areas that relate to the sub-capabilities included in the detailed syllabus. Subject areas are broken down into sub-headings that describe the detailed outcomes that could be assessed in examinations. These outcomes are described using verbs indicating what exams may require students to demonstrate, and the broad intellectual level at which these may need to be demonstrated (*see intellectual levels below).

Intellectual levels

The syllabus is designed to progressively broaden and deepen the knowledge, skills and professional values demonstrated by the student on their way through the qualification.

The specific capabilities within the detailed syllabuses and study guides are assessed at one of three intellectual or cognitive levels:

Level 1: Knowledge and comprehension

Level 2: Application and analysis

Level 3: Synthesis and evaluation

Very broadly, these intellectual levels relate to the three cognitive levels at which the Knowledge module, the Skills module and the Professional level are assessed.

Each subject area in the detailed study guide included in this document is given a 1, 2 or 3 superscript, denoting intellectual level, marked at the end of each relevant line. This gives an indication of the intellectual depth at which an area could be assessed within the examination. However, while level 1 broadly equates with the Knowledge module, level 2 equates to the Skills module and level 3 to the Professional level, some lower level skills can continue to be assessed as the student progresses through each module and level. This reflects that at each stage of study there will be a requirement to broaden, as well as deepen capabilities. It is also possible that occasionally some higher level capabilities may be assessed at lower levels.

Learning hours

The ACCA qualification does not prescribe or recommend any particular number of learning hours for examinations because study and learning patterns and styles vary greatly between people and organisations. This also recognises the wide diversity of personal, professional and educational circumstances in which ACCA students find themselves.

Each syllabus contains between 23 and 35 main subject area headings depending on the nature of the subject and how these areas have been broken down.

Guide to exam structure

The structure of examinations varies within and between modules and levels.

The Fundamentals level examinations contain 100% compulsory questions to encourage candidates to study across the breadth of each syllabus.

The Knowledge module is assessed by equivalent two-hour paper-based and computer based examinations.

The Skills module examinations are all paper-based three-hour papers. The structure of papers varies from ten questions in the Corporate and Business Law (F4) paper to four 25-mark questions in Performance Management (F5) and Financial Management (F9). Individual questions within all Skills module papers will attract between 10 and 30 marks.

The Professional level papers are all three-hour paper-based examinations, all containing two sections. Section A is compulsory, but there will be some choice offered in Section B.

For all three-hour examination papers, ACCA has introduced 15 minutes reading and planning time.

This additional time is allowed at the beginning of each three-hour examination to allow candidates to read the questions and to begin planning their answers before they start writing in their answer books. This time should be used to ensure that all the information and exam requirements are properly read and understood.

During reading and planning time candidates may only annotate their question paper. They may not write anything in their answer booklets until told to do so by the invigilator.

The Essentials module papers all have a Section A containing a major case study question with all requirements totalling 50 marks relating to this case. Section B gives students a choice of two from three 25-mark questions.

Section A of each of the Options papers contains 50–70 compulsory marks from two questions, each attracting between 25 and 40 marks. Section B will offer a choice of two from three questions totalling 30–50 marks, with each question attracting between 15 and 25 marks.

Guide to examination assessment

ACCA reserves the right to examine anything contained within the study guide at any examination session. This includes knowledge, techniques, principles, theories and concepts as specified.

For the financial accounting, audit and assurance, law and tax papers, ACCA will publish examinable documents every six months to indicate exactly what regulations and legislation could potentially be assessed at the following examination session. Knowledge of new examinable regulations will not be assessed until at least six calendar months after the last day of the month in which documents are issued or legislation is passed. The relevant cut-off date for the June examinations is 30 November of the previous year, and for the December examinations, it is 31 May of the same year.

The study guide offers more detailed guidance on the depth and level at which the examinable documents will be examined. The study guide should therefore be read in conjunction with the examinable documents list.

SYLLABUS

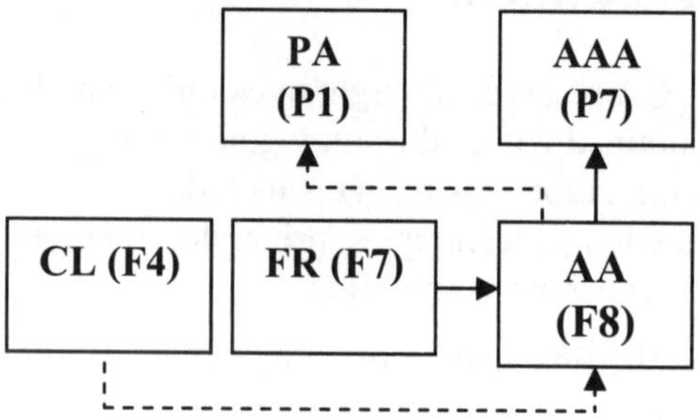

Aim

To develop knowledge and understanding of the process of carrying out the assurance engagement and its application in the context of the professional regulatory framework.

Main capabilities

On successful completion of this paper, candidates should be able to:

A Explain the nature, purpose and scope of assurance engagements including the role of the external audit and its regulatory and ethical framework

B Explain the nature of internal audit and describe its role as part of overall performance management and its relationship with the external audit

C Demonstrate how the auditor obtains an understanding of the entity and its environment, assesses the risk of material misstatement (whether arising from fraud or other irregularities) and plans an audit of financial statements

D Describe and evaluate information systems and internal controls to identify and communicate control risks and their potential consequences, making appropriate recommendations

E Identify and describe the work and evidence required to meet the objectives of audit engagements and the application of the International Standards on Auditing

F Evaluate findings and modify the audit plan as necessary

G Explain how the conclusions from audit work are reflected in different types of audit report, explain the elements of each type of report.

Relational diagram of main capabilities

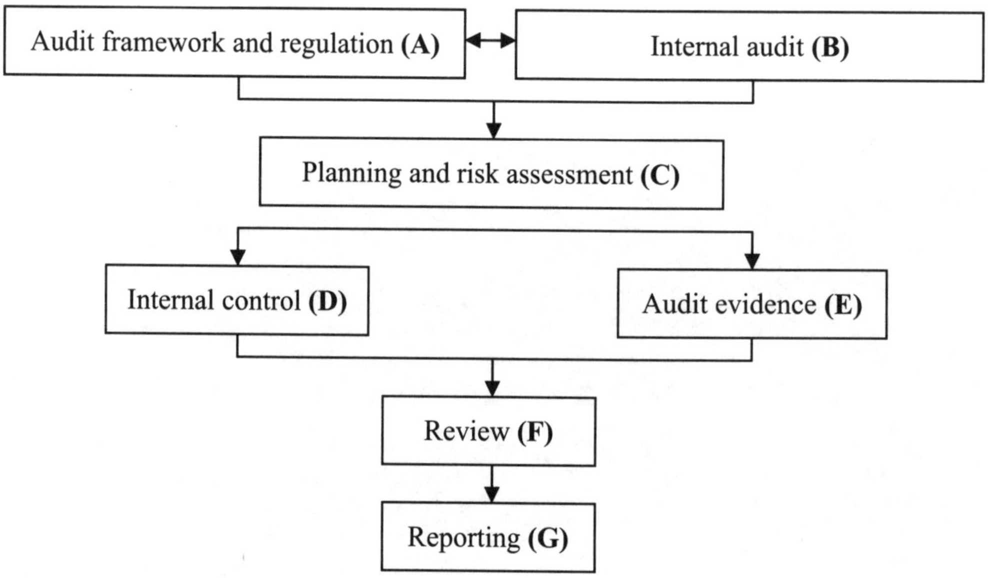

Rationale

The Audit and Assurance syllabus is essentially divided into seven areas. The syllabus starts with the nature, purpose and scope of assurance engagements, including the statutory audit, its regulatory environment, and introduces professional ethics relating to audit and assurance. It then leads into internal audit, including the scope of internal audit as well as the differences between internal audit and external audit. The syllabus then covers a range of areas relating to an audit of financial statements. These include planning and risk assessment, evaluating internal controls, audit evidence, and a review of the financial statements. The final section then deals with reporting, including statutory audit reports, management reports, and internal audit reports.

Detailed syllabus

A Audit Framework and Regulation

1. The concept of audit and other assurance engagements
2. Statutory audits
3. The regulatory environment and corporate governance
4. Professional ethics and ACCA's Code of Ethics and Conduct

B Internal audit

1. Internal audit and corporate governance
2. Differences between external and internal audit
3. The scope of the internal audit function
4. Outsourcing the internal audit department
5. Internal audit assignments

C Planning and risk assessment

1. Objective and general principles
2. Understanding the entity and knowledge of the business
3. Assessing the risks of material misstatement and fraud
4. Analytical procedures
5. Planning an audit
6. Audit documentation
7. The work of others

D Internal control

1. Internal control systems
2. The use of internal control systems by auditors
3. Transaction cycles
4. Tests of control
5. The evaluation of internal control components
6. Communication on internal control

E Audit evidence

1. The use of assertions by auditors
2. Audit procedures
3. The audit of specific items
4. Audit sampling and other means of testing
5. Computer-assisted audit techniques
6. Not-for-profit organisations

F Review

1. Subsequent events
2. Going concern
3. Management representations
4. Audit finalisation and the final review

G Reporting

1. Audit reports
2. Reports to management
3. Internal audit reports

Approach to examining the syllabus

The syllabus is assessed by a three-hour paper-based examination, consisting of five compulsory questions. The bulk of the questions will be discursive but some questions involving computational elements will be set from time to time.

The questions will cover all areas of the syllabus.

Question 1 will be a scenario-based question worth 30 marks. Question 2 will be a knowledge-based question worth 10 marks. Questions 3, 4 and 5 will be worth 20 marks each.

Study Guide

A AUDIT FRAMEWORK AND REGULATION

1 The concept of audit and other assurance engagements

(a) Identify and describe the objective and general principles of external audit engagements. [2]

(b) Explain the nature and development of audit and other assurance engagements. [1]

(c) Discuss the concepts of accountability, stewardship and agency. [2]

(d) Discuss the concepts of materiality, true and fair presentation and reasonable assurance. [2]

(e) Explain reporting as a means of communication to different stakeholders. [1]

(f) Explain the level of assurance provided by audit and other review assignments. [1]

2 Statutory audits

(a) Describe the regulatory environment within which statutory audits take place. [1]

(b) Discuss the reasons and mechanisms for the regulation of auditors. [2]

(c) Explain the statutory regulations governing the appointment, removal and resignation of auditors. [1]

(d) Discuss the types of opinion provided in statutory audits. [2]

(e) State the objectives and principle activities of statutory audit and assess its value (e. g. in assisting management to reduce risk and improve performance). [1]

(f) Describe the limitations of statutory audits. [1]

3 The regulatory environment and corporate governance

(a) Explain the development and status of International Standards on Auditing. [1]

(b) Explain the relationship between International Standards on Auditing and National Standards.[1]

(c) Discuss the objective, relevance and importance of corporate governance. [2]

(d) Discuss the need for auditors to communicate with those charged with governance. [2]

(e) Discuss the provisions of international codes of corporate governance (such as OECD) that are most relevant to auditors. [2]

(f) Describe good corporate governance requirements relating to directors' responsibilities (e. g. for risk management and internal control) and the reporting responsibilities of auditors. [1]

(g) Analyse the structure and roles of audit committees and discuss their drawbacks and limitations. [2]

(h) Explain the importance of internal control and risk management. [1]

(i) Compare the responsibilities of management and auditors for the design and operation of systems and controls. [2]

4 Professional ethics and ACCA's Code of Ethics and Conduct

(a) Define and apply the fundamental principles of professional ethics of integrity, objectivity, professional competence and due care, confidentiality and professional behaviour. [2]

(b) Define and apply the conceptual framework. [2]

(c) Discuss the sources of, and enforcement mechanisms associated with, ACCA's Code of Ethics and Conduct. [2]

(d) Discuss the requirements of professional ethics and other requirements in relation to the acceptance of new audit engagements. [2]

(e) Discuss the process by which an auditor obtains an audit engagement. [2]

(f) Explain the importance of engagement letters and state their contents. [1]

B INTERNAL AUDIT

1 Internal audit and corporate governance

(a) Discuss the factors to be taken into account when assessing the need for internal audit. [2]

(b) Discuss the elements of best practice in the structure and operations of internal audit with reference to appropriate international codes of corporate governance. [2]

2 Differences between external and internal audit

(a) Compare and contrast the role of external and internal audit regarding audit planning and the collection of audit evidence. [2]

(b) Compare and contrast the types of report provided by internal and external audit. [2]

3 The scope of the internal audit function

(a) Discuss the scope of internal audit and the limitations of the internal audit function. [2]

(b) Explain the types of audit report provided in internal audit assignments. [1]

(c) Discuss the responsibilities of internal and external auditors for the prevention and detection of fraud and error. [2]

4 Outsourcing the internal audit department

(a) Explain the advantages and disadvantages of outsourcing internal audit. [1]

5 Internal audit assignments

(a) Discuss the nature and purpose of internal audit assignments including value for money, IT, best value and financial. [2]

(b) Discuss the nature and purpose of operational internal audit assignments including procurement, marketing treasury and human resources management. [2]

C PLANNING AND RISK ASSESSMENT

1 Objective and general principles

(a) Identify and describe the need to plan and perform audits with an attitude of professional scepticism. [2]

(b) Identify and describe engagement risks affecting the audit of an entity. [1]

(c) Explain the components of audit risk.[1]

(d) Compare and contrast risk based, procedural and other approaches to audit work. [2]

(e) Discuss the importance of risk analysis. [2]

(f) Describe the use of information technology in risk analysis. [1]

2 Understanding the entity and knowledge of the business

(a) Explain how auditors obtain an initial understanding of the entity and knowledge of its business environment.[2]

3 Assessing the risks of material misstatement and fraud

(a) Define and explain the concepts of materiality and tolerable error. [2]

(b) Compute indicative materiality levels from financial information. [2]

(c) Discuss the effect of fraud and misstatements on the audit strategy and extent of audit work. [2]

4 Analytical procedures

(a) Describe and explain the nature and purpose of analytical procedures in planning. [2]

(b) Compute and interpret key ratios used in analytical procedures. [2]

5 Planning an audit

(a) Identify and explain the need for planning an audit. [2]

(b) Identify and describe the contents of the overall audit strategy and audit plan. [2]

(c) Explain and describe the relationship between the overall audit strategy and the audit plan. [2]

(d) Develop and document an audit plan. [2]

(e) Explain the difference between interim and final audit. [1]

6 Audit documentation

(a) Explain the need for and the importance of audit documentation. [1]

(b) Describe and prepare working papers and supporting documentation. [2]

(c) Explain the procedures to ensure safe custody and retention of working papers. [1]

7 The work of others

(a) Discuss the extent to which auditors are able to rely on the work of experts. [2]

(b) Discuss the extent to which external auditors are able to rely on the work of internal audit. [2]

(c) Discuss the audit considerations relating to entities using service organisations. [2]

(d) Discuss why auditors rely on the work of others. [2]

(e) Explain the extent to which reference to the work of others can be made in audit reports. [1]

D INTERNAL CONTROL

The following transaction cycles and account balances are relevant to this capability:

- revenue,
- purchases,
- inventory,
- revenue and capital expenditure,
- payroll
- bank and cash.

1 Internal control systems

(a) Explain why an auditor needs to obtain an understanding of internal control activities relevant to the audit. [1]

(b) Describe and explain the key components of an internal control system. [1]

(c) Identify and describe the important elements of internal control including the control environment and management control activities. [1]

(d) Discuss the difference between tests of control and substantive procedures. [2]

2 The use of internal control systems by auditors

(a) Explain the importance of internal control to auditors. [1]

(b) Explain how auditors identify weaknesses in internal control systems and how those weaknesses limit the extent of auditors' reliance on those systems. [2]

3 Transaction cycles

(a) Explain, analyse and provide examples of internal control procedures and control activities. [2]

(b) Provide examples of computer system controls. [2]

4 Tests of control

(a) Explain and tabulate tests of control suitable for inclusion in audit working papers. [2]

(b) List examples of application controls and general IT controls. [2]

5 The evaluation of internal control components

(a) Analyse the limitations of internal control components in the context of fraud and error. [2]

(b) Explain the need to modify the audit strategy and audit plan following the results of tests of control. [1]

(c) Identify and explain management's risk assessment process with reference to internal control components. [1]

6 Communication on internal control

(a) Discuss and provide examples of how the reporting of internal control weaknesses and recommendations to overcome those weaknesses are provided to management. [2]

E AUDIT EVIDENCE

1 The use of assertions by auditors

(a) Explain the assertions contained in the financial statements. [2]

(b) Explain the principles and objectives of transaction testing, account balance testing and disclosure testing. [1]

(c) Explain the use of assertions in obtaining audit evidence. [2]

2 Audit procedures

(a) Discuss the sources and relative merits of the different types of evidence available. [2]

(b) Discuss and provide examples of how analytical procedures are used as substantive procedures. [2]

(c) Discuss the problems associated with the audit and review of accounting estimates. [2]

(d) Describe why smaller entities may have different control environments and describe the types of evidence likely to be available in smaller entities. [1]

(e) Discuss the quality of evidence obtained. [2]

3 The audit of specific items

For each of the account balances stated in this sub-capability:

- explain the purpose of substantive procedures in relation to financial statement assertions,
- explain the substantive procedures used in auditing each balance,
- tabulate those substantive procedures in a work program.

(a) Receivables: [2]

(i) direct confirmation of accounts receivable

(ii) other evidence in relation to receivables and prepayments, and

(iii) the related income statement entries.

(b) Inventory: [2]

(i) inventory counting procedures in relation to year-end and continuous inventory systems

(ii) cut-off

(iii) auditor's attendance at inventory counting

(iv) direct confirmation of inventory held by third parties

(v) other evidence in relation to inventory.

(c) Payables and accruals: [2]

(i) supplier statement reconciliations and direct confirmation of accounts payable

(ii) obtain evidence in relation to payables and accruals, and

(iii) the related income statement entries.

(d) Bank and cash: [2]

(i) bank confirmation reports used in obtaining evidence in relation to bank and cash

(ii) other evidence in relation to bank and cash, and

(iii) the related income statement entries.

(e) Tangible non-current assets and long-term liabilities: [2]

(i) evidence in relation to non-current assets and

(ii) non-current liabilities and

(iii) the related income statement entries.

4 Audit sampling and others means of testing

(a) Define audit sampling and explain the need for sampling. [1]

(b) Identify and discuss the differences between statistical and non-statistical sampling. [2]

(c) Discuss and provide relevant examples of, the application of the basic principles of statistical sampling and other selective testing procedures. [2]

(d) Discuss the results of statistical sampling, including consideration of whether additional testing is required. [2]

5 Computer-assisted audit techniques

(a) Explain the use of computer-assisted audit techniques in the context of an audit. [1]

(b) Discuss and provide relevant examples of the use of test data and audit software for the transaction cycles and balances mentioned in sub-capability 3. [2]

(c) Discuss the use of computers in relation to the administration of the audit. [2]

6 Not-for-profit organisations

(a) Apply audit techniques to small not-for-profit organisations. [2]

(b) Explain how the audit of small not-for-profit organisations differs from the audit of for-profit organisations. [1]

F REVIEW

1 Subsequent events

(a) Explain the purpose of a subsequent events review. [1]

(b) Discuss the procedures to be undertaken in performing a subsequent events review. [2]

2 Going concern

(a) Define and discuss the significance of the concept of going concern. [2]

(b) Explain the importance of and the need for going concern reviews. [2]

(c) Explain the respective responsibilities of auditors and management regarding going concern. [1]

(d) Discuss the procedures to be applied in performing going concern reviews. [2]

(e) Discuss the disclosure requirements in relation to going concern issues. [2]

(f) Discuss the reporting implications of the findings of going concern reviews. [2]

3 Management representations

(a) Explain the purpose of and procedure for obtaining management representations. [2]

(b) Discuss the quality and reliability of management representations as audit evidence. [2]

(c) Discuss the circumstances where management representations are necessary and the matters on which representations are commonly obtained. [2]

4 Audit finalisation and the final review

(a) Discuss the importance of the overall review of evidence obtained. [2]

(b) Explain the significance of unadjusted differences. [1]

G REPORTING

1 Audit reports

(a) Describe and analyse the format and content of unmodified audit reports. [2]

(b) Describe and analyse the format and content of modified audit reports. [2]

2 Reports to management

(a) Identify and analyse internal control and system weaknesses and their potential effects and make appropriate recommendations to management. [2]

3 Internal audit reports

(a) Describe and explain the format and content of internal audit review reports and other reports dealing with the enhancement of performance. [1]

(b) Explain the process for producing an internal audit report. [1]

ANALYSIS OF PILOT PAPER

Question 1 – (30 marks)

Audit Evidence – audit of purchases cut-off and trade payables, computer assisted audit techniques

Internal Control – controls over standing data

Question 2 – (10 marks)

Audit Framework and Regulation – engagement letter

Audit Evidence - types of audit evidence

Reporting – Audit reports

Question 3 – (20 marks)

Audit Framework and Regulation – threats to independence, corporate governance, audit committees

Question 4 – (20 marks)

Internal Control – wages system

Internal Audit – responsibilities of internal and external auditors

Question 5 – (20 marks)

Review – subsequent events and affect on financial statements and audit report

REVISION GUIDANCE

Planning your revision

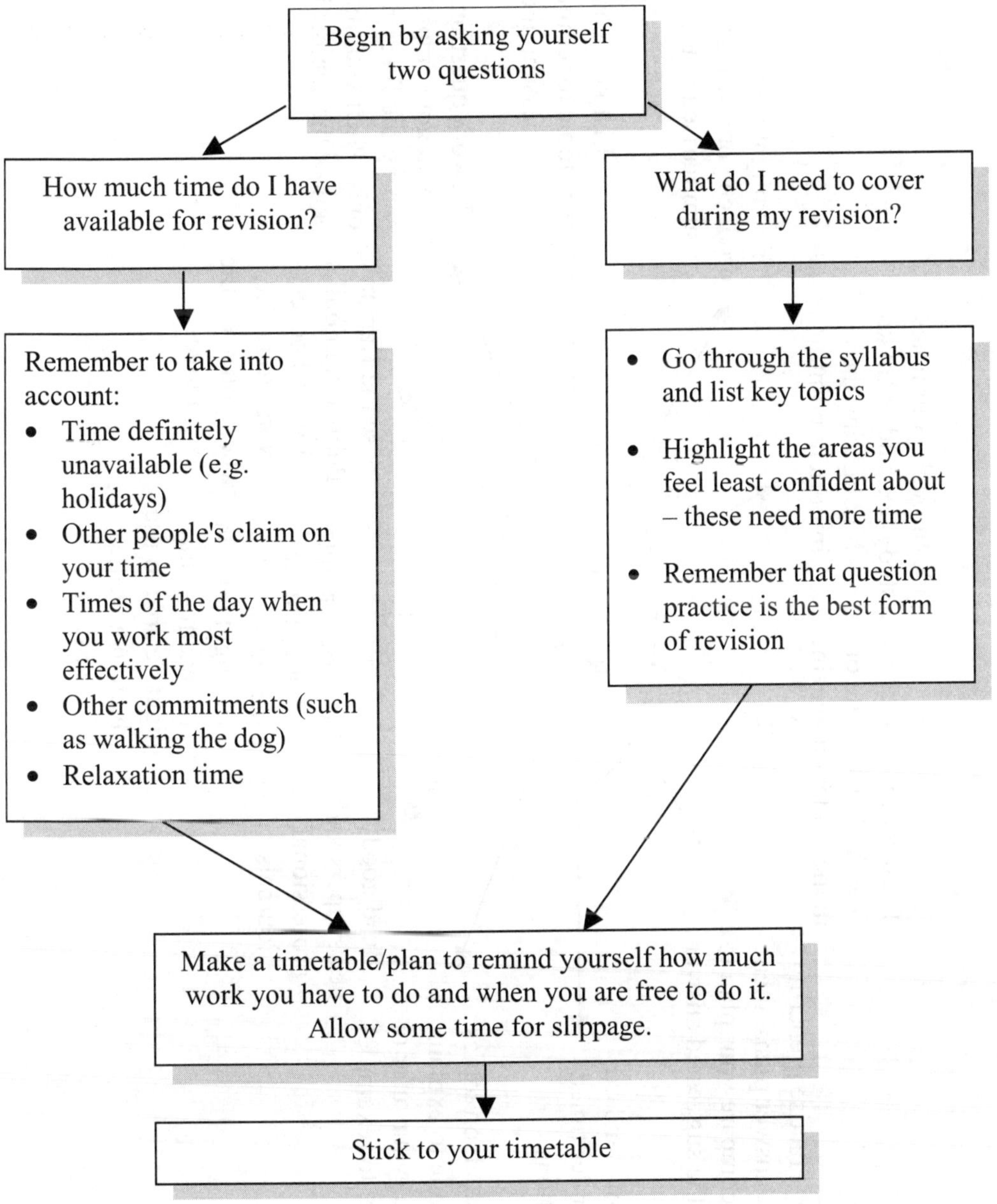

Revision techniques

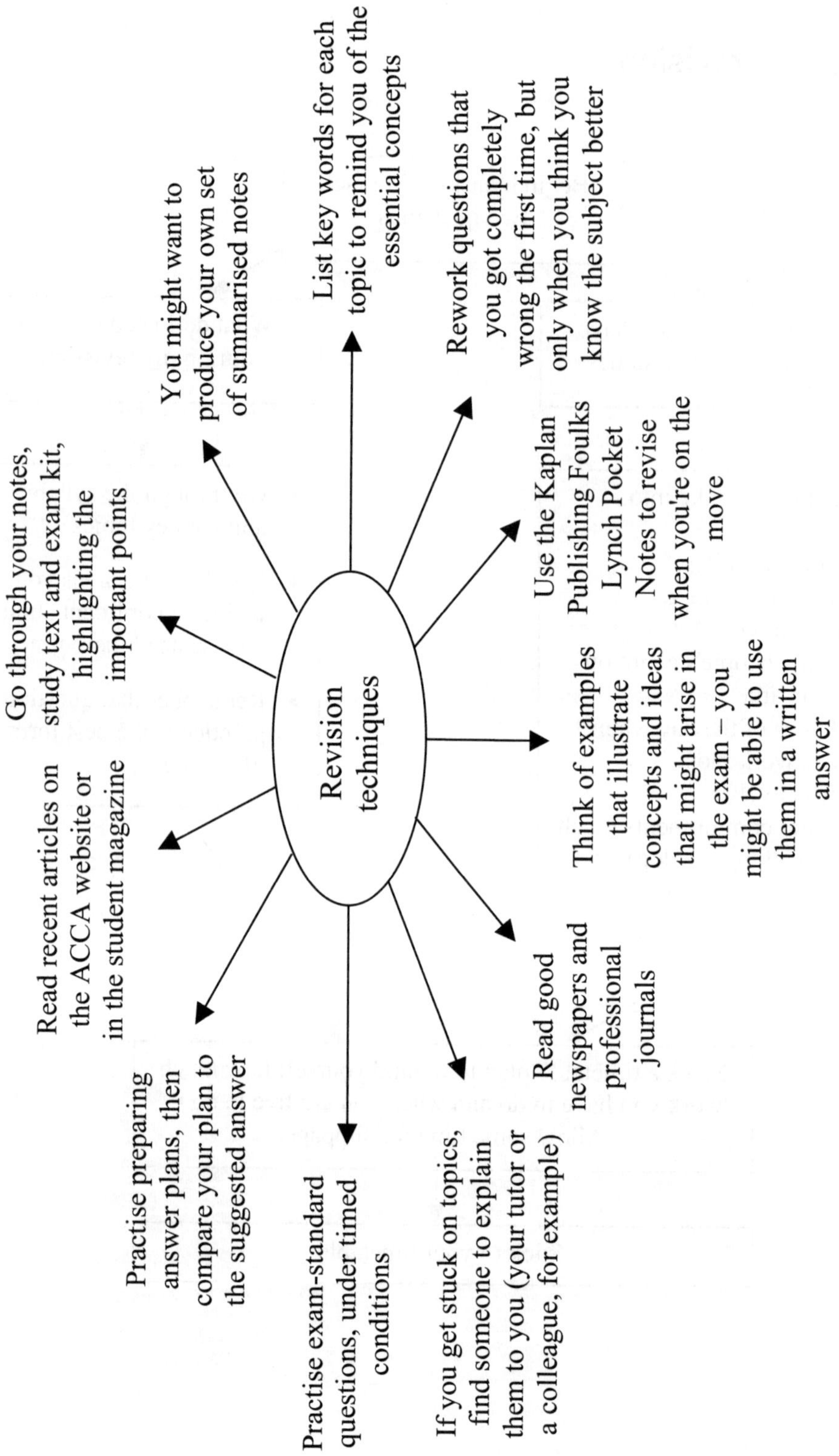

EXAM TECHNIQUES

- Use the allocated **15 minutes reading and planning time** at the beginning of the exam to read the questions and begin planning your answers.
- Where you have a **choice of question**, decide which questions you will do.
- Unless you know exactly how to answer the question, spend some time **planning** your answer.
- **Divide the time** you spend on questions in proportion to the marks on offer. One suggestion is to allocate 1½ minutes to each mark available, so a 10 mark question should be completed in 15 minutes.
- Spend the last **five minutes** reading through your answers and **making any additions or corrections**.
- If you **get completely stuck** with a question, leave space in your answer book and **return to it later.**
- Stick to the question and **tailor your answer** to what you are asked. Pay particular attention to the verbs in the question.
- If you do not understand what a question is asking, **state your assumptions**. Even if you do not answer in precisely the way the examiner hoped, you should be given some credit, if your assumptions are reasonable.
- You should do everything you can to make things easy for the marker. The marker will find it easier to identify the points you have made if your **answers are legible**.
- **Essay questions**: Your essay should have a clear structure. It should contain a brief introduction, a main section and a conclusion. Be concise. It is better to write a little about a lot of different points than a great deal about one or two points.
- **Computations**: It is essential to include all your workings in your answers. Many computational questions require the use of a standard format: company profit and loss account, balance sheet and cash flow statement for example. Be sure you know these formats thoroughly before the exam and use the layouts that you see in the answers given in this book and in model answers.
- **Case studies**: To write a good case study, first identify the area in which there is a problem, outline the main principles/theories you are going to use to answer the question, and then apply the principles/theories to the case.
- **Reports, memos and other documents**: Some questions ask you to present your answer in the form of a report or a memo or other document. So use the correct format - there could be easy marks to gain here.

Section 1

PRACTICE QUESTIONS

Chapter references refer to chapters in the Complete Text.

AUDIT FRAMEWORK AND REGULATION

1 EXTERNAL AUDIT
(DEC 04) (CHAPTER 1)

The purpose of an external audit and its role are not well understood. You have been asked to write some material for inclusion in your firm's training materials dealing with these issues in the audit of large companies.

Required:

(a) Draft an explanation dealing with the purpose of an external audit and its role in the audit of large companies, for inclusion in your firm's training materials. **(10 marks)**

(b) The external audit process for the audit of large entities generally involves two or more recognisable stages. One stage involves understanding the business and risk assessment, determining the response to assessed risk, testing of controls and a limited amount of substantive procedures. This stage is sometimes known as the interim audit. Another stage involves further tests of controls and substantive procedures and audit finalisation procedures. This stage is sometimes known as the final audit.

Describe and explain the main audit procedures and processes that take place during the interim and final audit of a large entity. **(10 marks)**

(Total: 20 marks)

2 BILLINGTON TRAVEL
(2.6 PILOT) (CHAPTER 5)

Professional ethics are relevant to both external auditors and internal auditors.

You work for a medium-sized firm of Chartered Certified Accountants with seven offices and 150 employees. Your firm has been asked to tender for the provision of statutory audit and other services to Billington Travel, a private company providing discounted package holiday services in the Mediterranean. The company is growing fast and would represent a substantial amount of fee income for your firm. The finance director has explained to you that the company would like the successful firm to provide a number of different services. These include the statutory audit and assistance with the preparation of the financial statements. The company is also struggling with a new computer system and the finance director considers that a systems review by your firm may be helpful. Your firm does not have much experience in the travel sector.

Required:

(a) Explain why it is necessary for external auditors to be and be seen to be independent of their audit clients. **(3 marks)**

(b) With reference to the ACCA's *Rules of Professional Conduct*, describe the ethical matters that should be considered in deciding on whether your firm should tender for:

(i) the statutory audit of Billington Travel **(4 marks)**

(ii) the provision of other services to Billington Travel **(4 marks)**

You are a student Chartered Certified Accountant and you are one of four assistant internal auditors in a large manufacturing company. You report to the chief internal auditor. You have been working on the review of the payables system and you have discovered what you consider to be several serious deficiencies in the structure and operation of the system. You have reported these matters in writing to the chief internal auditor but you are aware that none of these matters have been covered in his final report on the system which is due to be presented to management.

Required:

(c) List the actions you might take in these circumstances. **(6 marks)**

(d) Explain the dangers of doing nothing in these circumstances. **(3 marks)**

(Total: 20 marks)

3 TOUREX AND PUDCO

(JUN 03) (CHAPTER 5)

Your firm is the external auditor to two companies. One is a hotel, Tourex, the other is a food wholesaler, Pudco, that supplies the hotel. Both companies have the same year-end. Just before that year-end, a large number of guests became ill at a wedding reception at the hotel, possibly as a result of food poisoning.

The guests have taken legal action against the hotel and the hotel has taken action against the food wholesaler. Neither the hotel nor the food wholesaler have admitted liability. The hotel is negotiating out-of-court settlements with the ill guests, the food wholesaler is negotiating an out-of-court settlement with the hotel. At the balance sheet date, the public health authorities have not completed their investigations.

Lawyers for both the hotel and the food wholesaler say informally that negotiations are 'going well' but refuse to confirm this in writing. The amounts involved are material to the financial statements of both companies.

Required:

(a) Describe how ACCA's *Rules of Professional Conduct* apply to this situation and explain how the external auditors should manage this conflict of interest. **(6 marks)**

(b) Outline the main requirements of IAS 37 *Provisions, Contingent Liabilities and Contingent Assets* and apply them to this case. **(7 marks)**

(c) Assuming that your firm continues with the audit of both companies, for each company, describe the difficulties you foresee in obtaining sufficient audit evidence for potential provisions, contingent liabilities and contingent assets, and describe how this could affect your audit reports on their financial statements. **(7 marks)**

(Total: 20 marks)

4 CLIENT CONFIDENTIALITY

(DEC 03) (CHAPTER 5)

Client confidentiality underpins the relationship between Chartered Certified Accountants in practice and their clients.

It is a core element of ACCA's *Rules of Professional Conduct.*

Required:

(a) Explain the circumstances in which ACCA's Rules of Professional Conduct permit or require external auditors to disclose information relating to their clients to third parties without the knowledge or consent of the client. **(8 marks)**

(b) A waste disposal company has breached tax regulations, environmental regulations and health and safety regulations. The auditor has been approached by the tax authorities, the government body supervising the award of licences to such companies and a trade union representative. All of them have asked the auditor to provide them with information about the company. The auditor has also been approached by the police. They are investigating a suspected fraud perpetrated by the managing director of the company and they wish to ask the auditor certain questions about him.

Required:

Describe how the auditor should respond to these types of request. **(12 marks)**

(Total: 20 marks)

5 TELA & CO

(JUN 06) (CHAPTER 3)

You are the audit manager of Tela & Co, a medium sized firm of accountants. Your firm has just been asked for assistance from Jumper & Co, a firm of accountants in an adjacent country. This country has just implemented the internationally recognised codes on corporate governance and Jumper & Co has a number of clients where the codes are not being followed. One example of this, from SGCC, a listed company, is shown below. As your country already has appropriate corporate governance codes in place, Jumper & Co have asked for your advice regarding the changes necessary in SGCC to achieve appropriate compliance with corporate governance codes.

Extract from financial statements regarding corporate governance

Mr Sheppard is the Chief Executive Officer and board chairman of SGCC. He appoints and maintains a board of five executive and two non-executive directors. While the board sets performance targets for the senior managers in the company, no formal targets or review of board policies is carried out. Board salaries are therefore set and paid by Mr Sheppard based on his assessment of all the board members, including himself, and not their actual performance.

Internal controls in the company are monitored by the senior accountant, although detailed review is assumed to be carried out by the external auditors; SGCC does not have an internal audit department.

Annual financial statements are produced, providing detailed information on past performance.

Required:

Write a memo to Jumper & Co which:

(a) Explains why SGCC does not meet international codes of corporate governance

(b) Explains why not meeting the international codes may cause a problem for SGCC, and

(c) Recommends any changes necessary to implement those codes in the company.

(20 marks)

6 MCKAY & CO

(JUN 06) (CHAPTER 5)

(a) Explain the situations where an auditor may disclose confidential information about a client. **(8 marks)**

(b) You are an audit manager in McKay & Co, a firm of Chartered Certified Accountants. You are preparing the engagement letter for the audit of Ancients, a public limited company, for the year ending 30 June 2006.

Ancients has grown rapidly over the past few years, and is now one of your firm's most important clients.

Ancients has been an audit client for eight years and McKay & Co has provided audit, taxation and management consultancy advice during this time. The client has been satisfied with the services provided, although the taxation fee for the period to 31 December 2005 remains unpaid.

Audit personnel available for this year's audit are most of the staff from last year, including Mr Grace, an audit partner and Mr Jones, an audit senior. Mr Grace has been the audit partner since Ancients became an audit client. You are aware that Allyson Grace, the daughter of Mr Grace, has recently been appointed the financial director at Ancients.

To celebrate her new appointment, Allyson has suggested taking all of the audit staff out to an expensive restaurant prior to the start of the audit work for this year.

Required:

Identify and explain the risks to independence arising in carrying out your audit of Ancients for the year ending 30 June 2006, and suggest ways of mitigating each of the risks you identify. **(12 marks)**

(Total: 20 marks)

INTERNAL AUDIT

7 FRAUD AND ERROR

(DEC 04) (CHAPTER 4)

Fraud and error present risks to an entity. Both internal and external auditors are required to deal with risks to the entity. However, the responsibilities of internal and external auditors in relation to the risk of fraud and error differ.

Required:

(a) Explain how the internal audit function helps an entity deal with the risk of fraud and error. **(7 marks)**

(b) Explain the responsibilities of external auditors in respect of the risk of fraud and error in an audit of financial statements. **(7 marks)**

(c) Stone Holidays is an independent travel agency. It does not operate holidays itself. It takes commission on holidays sold to customers through its chain of high street shops. Staff are partly paid on a commission basis. Well-established tour operators run the holidays that Stone Holidays sells. The networked reservations system through which holidays are booked and the computerised accounting system are both well-established systems used by many independent travel agencies.

Payments by customers, including deposits, are accepted in cash and by debit and credit card. Stone Holidays is legally required to pay an amount of money (based on its total sales for the year) into a central fund maintained to compensate customers if the agency should cease operations.

Describe the nature of the risks to which Stone Holidays is subject arising from fraud and error. **(6 marks)**

(Total: 20 marks)

8 CLEANCO

(DEC 03) (CHAPTER 3)

Internal auditors often assist management in performing internal review assignments covering, for example, human resources, procurement (purchasing), marketing and treasury activities. Such reviews involve:

(i) the identification of risks;

(ii) the identification of control systems and procedures implemented to manage those risks;

(iii) tests of controls to ensure that internal controls are operating effectively; and

(iv) an evaluation of the overall effectiveness of the design and operation of controls in managing the risks identified.

You are the internal auditor for a private company, Cleanco. Cleanco provides cleaning services to shops and offices and has a reputation for high quality work. You have been asked to review the human resources, procurement and marketing functions within the company.

Cleanco employs about 500 cleaning staff, all of whom are on the payroll, and most of whom work part-time. Cleanco does not employ sub-contractors. Cleanco has a high turnover of staff.

The company buys its computers, office stationery and furniture, cleaning materials, equipment and work clothes for staff, from a variety of different suppliers. It processes its payroll in-house.

The company has recently decided to out-source its marketing to a large, aggressive, third party company that will advertise Cleanco's services by means of direct mail, sometimes by offering discounts; this company has been criticised in the past for breaching advertising regulations. There is growing price competition in Cleanco's market. Cleanco is struggling to maintain its profitability and would like to expand its client base.

Cleanco has three main functions:

(i) human resources;

(ii) procurement; and

(iii) marketing.

Required:

For each of the three main functions at Cleanco describe the:

(a) risks that you expect the company to face;

(b) controls you expect to be in place to manage the risks you have identified in (a), above; and

(c) tests of control you should perform to check that the controls you have identified in (b) above are operating properly.

Marks will be awarded as follows:

(i) Human resources. **(8 marks)**

(ii) Procurement. **(6 marks)**

(iii) Marketing. **(6 marks)**

You may present your answer in tabular format, if you wish. **(Total: 20 marks)**

9 ZX COMPANY

(JUN 05) (CHAPTER 3)

You are a recently qualified Chartered Certified Accountant in charge of the internal audit department of ZX, a rapidly expanding company. Turnover has increased by about 20% p.a. for the last five years, to the current level of $50 million. Net profits are also high, with an acceptable return being provided for the four shareholders.

The internal audit department was established last year to assist the board of directors in their control of the company and to prepare for a possible listing on the stock exchange. The Managing Director is keen to follow the principles of good corporate governance with respect to internal audit. However, he is also aware that the other board members do not have complete knowledge of corporate governance or detailed knowledge of International Auditing Standards.

Required:

Write a memo to the board of ZX that:

(a) Explains how the internal audit department can assist the board of directors in fulfilling their obligations under the principles of good corporate governance. **(10 marks)**

(b) Explains the advantages and disadvantages to ZX of an audit committee. **(10 marks)**

(Total: 20 marks)

10 OCTBALL

(DEC 05) (CHAPTER 3)

You are the senior manager in the internal audit department of Octball, a limited liability company. You report to the chief internal auditor and have a staff of six junior auditors to supervise, although the budget allows for up to ten junior staff.

In a recent meeting with the chief internal auditor, the difficulty of staff recruitment and retention was discussed. Over the past year, five junior internal audit staff have left the company, but only two have been recruited. Recruitment problems identified include location of Octball's head office in a small town over 150 kilometres from the nearest major city and extensive foreign travel, often to cold climates.

Together with the chief internal auditor you believe that outsourcing the internal audit department may be a way of alleviating the staffing problems. You would monitor the new outsourced department in a part-time role taking on additional responsibilities in other departments, and the chief internal auditor would accept the post of Finance Director (FD) on the board, replacing the retiring FD.

Two firms have been identified as being able to provide the internal audit service:

- The NFA Partnership, a local firm specialising in provision of accountancy and internal audit services. NFA does not audit financial statements or report to members, and
- T&M, Octball's external auditors, who have offices in 75 countries and employ in excess of 65,000 staff.

Required:

(a) Discuss the advantages and disadvantages of appointing NFA as internal auditors for Octball. **(8 marks)**

(b) Discuss the issues T&M need to consider before they could accept appointment as internal auditors for Octball. **(7 marks)**

(c) Assume that an outsourcing company has been chosen to provide internal audit services.

Describe the control activities that Octball should apply to ensure that the internal audit service is being maintained to a high standard. **(5 marks)**

(Total: 20 marks)

11 INTERNAL AUDIT AND CORPORATE GOVERNANCE

(DEC 01) (CHAPTER 3)

There are similarities and differences between the responsibilities of internal and external auditors. Both internal and external auditors have responsibilities relating to the prevention, detection and reporting of fraud, for example, but their responsibilities are not the same. Both internal and external audit are part of an organisation's overall corporate governance arrangements. Sometimes, the responsibilities of internal auditors are out-sourced to external organisations.

Required:

(a) Explain the difference between the responsibilities of internal auditors and external auditors for the prevention, detection and reporting of fraud and error. **(5 marks)**

(b) Explain the role of internal audit in the context of:

(i) corporate governance;

(ii) risk management;

(iii) organisational control. **(10 marks)**

Your answer should include one example of how an internal audit department in a manufacturing company might fulfil its role under each of the headings above.

(c) Outline the issues that should be considered when an organisation decides to out-source the internal audit function. **(5 marks)**

(Total: 20 marks)

12 ROXY HOTELS

(2.6 PILOT) (CHAPTER 3)

Roxy Hotels is a listed company which runs a chain of some 40 hotels. The company has an established internal audit department which is based at the head office and which makes regular visits to the hotels.

The hotels provide business and tourist class accommodation. They also provide restaurants, bars, and conference and leisure facilities which are open to the general public as well as residents. The company operates a computerised central booking and billing system and an inventory and asset control system, both of which can be accessed via terminals in the hotels. Access to the system is restricted by the use of passwords and all significant expenditure is authorised through head office. The payroll is operated through head office. Hotel and regional managers are actively involved in the setting of budgets and cash flow forecasting. On average, throughout the year, the chain has a 65% occupancy rate.

Required:

(a) Describe the role of internal audit in ensuring that organisations achieve their corporate objectives. **(5 marks)**

(b) List the types of activities normally carried out by internal audit department. **(5 marks)**

(c) Describe SIX areas in which the internal audit department at Roxy Hotels might check detailed transactions and balances. **(6 marks)**

(d) Describe FOUR areas in which the internal audit department at Roxy Hotels might perform reviews of systems or operational performance. **(4 marks)**

(Total: 20 marks)

PLANNING AND RISK ASSESSMENT

13 RELIANCE ON INTERNAL AUDIT

(JUN 03) (CHAPTER 10)

Your firm is the newly appointed external auditor to a large company that sells, maintains and leases office equipment and furniture to its customers and you have been asked to co-operate with internal audit to keep audit costs down. The company wants the external auditors to rely on some of the work already performed by internal audit.

The internal auditors provide the following services to the company:

(i) a cyclical audit of the operation of internal controls in the company's major functions (operations, finance, customer support and information services);

(ii) a review of the structure of internal controls in each major function every four years;

(iii) an annual review of the effectiveness of measures put in place by management to minimise the major risks facing the company.

During the current year, the company has gone through a major internal restructuring in its information services function and the internal auditors have been closely involved in the preparation of plans for restructuring, and in the related post-implementation review.

Required:

(a) Explain the extent to which your firm will seek to rely on the work of the internal auditors in each of the areas noted above. **(6 marks)**

(b) Describe the information your firm will seek from the internal auditors in order for you to determine the extent of your reliance. **(6 marks)**

(c) Describe the circumstances in which it would not be possible to rely on the work of the internal auditors. **(4 marks)**

(d) Explain why it will be necessary for your firm to perform its own work in certain audit areas in addition to relying on the work performed by internal audit. **(4 marks)**

(Total: 20 marks)

14 FLYLO

(JUN 04) (CHAPTER 10)

Flylo is an airline. The company owns some of its fleet of aircraft. Other aircraft are leased from third parties. Flylo has an internal audit function that has recently been expanded. Your firm is the external auditor to Flylo. Your firm has been asked to investigate the extent to which it may be able to rely on the work of internal audit in the following areas:

– sales and ticketing;

– fleet acquisition and maintenance;

– trade payables and long-term debt financing (borrowings).

The company outsources its in-flight catering and payroll functions to different service organisations.

Required:

(a) Explain why the work of the internal auditors, in the three areas noted above, is likely to be useful to you as the external auditor. **(9 marks)**

(b) Explain how the quality of the internal audit function is likely to influence the extent of your reliance on internal audit work. **(5 marks)**

(c) Describe the audit evidence you will seek relating to internal controls over the out-sourced functions (in-flight catering and payroll). **(6 marks)**

(Total: 20 marks)

15 E WHEELS

(2.6 PILOT) (CHAPTER 7)

Your firm has recently been appointed as external auditor to EWheels. EWheels is a private 'dot.com' company that operates an internet auction service for the sale of used motor vehicles. You are planning the audit of the financial statements. The company has been in existence for four years and has grown rapidly. It was founded by three individuals who are a former car auctioneer, an internet specialist with an interest in cars, and an accountant. The company now has three offices and some 100 employees. The on-line car auction market is very competitive. The company is the biggest provider of the service in the south of the country, but the directors have ambitious plans which include an aggressive marketing campaign, the take-over of a number of target competitors and additional office space and staff, all of which will require considerable additional finance.

The company is financed partly by private capital brought in by the three founders, and partly by bank loans. The three founders were all directors, but the accountant resigned six months ago and has commenced a legal action against the company for a considerable amount of money, claiming that he has effectively been excluded from management by the other two directors. The company's balance sheet shows net liabilities. The company has not yet made a profit although preliminary figures indicate that it has reached break-even point in the current year. Your firm has discovered that the previous auditors were not re-appointed because they refused to issue an unmodified audit opinion on the previous year's financial statements, and instead made reference to the going concern status of the company in their audit report. Your firm has made it clear to the directors that it may be necessary to make reference to the going concern status of the company again in the current year, but they have indicated that they would prefer an unmodified report if at all possible. You are also aware that loan facilities for this type of company are becoming more scarce, as there are too many companies seeking such finance.

The director who resigned six months ago was responsible for the day to day accounting function and for the preparation of the financial and management accounts. The company has been unsuccessful in recruiting a permanent replacement and has used a number of temporary accountants. Your initial investigations have highlighted a number of weaknesses in the operation of the accounting and internal control systems.

Required:

(a) Explain your understanding of audit risk. **(4 marks)**

(b) Describe the risks associated with the audit of EWheels. **(7 marks)**

(c) List the enquiries you will make and the procedures you will perform in deciding whether to make reference to the going concern status of Ewheels in your audit report on the financial statements. **(5 marks)**

(d) Describe the different ways in which your audit report might refer to the going concern status of the company. **(4 marks)**

(Total: 20 marks)

16 BONDI

(JUN 99) (CHAPTER 7)

You are a partner with a firm of Certified Public Accountants that has been invited, by the board of directors, to accept nomination as external auditors to Bondi. Bondi operates a number of car dealerships and has grown rapidly over the past two years through an aggressive take-over strategy.

You are aware that the company's existing directors, a much smaller firm, qualified their last auditor's report. Over lunch with a number of your firm's partners, the company's chief financial officer maintained that their existing auditors could not cope with the audit of a company their size and, in particular, were not equipped to audit the recently installed sophisticated computer accounting program. He also suggests that they need a firm of your reputation in order to reassure the market as they intend to seek a public listing within two years.

The existing auditors, in response to your inquiry, advise against accepting the audit on the following grounds:

– Insufficient consideration has been devoted by management to developing the accounting system in line with the expanding business. In particular there is a lack of concern as to control. They detected a number of petty employee frauds as a result of control weaknesses. No action was taken against the employees identified as engaged in fraud. The attitude seems to be to encourage risk taking employees who, if they make money on the side whilst securing good deals for the company, that is seen as a legitimate bonus.

– The newly installed computer accounting system is unreasonably complicated. Bondi claims this is necessary because of the need to maintain records to justify the company's claims for volume rebates, and bonuses under the complex incentive schemes by which car manufacturers reward dealers.

– They have no evidence of deliberate misrepresentation by the directors but audit staff were hindered in their audit work by a less than helpful attitude by senior management who adopted an aggressive stance whenever a query was raised. The chief financial officer was constantly on the phone to the partner claiming the audit staff were incompetent and accusing them of wasting his time asking unnecessary questions.

At a partner's meeting a majority of partners accepted the story that the existing auditors were out of their depth and that their complaints were merely an attempt to cover up their own shortcomings. Your firm accepted nomination and was duly appointed as auditors.

Required:

(a) State factors the partners should have considered for and against accepting nomination. **(7 marks)**

(b) Detail the matters to which you would pay particular attention in obtaining the required knowledge of the business and in developing your audit plan. **(7 marks)**

During the first audit your firm discovers that the reason for the complexity of the computer system is to falsify records in order to reduce the amount of tax payable to the government.

(c) Describe the action you would take on discovery of the fraud. **(6 marks)**

(Total: 20 marks)

17 NEPCO

(DEC 01) (CHAPTER 7)

Nepco is a European company that manufactures high quality computer components and assembles computer parts. It has existed for some years and is part of a vertical supply chain for a well-known brand of computer hardware. Profits are coming under increasing pressure from manufacturers in the Far East and Asia with lower labour costs, and from rising raw material costs. Nepco is listed on a stock exchange. There is pressure from institutional investors for better returns in the form of dividends and the main institutional investors are considering selling a proportion of their shares in the company. The directors of Nepco are considering whether to move into new market areas.

Nepco has good accounting and internal control systems. Inventory is material to the accounts, and there is a good set of permanent inventory records. No year-end inventory count is conducted. Operational compliance issues are important to Nepco as many countries have inflexible quality standards and some projects are being held up because of difficulties in obtaining approval from regulators for new components. All staff and directors of Nepco are remunerated (at least in part) on a performance-related basis, some with share options. Staff are generally highly qualified and well-paid.

This is your first year as auditors. Your firm has very little experience in this industry. External audit costs are tightly controlled and your firm has agreed to a budget that will allow very little flexibility.

Required:

(a) Describe the risks relating to Nepco under the headings of inherent risk, control risk and detection risk. **(12 marks)**

(b) In the light of the risks identified in (a) above, list the matters to which you will pay particular attention during the audit of Nepco and explain the work you will perform in relation to them. **(8 marks)**

(Total: 20 marks)

18 RISKS

(DEC 02) (CHAPTER 7)

Risk management involves the classification of risks. Internal auditors sometimes classify risks as:

(i) high impact, high likelihood – such as the risk that contaminated foodstuffs will enter the production process in a biscuit manufacturing business, or, that other entrants into the market will reduce the existing business' market share or profit margins;

(ii) high impact, low likelihood – such as the risk of the non-availability of a basic element of production such as sugar, for a biscuit manufacturing business, or, that there will be significant damage to property or injury to employees as a result of an earthquake in Northern Europe;

(iii) low impact, low likelihood – such as the risk that minor damage to property will be caused by snow in Australia;

(iv) low impact, high likelihood – such as the risk that drivers may be involved in vehicle accidents that will leave the business temporarily without the vehicle, or, that production employees may be ill and unable to work temporarily.

Companies may transfer, reduce, or accept risks, or adopt some combination of these approaches to risk.

Required:

(a) For each of the examples given above, describe how the business might transfer, reduce or accept the risk. **(12 marks)**

(b) Explain how the work of internal auditors on the classification of risks, as described above, could be used by external auditors. **(8 marks)**

(Total: 20 marks)

19 HIVEX

(JUN 03) (CHAPTER 6)

You have been presented with the following draft financial information about Hivex, a very successful company that develops and licenses specialist computer software and hardware. Its non-current assets mainly consist of property, computer hardware and investments, and there have been additions to these during the year. The company is experiencing increasing competition from rival companies, most of which specialise in hardware or software, but not both. There is pressure to advertise and to cut prices.

You are the audit manager. You are planning the audit and you are conducting a preliminary analytical review and associated risk analysis for this client for the year ended 31 May 20X3. You have been provided with a summarised draft income statement which has been produced very quickly and certain accounting ratios and percentages. You have been informed that the company accounts for research and development costs in accordance with IAS 38 *Intangible assets*.

Income statement

	Year ended 31 May	
	20X3	*20X2*
	$000	$000
Revenue	15,206	13,524
Cost of sales	3,009	3,007
Gross profit	12,197	10,517
Distribution costs	3,006	1,996
Administrative expenses	994	1,768
Selling expenses	3,002	274
Profit from operations	5,195	6,479
Net interest receivable	995	395

	Year ended 31 May	
	20X3	*20X2*
	$000	$000
Profit before tax	6,190	6,874
Corporation tax	3,104	1,452
Net profit	3,086	5,422
Dividends paid	1,469	1,439
Retained profits	1,617	3,983

Accounting ratios and percentages		
Earnings per share	0.43	1.04
Performance ratios include the following:		
Gross margin	0.80	0.78
Expenses as a percentage of sales:		
Distribution costs	0.20	0.15
Administrative expenses	0.07	0.13
Selling expenses	0.20	0.02
Operating profit	0.34	0.48

Required:

(a) Using the information above, comment briefly on the performance of the company for the two years. **(8 marks)**

(b) Use your answer to part (a) to identify the areas that are subject to increased audit risk and describe the further audit work you would perform in response to those risks. **(12 marks)**

(Total: 20 marks)

20 ROCK

(DEC 04) (CHAPTER 6)

You are an audit senior responsible for understanding the entity and its environment and assessing the risk of material misstatements for the audit of Rock for the year ending 31 December 20X4. Rock is a company listed on a stock exchange. Rock is engaged in the wholesale import, manufacture and distribution of basic cosmetics and toiletries for sale to a wide range of stores, under a variety of different brand names. You have worked on the audit of this client for several years as an audit junior.

Required:

(a) Describe the information you will seek, and procedures you will perform in order to understand the entity and its environment and assess risk for the audit of Rock for the year ending 31 December 20X4. **(10 marks)**

(b) You are now nearing the completion of the audit of Rock for the year ending 31 December 20X4. Draft financial statements have been produced. You have been given the responsibility of performing a review of the audit files before they are passed to the audit manager and the audit partner for their review. You have been asked to concentrate on the proper completion of the audit working papers. Some of the audit working papers have been produced electronically but all of them have been printed out for you.

Describe the types of audit working papers you should expect to see in the audit files and the features of those working papers that show that they have been properly completed. **(10 marks)**

(Total: 20 marks)

21 ANALYTICAL PROCEDURES

(JUN 02) (CHAPTER 6)

(a) Analytical procedures are an important and powerful tool for auditors in explaining the performance of a business.

They are used at the planning, testing and review stages of the audit.

Required:

Preliminary analytical procedures are often performed on accounting ratios. Explain the possible reasons for the following changes found at the planning stage of the audit:

(i) an increase in the current ratio;

(ii) a decrease in the gross profit margin;

(iii) an increase in the inventory holding period;

(iv) an increase in dividend cover;

(v) an increase in capital gearing (leverage). **(10 marks)**

Note: No marks will be awarded for showing the calculation of the ratio, all parts carry equal marks.

(b) The concept of materiality is fundamental to the work of auditors. Matters that are immaterial are not reported in financial statements.

Required:

(i) explain the concept of materiality **(4 marks)**

(ii) describe how materiality affects the audit work performed by auditors **(4 marks)**

(iii) give an example of qualitative materiality. **(2 marks)**

(Total: 20 marks)

22 WORKING PAPERS

(JUN 00) (CHAPTER 9)

The preparation of working papers is an important part of the audit process. You have been asked to prepare a session introducing new recruits to your firm of Chartered Certified Accountants to the use of working papers. Amongst the topics you have been asked to cover are the distinction between working papers held in the permanent and current audit files, the design and use of audit programmes and the concept of an audit trail with respect to the conduct of the audit itself.

Required:

(a) State four matters you would expect to find recorded in working papers in the permanent audit file and explain their purpose. **(8 marks)**

(b) Explain the design and use of audit programmes and discuss the merits of standard and tailored audit programmes. **(7 marks)**

(c) Explain the importance of recording details of the actual evidence examined in the course of the audit on which the conclusions are drawn. Your explanation should include consideration of the details to be recorded in the working papers and of the audit trail to be left in the books and records of the entity being audited. **(5 marks)**

(Total: 20 marks)

23 SPECS4YOU

(JUN 07) (CHAPTER 9)

ISA 230 *Audit Documentation (Revised)* establishes standards and provides guidance regarding documentation in the context of the audit of financial statements.

Required:

(a) List the purposes of audit working papers. **(3 marks)**

(b) You have recently been promoted to audit manager in the audit firm of Trums & Co. As part of your new responsibilities, you have been placed in charge of the audit of Specs4You Co, a long established audit client of Trums & Co. Specs4You Co sells spectacles; the company owns 42 stores where customers can have their eyes tested and choose from a range of frames.

Required:

List the documentation that should be of assistance to you in familiarising yourself with Specs4You Co. Describe the information you should expect to obtain from each document. **(8 marks)**

(c) The time is now towards the end of the audit, and you are reviewing working papers produced by the audit team. An example of a working paper you have just reviewed is shown below.

Client Name **Specs4You Co**	Year **end 30 April**	Page **xxxxxxx**
Working paper **Payables transaction testing**		
	Prepared by	Date
	Reviewed by **CW**	Date **12 June 2007**

Audit assertion: To make sure that the purchases day book is correct.

Method: Select a sample of 15 purchase orders recorded in the purchase order system. Trace details to the goods received note (GRN), purchase invoice (PI) and the purchase day book (PDB) ensuring that the quantities and prices recorded on the purchase order match those on the GRN, PI and PDB.

Test details: In accordance with audit risk, a sample of purchase orders were selected from a numerically sequenced purchase order system and details traced as stated in the method. Details of items tested can be found on another working paper.

Results: Details of purchase orders were normally correctly recorded through the system. Five purchase orders did not have any associated GRN, PI and were not recorded in the PDB. Further investigation showed that these orders had been cancelled due to a change in spectacle specification. However, this does not appear to be a system weakness as the internal controls do not allow for changes in specification.

Conclusion: Purchase orders are completely recorded in the purchase day book.

Required:

Explain why the working paper shown above does not meet the standards normally expected of a working paper. Note: You are not required to reproduce the working paper. **(9 marks)**

(Total: 20 marks)

24 TEMPEST

(DEC 05) (CHAPTER 6)

(a) International Standard on Auditing 300 (revised) *Planning an Audit of Financial Statements*, states that an auditor must plan the audit.

Explain why it is important to plan an audit. **(5 marks)**

(b) You are the audit manager in charge of the audit of Tempest, a limited liability company. The company's year end is 31 December, and Tempest has been a client for seven years. The company purchases and resells fittings for ships including anchors, compasses, rudders, sails etc. Clients vary in size from small businesses making yachts to large companies maintaining large luxury cruise ships. No manufacturing takes place in Tempest.

Information on the company's financial performance is available as follows:

	2005 Forecast	*2004 Actual*
	$000	$000
Revenue	45,928	40,825
Cost of sales	(37,998)	(31,874)
Gross profit	7,930	8,951
Administration costs	(4,994)	(4,758)
Distribution costs	(2,500)	(2,500)
Net profit	436	1,693

Non-current assets (at net book value)	3,600	4,500
Current assets		
Inventory	200	1,278
Receivables	6,000	4,052
Cash and bank	500	1,590
Total assets	10,300	11,420
Capital and reserves		
Share capital	1,000	1,000
Accumulated profits	5,300	5,764
Total shareholders' funds	6,300	6,764
Non-current liabilities	1,000	2,058
Current liabilities	3,000	2,598
	10,300	11,420

Other information

The industry that Tempest trades in has seen moderate growth of 7% over the last year.

- Non-current assets mainly relate to company premises for storing inventory. Ten delivery vehicles are owned with a net book value of $300,000.
- One of the directors purchased a yacht during the year.
- Inventory is stored in ten different locations across the country, with your firm again having offices close to seven of those locations.
- A computerised inventory control system was introduced in August 2005. Inventory balances are now obtainable directly from the computer system. The client does not intend to count inventory at the year end but rely instead on the computerised inventory control system.

Required:

Using the information provided above, prepare the audit strategy for Tempest for the year ending 31 December 2005. **(15 marks)**

(Total: 20 marks)

25 ZPM

(JUN 06) (CHAPTER 10)

ISA 610 *Considering the Work of Internal Auditing* states that 'when the external auditor intends to use specific work of internal auditing, the external auditor should evaluate and perform audit procedures on that work to confirm its adequacy for the external auditor's purposes.'

Required:

(a) In relation to ISA 610, explain the factors the external auditor will consider when evaluating the work of the internal auditor. **(5 marks)**

(b) ZPM is a listed limited liability company with a year end of 30 June. ZPM's main activity is selling home improvement or 'Do-It-Yourself' (DIY) products to the public. Products sold range from nails, paint and tools to doors and showers; some stores also sell garden tools and furniture. Products are purchased from approximately 200 different suppliers. ZPM has 103 stores in eight different countries.

ZPM has a well-staffed internal audit department, who report on a regular basis to the audit committee. Areas where the internal and external auditors may carry out work include:

1. Attending the year end inventory count in 30 stores annually. All stores are visited on a rotational basis.
2. Checking the internal controls over the procurement systems (e.g. ensuring a liability is only recorded when the inventory has been received).
3. Reviewing the operations of the marketing department.

Required:

For each of the above three areas, discuss

(i) the objectives of the internal auditor; **(5 marks)**

(ii) the objectives of the external auditor; and **(5 marks)**

(iii) whether the external auditor will rely on the internal auditor, and if reliance is required, the extent of that reliance. **(5 marks)**

(Total: 20 marks)

26 SMALLER ENTITIES

(DEC 04) (CHAPTER 9)

International Standards on Auditing (ISAs) apply equally to the audit of all entities, whatever their size. However, the manner in which ISAs are applied differs from entity to entity and depends on the use of the auditor's judgement. The characteristics of smaller entities may include:

(a) Common ownership and management;

(b) A control framework that is different to the control framework for larger entities;

(c) The use of standardised computer packages;

(d) Reliance on the auditor for accounting expertise;

(e) A lack of sufficient appropriate audit evidence to support financial statement assertions relating to income from cash transactions.

These characteristics have an effect on the way the audits of smaller entities are approached, how audit risk is assessed, how the audit is conducted, the auditor's report and the relationship between auditor and client.

Required:

Describe the nature and effect of each of the five characteristics listed in (a)–(e) above on the audit of smaller entities and on the relationship between auditor and client.

Note: The five characteristics (a)–(e) carry equal marks **(20 marks)**

INTERNAL CONTROL

27 BESTWOOD ENGINEERING

(DEC 98) (CHAPTER 8)

Your firm is the external auditor of Bestwood Engineering, a privately owned incorporated business, which manufactures components for motor vehicles and sells them to motor vehicle manufacturers and wholesalers. It has sales of $10 million and a profit before tax of $400,000.

The company has a new chief financial officer who has asked your advice on controls in the company's purchases and accounts payable system.

Bestwood Engineering has separate accounts, purchasing and goods received departments. Most purchases are required by the production department, but other departments are able to raise requisitions for goods and services. The purchasing department is responsible for obtaining goods and services for the company at the lowest price which is consistent with the required delivery date and quality, and for ensuring their prompt delivery.

The accounts department is responsible for obtaining authorisation of purchase invoices before they are input into the computer which posts them to the accounts payable ledger and the general ledger. The accounting records are kept on a microcomputer and the standard accounting software was obtained from an independent supplier. The accounting software maintains the accounts payable ledger, accounts receivable ledger, general ledger and payroll. The company does not maintain inventory records, as it believes the costs of maintaining these records outweigh the benefits.

The chief financial officer has explained that services include gas, electricity, telephone, repairs and short-term rental (hire) of equipment and vehicles.

You are required to:

(a) describe the procedures which should be in operation in the purchasing department to control the purchase and receipt of goods **(8 marks)**

(b) describe the controls the accounts department should exercise over obtaining authorisation of purchase invoices before posting them to the accounts payable ledger **(6 marks)**

(c) explain how controls over the purchase of services, from raising the purchase requisition to posting the invoice to the accounts payable ledger, might differ from the procedures for the purchase of goods, as described in your answers to parts (a) and (b) above. **(6 marks)**

(Total: 20 marks)

28 AUDIT RISK

(DEC 99) (CHAPTER 8)

ISA 200 *Objective and General Principles Governing an Audit of Financial Statements* defines the terms of 'audit risk', 'inherent risk', 'control risk' and 'detection risk'.

When developing the audit approach, the auditor considers the preliminary assessment of control risk (in conjunction with the assessment of inherent risk) to determine the appropriate detection risk to accept for the financial statement assertions.

Required:

(a) Distinguish between inherent risk at the entity level and at the account balance and class of transactions level. Identify factors, at each level, that will be considered by the auditors in arriving at their assessment of inherent risk. **(6 marks)**

(b) (i) Explain how the preliminary assessment of control risk affects:

– the mix of tests of control and substantive procedures

– the design of substantive procedures. **(5 marks)**

(ii) Identify other factors that affect the auditors' decision as to the extent of substantive procedures. **(3 marks)**

(c) Explain what is meant by the *control environment*, identify the factors contributing to the control environment and describe its effect on the assessment of control risk. **(6 marks)**

(Total: 20 marks)

29 XY CO

(DEC 00) (CHAPTER 8)

XY Co, Chartered Certified Accountants, have recently been appointed as the first external auditors to Fairlight on its incorporation after trading as a partnership for several years.

David Smith, the senior in charge of the audit, is in the process of obtaining the understanding of the accounting system. Fairlight's chief executive officer admits that the system has remained unchanged from when it was a small business. He tells David that he is particularly concerned about the purchasing system, which he describes as follows:

(i) department managers order goods and services for their own departments

(ii) suppliers' invoices are sent directly to the department managers who approve them for payment and pass them to the cashier to be paid

(iii) the cashier enters the invoices in the purchase journal and then files them by supplier

(iv) no accounts payable ledger is maintained. When suppliers' statements are received the invoices are attached to the statement. There are always a few invoices missing, mostly more recent ones, so, to avoid harming Fairlight's credit rating, suppliers are always paid the balance on their statement.

The chief executive officer also advises David that he intends to hire an experienced purchasing officer but he is not quite sure how best to use such a person. On further investigation, David discovers that the general ledger shows a debit balance for accounts payable.

David tells the chief executive officer that there are three types of problem with the existing purchases system.

(a) Occurrence:

such as paying for goods Fairlight has not ordered.

(b) Completeness:

for example, not all invoices for goods and services received may be recorded in Fairlight's accounting records (which probably accounts for the debit balance currently recorded as accounts payable).

(c) Measurement:

such as suppliers' invoices being incorrectly entered in the purchase journal.

David agrees that, as a matter of urgency, the audit firm will advise the chief executive officer of control weaknesses in the purchasing system and their consequences and will recommend changes, including how best to use the purchasing officer.

Required:

Draft paragraphs for inclusion in the section of a management letter to the chief executive officer dealing with the purchasing system, under three headings:

(a) Occurrence **(11 marks)**

(b) Completeness **(5 marks)**

(c) Measurement. **(4 marks)**

Notes: Do not draft the whole letter. Only draft those paragraphs dealing with the purchasing system. If one of your recommendations deals with matters under two or more of the headings it need not be repeated but reference should be made to the recommendation.

(Total: 20 marks)

30 INTERNAL CONTROL AND CASH

(JUN 02) (CHAPTER 8)

(a) Internal control systems are designed, amongst other things, to prevent error and misappropriation.

Required:

Describe the errors and misappropriations that may occur if the following are not properly controlled:

(i) receipts paid into bank accounts; **(2 marks)**

(ii) payments made out of bank accounts; **(3 marks)**

(iii) interest and charges debited and credited to bank accounts. **(2 marks)**

(b) A book-selling company has a head office and 25 shops, each of which holds cash (banknotes, coins, and credit card vouchers) at the balance sheet date. There are no receivables. Accounting records are held at shops. Shops make returns to head office and head office holds its own accounting records. Your firm has been the external auditor to the company for many years and has offices near to the location of some but not all of the shops.

Required:

List the audit objectives for the audit of cash and state how you would gain the audit evidence in relation to those objectives at the year-end. **(8 marks)**

(c) The external auditors of companies often write to companies' bankers asking for details of bank balances and other matters at the year-end.

Required:

Explain why auditors write to companies' bankers and list the matters you would expect banks to confirm. **(5 marks)**

(Total: 20 marks)

31 DINKO

(DEC 03) (CHAPTER 8)

ISA 315 *Understanding the Entity and its Environment and Assessing the Risks of Material Misstatement* deals with internal control objectives and internal controls. ISA 500 *Audit Evidence* deals with audit objectives and audit procedures. A proper understanding of internal controls is essential to auditors in order that they understand the business and are able to effectively plan and execute tests of controls and an appropriate level of substantive procedures.

You are the auditor of a small manufacturing company, Dinko, that pays its staff in cash and by bank transfer and maintains its payroll on a small stand-alone computer.

Required:

(a) For the payroll department at Dinko, describe the:

(i) internal control objectives that should be in place; **(4 marks)**

(ii) internal control environment and internal control procedures that should be in place to achieve the internal control objectives. **(6 marks)**

(b) For the payroll charges and payroll balances (including cash) in the financial statements of Dinko:

(i) describe the external auditor audit objectives; **(4 marks)**

(ii) list the tests of control and substantive procedures that will be applied in order to achieve the audit objectives identified in (b) (i) above. **(6 marks)**

(Total: 20 marks)

32 FLOWERS ANYWHERE

(DEC 02) (CHAPTER 8)

(a) There are a number of key procedures which auditors should perform if they wish to rely on internal controls and reduce the level of substantive testing they perform. These include:

(i) Documentation of accounting and internal control systems;

(ii) Walk-through tests;

(iii) Audit sampling;

(iv) Testing internal controls;

(v) Dealing with deviations from the application of control procedures.

Required:

Briefly explain each of the procedures listed above. **(10 marks)**

N.B. (i) to (v) above carry equal marks

(b) Flowers Anytime sells flowers wholesale. Customers telephone the company and their orders are taken by clerks who take details of the flowers to be delivered, the address to which they are to be delivered, and account details of the customer. The clerks input these details into the company's computer system (whilst the order is being taken) which is integrated with the company's inventory control system. The company's standard credit terms are payment one month from the order (all orders are despatched within 48 hours) and most customers pay by bank transfer. An accounts receivable ledger is maintained and statements are sent to customers once a month. Credit limits are set by the credit controller according to a standard formula and are automatically applied by the computer system, as are the prices of flowers.

Required:

Describe and explain the purpose of the internal controls you might expect to see in the sales system at Flowers Anytime over the:

(i) Receipt, processing and recording of orders. **(6 marks)**

(ii) Collection of cash. **(4 marks)**

(Total: 20 marks)

33 TWINKLETOES

(JUN 04) (CHAPTER 8)

Required:

(a) Explain how the classification of risks into categories such as 'high', 'medium' or 'low', helps entities manage their businesses. **(4 marks)**

You are the internal auditor of a large private company, Twinkletoes. Twinkletoes manufactures a high volume of reasonably priced shoes for elderly people. The company has a trade receivables ledger that is material to the financial statements containing four different categories of account. The categories of account, and the risks associated with them, are as follows:

(i) small retail shoe shops. These accounts represent nearly two thirds of the accounts on the ledger by number, and one third of the receivables by value. Some of these customers pay promptly, others are very slow;

(ii) large retail shoe shops (including a number of overseas accounts) that sell a wide range of shoes. Some of these accounts are large and overdue;

(iii) chains of discount shoe shops that buy their inventory centrally. These accounts are mostly well-established 'high street' chains. Again, some of these accounts are large and overdue; and

(iv) mail order companies who sell the company's shoes. There have been a number of large new accounts in this category, although there is no history of bad debts in this category.

Receivables listed under (ii) to (iv) are roughly evenly split by both value and number. All receivables are dealt with by the same managers and staff and the same internal controls are applied to each category of receivables. You do not consider that using the same managers and staff, and the same controls, is necessarily the best method of managing the receivables ledger.

Twinkletoes has suffered an increasing level of bad debts and slow payers in recent years, mostly as a result of small shoe shops becoming insolvent. The company has also lost several overseas accounts because of a requirement for them to pay in advance. Management wishes to expand the overseas market and has decided that overseas customers will in future be allowed credit terms.

Management has asked you to classify the risks associated with the receivables ledger in order to manage trade receivables as a whole more efficiently. You have been asked to classify accounts as high, medium or low risk.

Required:

(b) Classify the risks relating to the four categories of trade receivables as high, medium or low and explain your classification. **(8 marks)**

Note: More than one risk classification may be appropriate within each account category.

(c) Describe the internal controls that you would recommend to Twinkletoes to manage the risks associated with the receivables ledger under the headings: *all* customers, *slow paying* customers, *larger* accounts, and *overseas* customers. **(8 marks)**

(Total: 20 marks)

34 CLIFF

(DEC 04) (CHAPTER 8)

Day-to-day internal controls are important for all businesses to maximise the efficient use of resources and profitability.

Your firm has recently been appointed as auditor to Cliff, a private company that runs a chain of small supermarkets selling fresh and frozen food, and canned and dry food. Cliff has very few controls over inventory because the company trusts local managers to make good decisions regarding the purchase, sale and control of inventory, all of which is done locally. Pricing is generally performed on a cost-plus basis.

Each supermarket has a stand-alone computer system on which monthly accounts are prepared. These accounts are mailed to head office every quarter. There is no integrated inventory control, sale or purchasing system and no regular system for inventory counting. Management accounts are produced twice a year.

Trade at the supermarkets has increased in recent years and the number of supermarkets has increased. However, the quality of staff that has been recruited has fallen. Senior management at Cliff are now prepared to invest in more up-to-date systems.

Required:

(a) Describe the problems that you might expect to find at Cliff resulting from poor internal controls. **(8 marks)**

(b) Make FOUR recommendations to the senior management of Cliff for the improvement of internal controls, and explain the advantages and disadvantages of each recommendation. **(12 marks)**

(Total: 20 marks)

AUDIT EVIDENCE

35 WALSH

(DEC 07) (CHAPTER 10)

Walsh Co sells motor vehicle fuel, accessories and spares to retail customers. The company owns 25 shops.

The company has recently implemented a new computerised wages system. Employees work a standard eight hour day. Hours are recorded using a magnetic card system; when each employee arrives for work, they hold their card close to the card reader; the reader recognises the magnetic information on the card identifying the employee as being 'at work'. When the employee leaves work at the end of the day the process is reversed showing that the employee has left work.

Hours worked are calculated each week by the computer system using the magnetic card information. Overtime is calculated as any excess over the standard hours worked. Any overtime over 10% of standard hours is sent on a computer generated report by e-mail to the financial accountant. If necessary, the accountant overrides overtime payments if the hours worked are incorrect. Statutory deductions and net pay are also computer calculated with payments being made directly into the employee's bank account. The only other manual check is the financial accountant authorising the net pay from Walsh's bank account, having reviewed the list of wages to be paid.

Required:

(a) Using examples from Walsh Co, explain the benefits of using Computer-Assisted Audit Techniques to help the auditor to obtain sufficient appropriate audit evidence to be able to draw reasonable conclusions on which to base the audit opinion. **(8 marks)**

(b) List SIX examples of audit tests on Walsh Co's wages system using audit software. **(6 marks)**

(c) Explain how using test data should help in the audit of Walsh Co's wages system, noting any problems with this audit technique. **(6 marks)**

(Total: 20 marks)

36 PORTHOS

(DEC 05) (CHAPTER 10)

(a) Computer-Assisted Audit Techniques (CAATs) are used to assist an auditor in the collection of audit evidence from computerised systems.

Required:

List and briefly explain four advantages of CAATs. **(4 marks)**

(b) Porthos, a limited liability company, is a reseller of sports equipment, specialising in racquet sports such as tennis, squash and badminton. The company purchases equipment from a variety of different suppliers and then resells this using the Internet as the only selling media. The company has over 150 different types of racquets available in inventory, each identified via a unique product code.

Customers place their orders directly on the Internet site. Most orders are for one or two racquets only. The ordering/sales software automatically verifies the order details, customer address and credit card information prior to orders being verified and goods being despatched. The integrity of the ordering system is checked regularly by ArcherWeb, an independent Internet service company.

You are the audit manager working for the external auditors of Porthos, and you have just started planning the audit of the sales system of the company. You have decided to use test data to check the input of details into the sales system. This will involve entering dummy orders into the Porthos system from an online terminal.

Required:

List the test data you will use in your audit of the financial statements of Porthos to confirm the completeness and accuracy of input into the sales system, clearly explaining the reason for each item of data. **(6 marks)**

(c) You are also considering using audit software as part of your substantive testing of the data files in the sales and inventory systems of Porthos.

(i) List and briefly explain some of the difficulties of using audit software; **(4 marks)**

(ii) List the audit tests that you can program into your audit software for the sales and inventory system in Porthos, explaining the reason for each test. **(6 marks)**

(Total: 20 marks)

37 TAM
(DEC 06) (CHAPTER 9)

(a) (i) In the context of ISA 530 *Audit Sampling and Other Means of Testing*, explain and provide examples of the terms 'sampling risk' and 'non-sampling' risk. **(4 marks)**

(ii) Briefly explain how sampling and non-sampling risk can be controlled by the audit firm. **(2 marks)**

(b) Tam Co, is owned and managed by two brothers with equal shareholdings. The company specialises in the sale of expensive motor vehicles. Annual revenue is in the region of $70,000,000 and the company requires an audit under local legislation. About 500 cars are sold each year, with an average value of $140,000, although the range of values is from $130,000 to $160,000. Invoices are completed manually with one director signing all invoices to confirm the sales value is correct. All accounting and financial statement preparation is carried out by the directors. A recent expansion of the company's showroom was financed by a bank loan, repayable over the next five years.

The audit manager is starting to plan the audit of Tam Co. The audit senior and audit junior assigned to the audit are helping the manager as a training exercise.

Comments are being made about how to select a sample of sales invoices for testing. Audit procedures are needed to ensure that the managing director has signed them and then to trace details into the sales day book and sales ledger.

'We should check all invoices' suggests the audit manager.

'How about selecting a sample using statistical sampling techniques' adds the audit senior.

'Why waste time obtaining a sample?' asks the audit junior. He adds 'taking a random sample of invoices by reviewing the invoice file and manually choosing a few important invoices will be much quicker.'

Required:

Briefly explain each of the sample selection methods suggested by the audit manager, audit senior and audit junior, and discuss whether or not they are appropriate for obtaining a representative sample of sales invoices. **(9 marks)**

(c) Define 'materiality' and explain why the auditors of Tam Co must form an opinion on whether the financial statements are free from material misstatement. **(5 marks)**

(Total: 20 marks)

38 STRATHFIELD
(DEC 99) (CHAPTER 9)

The recorded value of Strathfield's accounts receivable, as at 31 October 20X2, was $2,350,000.

Out of the 5,350 accounts receivable, Sarah Jones selected 120 accounts for confirmation as part of the external audit of the company.

In selecting accounts for confirmation Sarah picked the 10 largest accounts totalling $205,000 and 110 other accounts selected haphazardly. Her working paper states that she rejected any accounts that were less than $100 as not being worth confirming and accounts with government bodies since she knew they never bother replying to confirmation requests.

Each of the 10 largest accounts was satisfactorily confirmed. Sarah analysed the responses to the confirmation of the other 110 accounts as follows:

Result of confirmation	*Number of accounts*	*Recorded amount*	*Amount confirmed*
		$	$
Satisfactorily confirmed	75	245,000	245,000
Confirmation returned marked 'gone away – address unknown'	4	950	0
Cut-off differences due to cash or goods in transit	8	6,800	5,750
Invoicing errors	4	2,800	2,200
Invoices posted to the wrong customer's account	2	1,300	980
Disputed as to price or quantity or quality of goods	3	2,800	1,300
Not confirmed – verified by alternative procedures	14	5,800	5,800
Totals	110	265,450	261,030

Sarah is about to draw up her working paper in which she reaches a conclusion as to whether the results of the confirmation of accounts receivable enables her to conclude that the recorded balance is not materially misstated. She is aware that ISA 530 *Audit Sampling and Other Means of Testing* requires her to:

1 consider the qualitative aspects of errors and whether any of these relate to a sub-population and not to accounts receivable as a whole; and

2 project the error results of the sample to the population from which the sample was selected.

Required:

(a) Discuss Sarah's method of selecting items to be confirmed. Your answer should:

(i) identify any aspects of her approach that might be considered inconsistent with sampling

(ii) suggest alternative means of selecting a sample ensuring that the more material balances stand the greatest chance of selection

(iii) compare and contrast the haphazard method of selection with random selection and systematic selection. **(10 marks)**

(b) Consider qualitative aspects of each of the five categories of error or other reported differences analysed by Sarah. Suggest which of them should be included in arriving at an estimate of population error. (6 marks)

(c) Calculate the projected error in accounts receivable based on the results of the sample test consistent with the qualitative considerations in your answer to (b). (4 marks)

(Total: 20 marks)

39 INTERNAL CONTROL AND SAMPLING

(JUN 03) (CHAPTER 9)

(a) Internal controls over non-current assets are designed to ensure the orderly and efficient running of the business, adherence to management policies, safeguarding of assets, the prevention of fraud and error and the completeness and accuracy of the accounting records.

Required:

List the internal controls that a small printing company with office equipment, motor vehicles and plant and machinery should have in place to achieve the objectives described above. **(10 marks)**

(b) Audit sampling is a technique for drawing conclusions about the characteristics of a population by testing a sample drawn therefrom. Internal and external auditors use it for both tests of controls and substantive testing.

Required:

Describe the following:

(i) Judgement sampling and statistical sampling;

(ii) A representative sample;

(iii) Tolerable error;

(iv) Two different methods of selecting a representative sample;

(v) The extrapolation of errors.

Note: Parts (i) – (v) carry equal marks. **(10 marks)**

(Total: 20 marks)

40 ISA 500 ASSERTIONS

(DEC 04) (CHAPTER 10)

ISA 500 *Audit Evidence (Revised)* states that management implicitly or explicitly makes assertions relating to the various elements of financial statements including related disclosures. Auditors may use three categories of assertions to form a basis for risk assessments and the design and performance of further audit procedures. The three categories suggested by ISA 500 relate to (i) classes of transactions, (ii) account balances, and (iii) presentation and disclosure. One assertion applicable to all three categories is completeness: that all transactions, events, assets, liabilities, equity interests and disclosures that should be included, are included in the financial statements.

Required:

(a) List and describe SIX financial statement assertions, other than completeness, used by auditors in the audit of financial statements. **(6 marks)**

(b) Boulder is a small company that manufactures hosiery products. It employs approximately 150 staff, all of whom are paid by bank transfer.

Temporary factory staff are hired through an agency and are paid on piece rates (i.e. for the number of items that they produce or process) on a weekly basis. Supervisors at Boulder authorise documentation indicating the number of items produced or processed by agency staff. The agency is paid by bank transfer and it, not Boulder, is responsible for the deduction of tax and social insurance.

Permanent factory staff are paid on a weekly basis on the basis of hours worked as evidenced by clock cards. Administration and sales staff are paid a monthly salary. The two directors of the company are also paid a monthly salary.

Sales staff are paid a quarterly bonus calculated on the basis of sales. Directors are paid an annual bonus based on profits.

You will be performing the audit of the financial statements for the year ending 31 December 20X4 and you will be responsible for the figures in the financial statements relating to payroll.

Required:

Describe the substantive audit procedures you will perform on:

(i) the payroll balances in the balance sheet of Boulder; **(10 marks)**

(ii) the payroll transactions in the income statement of Boulder. **(4 marks)**

(Total: 20 marks)

41 VILLAWOOD COMPUTERS

(DEC 99) (CHAPTER 10)

The firm of Chartered Certified Accountants you are employed by is the external auditor of Villawood Computers, a privately owned incorporated business.

Accounting records are maintained on a computer using proprietary software.

You have worked on the audit for three years and this year you are in charge of the audit. Your assistant is a newly recruited business graduate who has done an accounting course but has no practical experience.

Because of the small size of the company there is limited opportunity for segregation of duties. You decide, as in previous years, that the appropriate audit strategy is to obtain evidence primarily through the performance of substantive procedures. You also plan to perform the audit around the computer as the proprietary software is known to be reliable and details of all transactions and balances can be readily printed out.

On arriving at the company's premises in December 20X2 to perform the final audit on the 31 October 20X2 financial statements, you obtain a copy of the year end bank reconciliation prepared by the bookkeeper and checked by the managing director. This is reproduced below.

Villawood Computers
Bank Reconciliation 31 October 20X2

	$	$
Balance per bank statement 31 October 20X2		18,375.91
Deposits outstanding		
30 October	1,887.00	
31 October	1,973.00	3,860.00
		22,235.91

Villawood Computers
Bank Reconciliation 31 October 20X2

	$	$
Outstanding cheques		
2696	25.00	
2724	289.40	
2725	569.00	
2728	724.25	
2729	1,900.00	
2730	398.00	
2731	53.50	
2732	1,776.00	
2733	255.65	5,990.80
		16,245.11
Cheque returned 'not sufficient funds' 29 October		348.00
Bank charges October		90.00
Balance per books 31 October 20X2		$16,683.11

You have already obtained the bank confirmation and lists of cash (and cheque) receipts and payments printed out from the computer. These lists have been added and the totals agreed with ledger postings. You decide the first task to set for your assistant is the verification of the bank reconciliation.

Required:

(a) (i) List the audit procedures to be followed by your assistant in verifying the bank reconciliation in sufficient detail for an inexperienced staff member to follow. **(6 marks)**

(ii) Explain the purpose of each procedure in terms of audit objectives. **(5 marks)**

(b) Discuss the reliability of bank statements as audit evidence. What steps can be taken if it is considered desirable to increase their reliability? **(3 marks)**

(c) (i) Distinguish between 'auditing around the computer' and 'auditing through the computer'. **(3 marks)**

(ii) Explain the circumstances when it would be inappropriate for the auditor to rely on auditing around the computer. **(3 marks)**

(Total: 20 marks)

42 OATLEY

(DEC 99) (CHAPTER 10)

Oatley is a small privately incorporated manufacturing company of which your firm of Chartered Certified Accountants is the external auditor. You have been assigned to the audit of accounts payable.

The audit file indicates that control risk for purchase and payments transactions is assessed as slightly less than high because of limitations in the extent of segregation of duties due to the small number of accounts personnel. There are no other identified control problems or prior year audit problems.

Narrative notes on the accounting system contain the following description:

- Purchases are requisitioned by the user department and ordered, using prenumbered order forms, by the purchasing manager.
- Raw materials and manufacturing supplies are delivered to the receiving department of the factory where the receiver issues prenumbered goods received notes (GRNs).
- Purchases of other goods and services are delivered directly to the requisitioning department and no GRNs are issued.
- The accounts department checks suppliers' invoices with purchase orders, and:
  - for production department purchases, with GRNs
  - for other purchases, sends the invoices to the requisitioning department manager who initials the invoice to indicate that it is appropriate to pay.
- Invoices are then processed to the accounting records using proprietary software.
- All accounts payable are paid at the end of the month following the month of receipt of the invoice.

Accounts payable at 31 October 20X2, therefore, represent goods and services invoiced in October. In addition, invoices received between 1 and 15 November were divided into those relating to goods received or services provided before and after 31 October, the former being recorded in the accounting records before the October trial balance was produced. On 15 November, any unmatched GRNs relating to deliveries before 31 October were posted to the accounts as at 31 October at the estimated amounts of the invoices.

Suppliers' invoices are filed alphabetically with supporting documentation, all of which is cancelled with the date of payment when the cheque is issued. Suppliers' monthly statements are also filed with the invoices. These are scrutinised by the accounts department for unusual items, such as overdue invoices, but are not regularly reconciled with the company's own records.

Required:

(a) In your audit of accounts payable in the 31 October 20X2 financial statements explain which of the financial statement assertions you would regard as presenting the greatest inherent risk. **(4 marks)**

(b) Discuss the reasons for undertaking or not undertaking an accounts payable circularisation. **(4 marks)**

(c) Outline substantive procedures you would apply in your audit of accounts payable relating to production department purchases. **(6 marks)**

(d) Explain additional procedures you would perform in verifying the completeness of non-production department payables. **(6 marks)**

(Total: 20 marks)

43 REDFERN

(JUN 00) (CHAPTER 10)

As a staff member of Reddy and Abel, Chartered Certified Accountants you are assigned to the audit of property, plant and equipment of Redfern Limited for the year ended 31 March 20X2. Reddy and Abel have been the auditors of Redfern for many years. You obtain the following schedule of non-current asset movements and analysis of additions from the company's accountant:

	Property	*Plant and machinery*	*Total*
Cost or valuation	$000	$000	$000
1 April 20X1	340	275	615
Additions		123	123
Disposals		(72)	(72)
Revaluations	120		120
31 March 20X2	460	326	786
Accumulated depreciation	$000	$000	$000
1 April 20X1	24	213	237
Charge	5	30	35
Written back on disposal		(65)	(65)
Adjustment on revaluation	(24)		(24)
31 March 20X2	5	178	183
Written down value	455	148	603

Schedule of additions (Plant and machinery)

Supplier	*Description*	*Cost*
		$
New Models Ltd	Milling machine Model 38	55,000
Drill Suppliers	Power drill Type 45C	34,000
Hoist Co Ltd	Electric hoist no 722	18,000
	Sundry below $1,000	16,000
		123,000

The company's accountant also advises you that the property was revalued following a valuation by the company's property manager who is a professionally qualified valuer.

During your verification of depreciation you discover that most plant and machinery is fully depreciated. Moreover you discover that, due to oversight, depreciation has continued to be provided on fully depreciated items. As at the beginning of the year the amount of overstatement was $43,000. The accountant suggests the correction be made by reducing the current year's charge for depreciation.

Required:

(a) State, with reasons, the initial audit procedures you would perform on the schedules provided by the company's accountant. **(3 marks)**

(b) Outline the substantive audit procedures you would apply in verifying additions to plant and equipment. Your answer should identify procedures applicable to each of the financial statement assertions. **(8 marks)**

(c) Describe the audit procedures applicable to verifying the revaluation of property. **(5 marks)**

(d) With respect to the correction to accumulated depreciation, and assuming the amount to be material, discuss the accountant's proposed treatment. If you disagree with the accountant's proposal, state, with reasons, the correct accounting treatment. **(4 marks)**

(Total: 20 marks)

44 TRACEY TRANSPORTERS

(JUN 05) (CHAPTER 10)

You are the external auditor of Tracey Transporters, a public limited company (TT). The company's year end is 31 March. You have been the auditor since the company was formed 24 years ago to take advantage of the increase in goods being transported by road. Many companies needed to transport their products but did not always have sufficient vehicles to move them. TT therefore purchased ten vehicles and hired these to haulage companies for amounts of time ranging from three days to six months.

The business has grown in size and profitability and now has over 550 vehicles on hire to many different companies. At any one time, between five and 20 vehicles are located at the company premises where they are being repaired; the rest could be anywhere on the extensive road network of the country it operates in. Full details of all vehicles are maintained in a non-current asset register.

Bookings for hire of vehicles are received either over the telephone or via e-mail in TT's offices. A booking clerk checks the customer's credit status on the receivables ledger and then the availability of vehicles using the Vehicle Management System (VMS) software on TT's computer network. E-mails are filed electronically by customer name in the e-mail program used by TT. If the customer's credit rating is acceptable and a vehicle is available, the booking is entered into the VMS and confirmed to the customer using the telephone or e-mail. Booking information is then transferred within the network from the VMS to the receivables ledger program, where a sales invoice is raised. Standard rental amounts are allocated to each booking depending on the amount of time the vehicle is being hired for. Hard copy invoices are sent in the post for telephone orders or via e-mail for e-mail orders.

The main class of asset on TT's balance sheet is the vehicles. The net book value of the vehicles is $6 million out of total shareholders' funds of $15 million as at 31 March 20X5.

Required:

(a) List and explain the reason for the audit tests you should perform to check the completeness and accuracy of the sales figure in TT's financial statements. **(10 marks)**

(b) List and describe the audit work you should perform on the balance sheet figure for vehicles in TT's financial statements for the year ended 31 March 20X5. **(10 marks)**

(Total: 20 marks)

45 LIDCOMBE

(DEC 00) (CHAPTER 10)

Lidcombe is a privately owned incorporated business whose accounting system is based on a well known accounting software package. The company maintains two accounts receivables ledgers, the Home ledger for customers in the same country and the Export ledger for customers in other countries. As at 31 October 20X2 there were 220 accounts in the Home ledger with balances totalling $350,000 and 90 accounts in the Export ledger with balances totalling $120,000.

Henry Jones and Mary Green, members of Lidcombe's firm of external auditors, have been given responsibility for the audit of accounts receivable.

Henry decides to undertake a positive circularisation of a sample of balances on the Home ledger. Because of poor response rates in prior audits, Mary decides to use alternative procedures in verifying the balance on the Export ledger.

Mary produces the following working paper:

A B Partners

D-3

Client Lidcome		**Prepared by** MG	**Date** 3/12/X2
Year end 31 October 20X2		**Reviewed by**	**Date**

Total export debtors

Audit test

5 customers' accounts selected for testing.

Customer	*Balance*	*Comment*
Doh	20,000	1
Ray	2,500	2
Mee	120	3
Fah	1,000	4
Soh	750	5

Total $24,370 = 20% of total export debtors.

Notes:

1. Made up of many small invoices. Checked a sample to copy invoice in Lidcombe's files.
2. In dispute. Customer claims goods were faulty.
3. Vouched to original customer order and goods delivered note signed by customer.
4. Balance incorrect. Credit note for $500 issued in November 20X2. Noted on A-4, Schedule of uncorrected differences.
5. Paid 15 November 20X2. Agreed to remittance advice and deposit slip date stamped by the bank.

% – agreed to general ledger trial balance.

Required:

(a) Describe the procedures Henry should perform from arrival at Lidcombe's premises to undertake the circularisation up to his mailing of the requests for confirmation.

(6 marks)

(b) Explain how Henry can use computer audit software (CAS) to assist him in the process of confirming accounts receivable. **(5 marks)**

(c) State the matters that you would expect to be raised by the audit manager on reviewing Mary's working paper. **(9 marks)**

(Total: 20 marks)

46 COMPANY A AND COMPANY B – LIABILITIES

(DEC 02) (CHAPTER 10)

(a) Company A has a number of long and short-term payables, accruals and provisions in its balance sheet.

Required:

Describe the audit procedures you would apply to each of the three items listed below, including those relating to disclosure.

(i) A 10-year bank loan with a variable interest rate and an overdraft (a bank account with a debit balance on the bank statement), both from the same bank. **(5 marks)**

(ii) Expense accruals. **(4 marks)**

(iii) Trade payables and purchase accruals. **(6 marks)**

(b) Company B has a provision in its balance sheet for claims made by customers for product defects under 1-year company warranties.

Required:

Describe the matters you would consider and the audit evidence you would require for the provision. **(5 marks)**

(Total: 20 marks)

47 BARDWELL

(JUN 01) (CHAPTER 10)

Bardwell is a privately owned incorporated business that operates a garage which repairs and services motor vehicles. Most customers are required to pay by cash or cheque on collecting their vehicle. Credit accounts are available to business customers. These customers sign the invoice on collection of the vehicle and their business is billed monthly. Separate series of prenumbered invoices are drawn up by the foreman for cash sales and for credit sales. All customer accounts are maintained by the receptionist. His duties include the following:

Cash sales

- Collect cash or cheques from customers on collecting their vehicle.
- At the end of the day, check the numerical sequence of cash sales invoices, add the sales total and agree the total to the amount of cash and cheques received.
- Record the total cash sales in the cash receipts book.

Credit sales

- Obtain the customer's signature on the copy invoice of business account customers.
- Enter the invoices in numerical sequence in the sales journal and post the customer's account in the accounts receivable ledger.
- Send monthly statements to credit account customers and follow up overdue accounts.

- List the balances on the accounts receivable ledger at the end of the month and reconcile the total with the control account in the general ledger.
- Write off uncollectable balances to bad debts.

Cash receipts

- Open the mail, extract cheques from credit account customers, record them in the cash receipts book and post the accounts receivable ledger.
- Make up the day's banking cash (and cheques) from both cash and credit sales, prepare the deposit slip and bank the cash (and cheques).

All other accounting duties are the responsibility of two further accounts clerks and all are subject to supervision by the garage manager.

Required:

(a) (i) Explain why the functions assigned to the receptionist result in an inadequate segregation of duties. Your explanation should identify misstatements that could occur and indicate how those duties could be reassigned to other staff members; **(8 marks)**

(ii) Identify other control procedures you would consider necessary to ensure the completeness of the recorded cash receipts and accounts receivable **(4 marks)**

(b) As a member of the audit staff of the company's external auditors, you visit the garage and make a count of cash on hand. You subsequently compare details of unbanked cash receipts that you counted with the entry in the cash receipts book for that date. Although the total in the cash receipts book is the same, the amount of banknotes and coins is less and there is a cheque from a business customer that you did not record.

(i) Explain the procedures to be followed in making a cash count for audit purposes; **(4 marks)**

(ii) Explain the irregularity that the discrepancy between cash count and cash receipts book might lead you to suspect, and describe how you would investigate the discrepancy. **(4 marks)**

(Total: 20 marks)

48 INVENTORY COUNTS

(JUN 03) (CHAPTER 10)

Some organisations conduct inventory counts once a year and external auditors attend those counts. Other organisations have continuous inventory counting procedures and do not conduct a year-end count.

Required:

(a) Explain why year-end inventory counting is important to the auditors of organisations that do not have continuous inventory counting procedures. **(4 marks)**

(b) Describe audit procedures you would perform in order to rely on continuous inventory counting procedures in a large, dispersed organisation. **(4 marks)**

(c) Snu is a family-owned company which retails beds, mattresses and other bedroom furniture items. The company's year-end is 31 December 20X3. The only full inventory count takes place at the year-end. The company maintains up-to-date computerised inventory records.

Where the company delivers goods to customers, a deposit is taken from the customer and customers are invoiced for the balance after the delivery. Some goods that are in inventory at the year-end have already been paid for in full – customers who collect goods themselves pay by cash or credit card.

Staff at the company's warehouse and shop will conduct the year-end count. The shop and warehouse are open seven days a week except for two public holidays during the year, one of which is 1 January. The company is very busy in the week prior to the inventory count but the shops will close at 15.00 hours on 31 December and staff will work until 17.00 hours to prepare the inventory for counting. The company has a high turnover of staff.

The following inventory counting instructions have been provided to staff at Snu:

(i) The inventory count will take place on 1 January 20X4 commencing at 09.00 hours. No movement of inventory will take place on that day.

(ii) The count will be supervised by Mr Sneg, the inventory controller. All staff will be provided with pre-printed, pre-numbered inventory counting sheets that are produced by the computerised system. Mr Sneg will ensure that all sheets are issued, and that all are collected at the end of the count.

(iii) Counters will work on their own, because there are insufficient staff for them to work in pairs, but they will be supervised by Mr Sneg and Mrs Zapad, an experienced shop manager who will make checks on the work performed by counters. Staff will count inventory with which they are most familiar in order to ensure that the count is completed as quickly and efficiently as possible.

(iv) Any inventory that is known to be old, slow-moving or already sold will be highlighted on the sheets. Staff are required to highlight any inventory that appears to be soiled or damaged.

(v) All inventory items counted will have a piece of paper attached to them that will show that they have been counted.

(vi) All inventory that has been delivered to customers but that has not yet been paid for in full will be added back to the inventory quantities by Mr Sneg.

Required:

Describe the weaknesses in Snu's inventory counting instructions and explain why these weaknesses are difficult to overcome. **(12 marks)**

(Total: 20 marks)

49 AJIO

(DEC 03) (CHAPTER 10)

Ajio is a charity whose constitution requires that it raises funds for educational projects. These projects seek to educate children and support teachers in certain countries. Charities in the country from which Ajio operates have recently become subject to new audit and accounting regulations. Charity income consists of cash collections at fund raising events, telephone appeals, and bequests (money left to the charity by deceased persons). The charity is small and the trustees do not consider that the charity can afford to employ a qualified accountant. The charity employs a part-time bookkeeper and relies on volunteers for fund raising. Your firm has been appointed as accountants and auditors to this charity because of the new regulations. Accounts have been prepared (but not audited) in the past by a volunteer who is a recently retired Chartered Certified Accountant.

Required:

(a) Describe the risks associated with the audit of Ajio under the headings inherent risk, control risk and detection risk and explain the implications of these risks for overall audit risk. **(10 marks)**

(b) List and explain the audit tests to be performed on income and expenditure from fund raising events. **(10 marks)**

Note: In part (a) you may deal with inherent risk and control risk together. You are not required to deal with the detail of accounting for charities in either part of the question. **(Total: 20 marks)**

50 FIZZIPOP

(JUN 04) (CHAPTER 10)

Fizzipop manufactures and distributes soft drinks. Its inventories are controlled using a real-time system which provides accurate records of quantities and costs of inventories held at any point in time. This system is known within the company as the 'Stockpop' system and it is integrated with the purchases and sales system. Fizzipop has an internal audit department whose activities encompass inventories.

No year-end inventory count takes place. Inventories are held in several large warehouses where non-stop production takes place.

Your firm is the external auditor to Fizzipop and you have been asked to perform the audit of inventories. Inventories include finished goods and raw materials (water, sugar, sweeteners, carbonating materials, flavourings, cans, bottles, bottle tops, fastenings and packaging materials).

Your firm, which has several offices, wishes to rely on the 'Stockpop' system to provide the basis of the figure to be included in the financial statements for inventories. Your firm does not wish to ask the company to conduct a year-end inventory count.

Required:

(a) Describe the audit tests that you would perform on the 'Stockpop' system during the year in order to determine whether to rely on it as a basis for the raw materials and finished goods figures to be included in the financial statements. **(11 marks)**

Note: You are not required to deal with work in progress.

(b) Describe the audit tests you would perform on the records held by Fizzipop at the year-end to ensure that raw materials and finished goods are fairly stated in the financial statements. **(9 marks)**

(Total: 20 marks)

51 CURDCO

(JUN 04) (CHAPTER 10)

Curdco is a company that runs a chain of fast food restaurants. The company has a centralised operating style and managers of individual restaurants have very limited decision-making powers on day-to-day operational matters. The company's centralised administration is responsible for the buying of food, the payment of staff, the maintenance and cleaning of restaurants by staff employed by a national agency, and all other matters relating to the running of the business. The company has good internal controls over purchasing. Inventory counts are conducted at each restaurant at the year-end. Your firm has recently been appointed as auditor to Curdco.

Required:

(a) List the account headings you would expect to find in Curdco's schedule of accounts payable and accrued expenditure. **(3 marks)**

(b) Describe and give reasons for the audit tests you would carry out to obtain audit evidence for Curdco's accounts payable and accrued expenditure. **(12 marks)**

(c) Explain the difficulties faced by auditors, and the decisions that auditors have to make, in conducting direct confirmations of accounts payable. **(5 marks)**

(Total: 20 marks)

52 BEARSWORLD
(JUN 05) (CHAPTER 10)

You are the auditor of BearsWorld, a limited liability company which manufactures and sells small cuddly toys by mail order. The company is managed by Mr Kyto and two assistants. Mr Kyto authorises important transactions such as wages and large orders, one assistant maintains the payables ledger and orders inventory and pays suppliers, and the other assistant receives customer orders and despatches cuddly toys. Due to other business commitments Mr Kyto only visits the office once per week.

At any time, about 100 different types of cuddly toys are available for sale. All sales are made cash with order – there are no receivables. Customers pay using credit cards and occasionally by sending cash. Turnover is over $5.2 million.

You are planning the audit of BearsWorld and are considering using some of the procedures for gathering audit evidence recommended by ISA 500 as follows:

(i) Analytical Procedures

(ii) Inquiry

(iii) Inspection

(iv) Observation

(v) Re-calculation

Required:

(a) For EACH of the above procedures:

(i) Explain its use in gathering audit evidence. **(5 marks)**

(ii) Describe one example for the audit of BearsWorld. **(5 marks)**

(b) Discuss the suitability of each procedure for BearsWorld, explaining the limitations of each. **(10 marks)**

(Total: 20 marks)

53 ATLANTIS
(JUN 06) (CHAPTER 10)

(a) State the control objectives for the ordering, despatch and invoicing of goods. **(5 marks)**

(b) Atlantis Standard Goods (ASG) Co has a year end of 30 June 2006. ASG is a retailer of kitchen appliances such as washing machines, fridges and microwaves. All sales are made via the company's Internet site with despatch and delivery of goods to the customer's house made using ASG's vehicles. Appliances are purchased from many different manufacturers.

The process of making a sale is as follows:

(1) Potential customers visit ASG's website and select the kitchen appliance that they require. The website ordering system accesses the inventory specification file to obtain details of products ASG sells.

(2) When the customer chooses an appliance, order information including price, item and quantity required are stored in the orders pending file.

(3) Online authorisation of credit card details is obtained from the customer's credit card company automatically by ASG's computer systems.

(4) Following authorisation, the sales amount is transferred to the computerised sales day book. At the end of each day the total from this ledger is transferred to the general ledger.

(5) Reimbursement of the sales amount is obtained from each credit card company monthly, less the appropriate commission charged by the credit card company.

(6) Following authorisation of the credit card, order details are transferred to a goods awaiting despatch file and allocated a unique order reference code. Order details are automatically transferred to the despatch department's computer system.

(7) In the despatch department, goods are obtained from the physical inventory, placed on ASG vehicles and the computerised inventory system updated. Order information is downloaded on a hand held computer with a writable screen.

(8) On delivery, the customer signs for the goods on the hand held computer. On return to ASG's warehouse, images of the customer signature are uploaded to the orders file which is then flagged as 'order complete'.

This year's audit planning documentation states that a substantive approach will be taken on the audit.

Required:

Tabulate the audit tests you should carry out on the sales and despatch system, explaining the reason for each test. **(15 marks)**

(Total: 20 marks)

54 JAYNE

(DEC 06) (CHAPTER 10)

(a) ISA 505, *External Confirmations*, states that 'the auditor should determine whether the use of external confirmations is necessary to obtain sufficient appropriate audit evidence at the assertion level'.

Required:

(i) List FOUR examples of external confirmations. **(2 marks)**

(ii) For EACH of the examples in (i) above explain:

ONE audit assertion that the external confirmation supports, and

ONE audit assertion that the external confirmation does NOT support. **(8 marks)**

(b) Jayne Co has a significant number of cash transactions and recent non-current asset purchases have been financed by a bank loan. This loan is repayable in equal annual instalments for the next five years.

Required:

(i) Explain the procedures to obtain a bank report for audit purposes from Jayne Co's bank and the substantive procedures that should be carried out on that report. **(5 marks)**

(ii) List the further substantive procedures that should be carried out on the bank balances in Jayne Co's financial statements. **(5 marks)**

(Total: 20 marks)

55 FIREFLY TENNIS CLUB

(DEC 06) (CHAPTER 10)

The FireFly Tennis Club owns 12 tennis courts. The club uses 'all weather' tarmac tennis courts, which have floodlights for night-time use. The club's year end is 30 September.

Members pay an annual fee to use the courts and participate in club championships. The club had 430 members as at 1 October 2005.

Income is derived from two main sources:

1. Membership fees. Each member pays a fee of $200 per annum. Fees for the new financial year are payable within one month of the club year end. Approximately 10% of members do not renew their membership. New members joining during the year pay 50% of the total fees that would have been payable had they been members for a full year. During 2006, 50 new members joined the club. No members pay their fees before they are due.

2. Court hire fees: Non-members pay $5 per hour to hire a court. Non-members have to sign a list in the club house showing courts hired. Money is placed in a cash box in the club house for collection by the club secretary.

All fees (membership and court hire) are paid in cash. They are collected by the club secretary and banked on a regular basis. The paying-in slip shows the analysis between fees and court hire income. The secretary provides the treasurer with a list of bankings showing member's names (for membership fees) and the amount banked. Details of all bankings are entered into the cash book by the treasurer.

Main items of expenditure are:

1. Court maintenance including repainting lines on a regular basis.

2. Power costs for floodlights.

3. Tennis balls for club championships. Each match in the championship uses 12 tennis balls.

The treasurer pays for all expenditure using the club's debit card. Receipts are obtained for all expenses and these are maintained in date order in an expenses file. The treasurer also prepares the annual financial statements.

Under the rules of the club, the annual accounts must be audited by an independent auditor. The date is now 13 December 2006 and the treasurer has just prepared the financial statements for audit.

Required:

(a) Describe the audit work that should be performed to determine the completeness of income for the FireFly Tennis Club. **(10 marks)**

(b) Describe the audit procedures that should be performed to check the completeness and accuracy of expenditure for the FireFly Tennis Club. **(5 marks)**

(c) Discuss why internal control testing has limited value when auditing not-for-profit entities such as the FireFly Tennis Club. **(5 marks)**

(Total: 20 marks)

56 DECE & CO
(DEC 05) (CHAPTER 10)

You are the audit manager in the firm of DeCe & Co, an audit firm with ten national offices.

One of your clients, Rocks Forever, purchases diamond jewellery from three manufacturers. The jewellery is then sold from Rocks Forever's four shops. This is the only client your firm has in the diamond industry.

You are planning to attend the physical inventory count for Rocks Forever. Inventory is the largest account on the balance sheet with each of the four shops holding material amounts. Due to the high value of the inventory, all shops will be visited and test counts performed.

With the permission of the directors of Rocks Forever, you have employed UJ, a firm of specialist diamond valuers who will also be in attendance. UJ will verify that the jewellery is, in fact, made from diamonds and that the jewellery is saleable with respect to current trends in fashion. UJ will also suggest, on a sample basis, the value of specific items of jewellery.

Counting will be carried out by shop staff in teams of two using pre-numbered count sheets.

Required:

(a) List and explain the reason for the audit procedures used in obtaining evidence in relation to the inventory count of inventory held in the shops. **(10 marks)**

(b) Explain the factors you should consider when placing reliance on the work of UJ. **(5 marks)**

(c) Describe the audit procedures you should perform to ensure that jewellery inventory is valued correctly. **(5 marks)**

(Total: 20 marks)

REVIEW

57 ISA 210/ 580/260
(JUN 01) (CHAPTER 11)

Two important communications between the auditors and the management or Board of Directors of the client entity are commonly referred to as *Letter of Representation* and the *Management Report* (or Letter of Weaknesses). Both communications are referred to in ISA 210 *Terms of Audit Engagements*. The letter of representation is, additionally, the subject of ISA 580 *Management Representations* and the management report is referred to in ISA 260 *Communication of Audit Matters with those Charged with Governance*.

Required:

(a) Letter of representation:

(i) Explain the purpose of the letter of representation and the extent to which it constitutes sufficient appropriate audit evidence. **(5 marks)**

(ii) Describe three matters you might find in a letter of representation (other than the acknowledgement by management of its responsibility for the financial statements). **(3 marks)**

(iii) Explain the effect, on the audit, if management refuse to make one or more of the representations requested. **(3 marks)**

(b) Management report:

(i) Describe the procedures associated with the communication of control weaknesses to management relating to:

– timing of the communication

– method of communication

– level of management to which communication should be made. **(4 marks)**

(ii) Discuss the extent of the auditors' responsibility for detecting and reporting internal control weaknesses. **(5 marks)**

(Total: 20 marks)

58 CRIGHTON-WARD

(JUN 05) (CHAPTER 11)

(a) Explain the purpose of a management representation letter. **(5 marks)**

(b) You are the manager in charge of the audit of Crighton-Ward, a public limited liability company which manufactures specialist cars and other motor vehicles for use in films. Audited turnover is $140 million with profit before tax of $7.5 million.

All audit work up to, but not including, the obtaining of management representations has been completed. A review of the audit file has disclosed the following outstanding points:

Lion's Roar

The company is facing a potential legal claim from the Lion's Roar company in respect of a defective vehicle that was supplied for one of their films. Lion's Roar maintains that the vehicle was not built strongly enough while the directors of Crighton-Ward argue that the specification was not sufficiently detailed. Dropping a vehicle 50 metres into a river and expecting it to continue to remain in working condition would be unusual, but this is what Lion's Roar expected. Solicitors are unable to determine liability at the present time. A claim for $4 million being the cost of a replacement vehicle and lost production time has been received by Crighton-Ward from Lions' Roar. The directors' opinion is that the claim is not justified.

Depreciation

Depreciation of specialist production equipment has been included in the financial statements at the amount of 10% pa based on reducing balance. The treatment is consistent with prior accounting periods (which received an unmodified auditor's report) and other companies in the same industry and sales of old equipment show negligible profit or loss on sale. The audit senior, who is new to the audit, feels that depreciation is being undercharged in the financial statements.

Required:

For each of the above matters:

(i) discuss whether or not a paragraph is required in the representation letter; and

(ii) if appropriate, draft the paragraph for inclusion in the representation letter. **(10 marks)**

(c) A suggested format for the letter of representation has been sent by the auditors to the directors of Crighton-Ward. The directors have stated that they will not sign the letter of representation this year on the grounds that they believe the additional evidence that it provides is not required by the auditor.

Required:

Discuss the actions the auditor may take as a result of the decision made by the directors not to sign the letter of representation. **(5 marks)**

(Total: 20 marks)

59 LALD

(DEC 05) (CHAPTER 11)

You are the auditor of LALD, a limited liability company. The main activity of the company is the construction of buildings ranging in size from individual houses to large offices and blocks of flats.

Under the laws of the country LALD operates in, LALD must add sales tax to all buildings sold and they pay this tax to the government at the end of each month.

The largest non-current asset on LALD's balance sheet is the plant and machinery used in the construction of buildings. Due to the variety of different assets used, four different sub-classes of plant and machinery are recognised, each with its own rate of depreciation.

You are now reaching the end of the audit work for the year ended 30 September 2005. There are two specific matters where additional audit work is required:

(i) The sales tax for the month of August was not paid to the government. This appears to have been an accidental error and the amount involved is not material to the financial statements.

(ii) The complicated method of calculating depreciation for plant and machinery appears to have resulted in depreciation being calculated incorrectly, with the result that depreciation may have been under-provided in the financial statements.

Required:

(a) Explain the additional audit procedures you should take regarding the accidental underpayment of sales tax. **(7 marks)**

(b) Explain the additional audit procedures you should take regarding the possible underprovision of depreciation. **(7 marks)**

(c) You have determined that the under-provision is material to the financial statements and therefore need to modify the audit report. The directors have informed you that they do not intend to take any action regarding the underprovision of depreciation. They also disagree with your action and have threatened to remove your company as the auditors of LALD unless you agree not to modify your report.

Required:

Explain the procedures that the directors must follow in order to remove your company as the auditors of LALD. **(6 marks)**

(Total: 20 marks)

60 GREEN CO

(JUN 07) (CHAPTER 11)

Green Co grows crops on a large farm according to strict organic principles that prohibits the use of artificial pesticides and fertilizers. The farm has an 'organic certification', which guarantees its products are to be organic. The certification has increased its sales of flour, potatoes and other products, as customers seek to eat more healthily.

Green Co is run by two managers who are the only shareholders. Annual revenue is $50 million with a net profit of 5%. Both managers have run other businesses in the last 10 years. One business was closed due to suspected tax fraud (although no case was ever brought to court).

Green Co's current auditors provide audit services. Additional assurance on business controls and the preparation of financial statements are provided by a different accountancy firm.

Last year, a neighbouring farm, Black Co started growing genetically modified (GM) crops, the pollen from which blows over Green Co's fields on a regular basis. This is a threat to Green Co's organic status because organic crops must not be contaminated with GM material. Green Co is considering court action against Black Co for loss of income and to stop Black Co growing GM crops.

You are an audit partner in Lime & Co, a 15 partner firm of auditors and business advisors. You have been friends with the managers of Green Co for the last 15 years, advising them on an informal basis. The managers of Green Co have indicated that the audit will be put out to tender next month and have asked your audit firm to tender for the audit and the provision of other professional services.

Required:

(a) Using the information provided, identify and explain the ethical threats that could affect Lime & Co. **(8 marks)**

(b) In respect of the going concern concept:

(i) Define 'going concern' and state two situations in which it should NOT be applied in the preparation of financial statements; **(3 marks)**

(ii) Explain the directors' responsibilities and the auditors' responsibilities regarding financial statements prepared on the going concern principle. **(4 marks)**

(c) List the audit procedures that should be carried out to determine whether or not the going concern basis is appropriate for Green Co. **(5 marks)**

(Total: 20 marks)

61 NEWBRIDGE TRADING

(DEC 97) (CHAPTER 11)

There is an auditing standard on subsequent events.

You are auditing the financial statements of Newbridge Trading, for the year ended 31 October 1997.

The senior partner of your audit firm has asked you to consider the auditor's responsibilities for identifying subsequent events. Also, he has asked you to describe the audit procedures which examine subsequent events. He has suggested that an example of one point in answer to part (b) below would be:

'checking sales ledger cash received after the year end to determine the realisability of debtors at the year end and highlight doubtful debts.'

The detailed audit work was completed on Friday 5 December 1997. It is proposed that:

(a) the audit report is signed on Friday 19 December

(b) the financial statements are sent to shareholders on Monday 5 January 1998, and

(c) the company's annual general meeting will be held on Wednesday 28 January 1998.

You are required to:

(a) consider the auditor's responsibilities for detecting material subsequent events in the periods:

(i) 31 October to 5 December 1997

(ii) 5 December to 19 December 1997

(iii) 19 December 1997 to 5 January 1998

(iv) 5 January 1998 to 28 January 1998

(v) after 28 January 1998 **(7 marks)**

(b) list and briefly explain audit procedures which involve examination of subsequent events. **(10 marks)**

(c) describe the audit work you will carry out in period (a)(ii) above. **(3 marks)**

(Total: 20 marks)

REPORTING

62 JONES, ROBERTS, WILLIAMS, GRIFFITHS AND EVANS (CHAPTER 12)

You are currently engaged in reviewing the working papers of several audit assignments recently carried out by your audit practice. Each of the audit assignments is nearing completion, but certain matters have recently come to light which may affect your audit opinion on each of the assignments. In each case the year end of the company is 30 September 20X2.

(a) **Jones** (Profit before tax $150,000)

On 3 October 20X2 a letter was received informing the company that a customer, who owed the company $30,000 as at the year end had been declared bankrupt on 30 September. At the time of the audit it was expected that unsecured creditors, such as Jones, would receive nothing in respect of this debt. The directors refuse to change the financial statements to provide for the loss, on the grounds that the notification was not received by the balance sheet date.

Total debts shown in the balance sheet amounted to $700,000. **(4 marks)**

(b) **Roberts** (Profit before tax $500,000)

On 31 July 20X2 a customer sued the company for personal damages arising from an unexpected defect in one of its products. Shortly before the year end the company made an out-of-court settlement with the customer of $10,000, although this agreement is not reflected in the financial statements as at 30 September 20X2. Further, the matter subsequently became known to the press and was extensively reported. The company's legal advisers have now informed you that further claims have been received following the publicity, although they are unable to place a figure on the potential liability arising from such claims which have not yet been received. The company had referred to the claims in a note to the financial statements stating, however, that no provision had been made to cover them because the claims were not expected to be material. **(4 marks)**

(c) **Williams** (Net loss for the year $75,000)

Three directors of this manufacturing company owed amounts totalling $50,000 at the end of the financial year, and you have ascertained that such loans were not of a type permissible under the local legislation. These amounts had been included in the balance sheet with other items under the heading 'Receivables collectable within one year'. The directors did not wish to disclose these loans separately in the financial statements as they were repaid shortly after the year end, as soon as they were made aware that the loans were not permissible. The directors have argued that the disclosures could prove embarrassing and that no purpose would be served by revealing this information in the financial statements. **(4 marks)**

(d) **Griffiths** (Net profit before tax $250,000)

The audit work revealed that a trade investment stated in the balance sheet at $500,000 had suffered a permanent fall in value of $300,000. The company admitted that the loss had occurred, but refused to make an allowance for it on the grounds that other trade investments (not held for resale) had risen in value and were stated at amounts considerably below their realisable values. **(4 marks)**

(e) **Evans** (Net profit before tax $100,000)

This client is a construction company, currently building a warehouse on its own premises, and using some of its own workforce. The cost of labour and materials has been included in the cost of the non-current asset in the balance sheet, the total figure being based on the company's costing records. The warehouse is almost complete and the cost shown in the balance sheet includes direct labour costs of $10,000. However, during audit testing it was discovered that the costing records, showing the direct labour costs for the warehouse in the early part of the year, had been destroyed accidentally. **(4 marks)**

You are required to:

Discuss each of the cases outlined above, referring to materiality considerations and, where appropriate, relevant accounting principles and appropriate accounting standards. You should also indicate, with reasons, the kind of audit report (including the type of qualification, if necessary) which you consider would be appropriate in each case.

You are not required to produce the full audit reports, and you may assume that all matters other than those specifically mentioned are considered satisfactory. **(Total: 20 marks)**

63 AUDIT REPORT AND REVIEW REPORT

(DEC 01) (CHAPTER 12)

The reports below are an audit report and a review report respectively.

INDEPENDENT AUDITOR'S REPORT

To the shareholders of ABC Company

We have audited the accompanying financial statements of ABC Company, which comprise the balance sheet as at December 31, 20X1, and the income statement, statement of changes in equity and cash flow statement for the year then ended, and a summary of significant accounting policies and other explanatory notes.

Management's Responsibility for the Financial Statements

Management is responsible for the preparation and fair presentation of these financial statements in accordance with International Financial Reporting Standards. This responsibility includes: designing, implementing and maintaining internal control relevant to the preparation and fair presentation of financial statements that are free from material misstatement, whether due to fraud or error; selecting and applying appropriate accounting policies; and making accounting estimates that are reasonable in the circumstances.

Auditor's Responsibility

Our responsibility is to express an opinion on these financial statements based on our audit. We conducted our audit in accordance with International Standards on Auditing. Those standards require that we comply with ethical requirements and plan and perform the audit to obtain reasonable assurance whether the financial statements are free from material misstatement.

An audit involves performing procedures to obtain audit evidence about the amounts and disclosures in the financial statements. The procedures selected depend on the auditor's judgment, including the assessment of the risks of material misstatement of the financial statements, whether due to fraud or error. In making those risk assessments, the auditor considers internal control relevant to the entity's preparation and fair presentation of the financial statements in order to design audit procedures that are appropriate in the circumstances, but not for the purpose of expressing an opinion on the effectiveness of the entity's internal control. An audit also includes evaluating the appropriateness of accounting policies used and the reasonableness of accounting estimates made by management, as well as evaluating the overall presentation of the financial statements. We believe that the audit evidence we have obtained is sufficient and appropriate to provide a basis for our audit opinion.

Opinion

In our opinion, the financial statements give a true and fair view of the financial position of ABC Company as of December 31, 20X1, and of its financial performance and its cash flows for the year then ended in accordance with International Financial Reporting Standards.

REVIEW REPORT

To the Directors of ABC Company

We have reviewed the accompanying balance sheet of ABC Company at 31 December 20X1, and the related statements of income and cash flows for the year then ended. These financial statements are the responsibility of the Company's management. Our responsibility is to issue a report on these financial statements based on our review.

We conducted our review in accordance with the International Standard on Review Engagements 2400. This Standard requires that we plan and perform the review to obtain moderate assurance as to whether the financial statements are free of material misstatement. A review is limited primarily to inquiries of company personnel and analytical procedures applied to financial data and thus provides less assurance than an audit. We have not performed an audit and, accordingly, we do not express an audit opinion.

Based on our review, nothing has come to our attention that causes us to believe that the accompanying financial statements do not give a true and fair view in accordance with International Accounting Standards.

XYZ & Co
30 March 20X2

Required:

(a) Compare and contrast the audit report and the review report shown above. Your answer should cover:

(i) the work performed; **(3 marks)**

(ii) the assurance provided; **(3 marks)**

(iii) the addressee of the report; **(4 marks)**

(iv) responsibility for the financial information; **(3 marks)**

(v) the opinion given. **(4 marks)**

(b) Explain the difference between a direct reporting engagement and an attest engagement. **(3 marks)**

(Total: 20 marks)

64 HOOD ENTERPRISES

(JUN 05) (CHAPTER 12)

You are the audit manager of Hood Enterprises, a limited liability company. The company's annual turnover is over $10 million.

Required:

(a) Compare the responsibilities of the directors and auditors regarding the published financial statements of Hood Enterprises. **(6 marks)**

(b) An extract from the draft audit report produced by an audit junior is given below:

Basis of Opinion

'We conducted our audit in accordance with Auditing Standards. An audit includes examination, on a test basis, of evidence relevant to the amounts and disclosures in the financial statements. It also includes an assessment of all the estimates and judgements made by the directors in the preparation of the financial statements, and of whether the accounting policies are appropriate to the company's circumstances, consistently applied and adequately disclosed.

'We planned and performed our audit so as to obtain as much information and explanation as possible given the time available for the audit. We confirm that the financial statements are free from material misstatement, whether caused by fraud or other irregularity or error. The directors however are wholly responsible for the accuracy of the financial statements and no liability for errors can be accepted by the auditor. In forming our opinion we also evaluated the overall adequacy of the presentation of information in the company's annual report.'

Required:

Identify and explain the errors in the above extract.

NOTE you are not required to redraft the report. **(10 marks)**

(c) The directors of Hood Enterprises have prepared a cash flow forecast for submission to the bank. They have asked you as the auditor to provide a negative assurance report on this forecast.

Required:

Briefly explain the difference between positive and negative assurance, outlining the advantages to the directors of providing negative assurance on their cash flow forecast. **(4 marks)**

(Total: 20 marks)

65 MSV

(JUN 07) (CHAPTER 12)

(a) ISA 700 *The Independent Auditor's Report on a Complete Set of General Purpose Financial Statements* indicates the basic elements that will ordinarily be included in the audit report.

Required:

List SIX basic elements of an auditor's report. Briefly explain why each element is included in the report. **(6 marks)**

(b) You are the audit manager in charge of the audit of MSV Co for the year ended 28 February 2007. MSV Co is based in a seaside town and hires motor boats and yachts to individuals for amounts of time between one day and one week. The majority of receipts are in cash, with a few customers paying by debit card. Consequently, there are no receivables on the balance sheet. The main non-current assets are the motor boats and yachts. The company is run by four directors who are also the major shareholders. Total income for the year was about $10m.

The following issues have been identified during the audit:

Issue 1

Audit tests on sales indicate a weakness in the internal control system, with a potential understatement of income in the region of $500,000. The weakness occurred because sales invoices are not sequentially numbered, allowing one of the directors to remove cash sales prior to recording in the sales day book. This was identified during analytical procedures of sales, when the audit senior noted that on the days when this director was working, sales were always lower than on the days when the director was not working. **(8 marks)**

Issue 2

During testing of non-current assets, one yacht was found to be located at the property of one of the directors. This yacht has not been hired out during the year and enquiries indicate that the director makes personal use of it. The yacht is included in the non-current assets balance in the financial statements. **(6 marks)**

Required:

For each of the issues above:

(i) List the audit procedures you should conduct to reach a conclusion on these issues;

(ii) Assuming that you have performed all the audit procedures that you can, but the issues are still unresolved, explain the potential effect (if any) on the audit report.

Note: The mark allocation is shown against each of the two issues. **(Total: 20 marks)**

Section 2

ANSWERS TO PRACTICE QUESTIONS

AUDIT FRAMEWORK AND REGULATION

1 EXTERNAL AUDIT

Key answer tips

This question focuses on the purpose and role of external audit in part (a), which is a fundamental part of your studies and therefore should not present any problems. Avoid presenting your answer in a long paragraph; where you are making several points it is always helpful to consider the points separately and it can ensure you focus on the question's requirements. Use of bullets/numbering in your answer would improve presentation.

In part (b) you have to demonstrate that you are clear as to the differences between the interim and final audit in terms of the main audit processes and procedures. You are provided with an outline in the question itself as to the main difference in approach and therefore you only need to extend this and provide the relevant detail.

(a) **Training material: purpose of external audit and its role**

(i) The external audit has a long history that derives largely from the separation of the ownership and management of assets. Those who own assets wish to ensure that those to whom they have entrusted control are using those assets wisely. This is known as the 'stewardship' function.

(ii) The requirement for an independent audit helps ensure that financial statements are free of bias and manipulation for the benefit of users of financial information.

(iii) Companies are owned by shareholders but they are managed by directors (in very small companies, owners and managers are the same, but many such companies are not subject to statutory audit requirements).

(iv) The requirement for a statutory audit is a public interest issue: the public is invited to invest in enterprises, it is in the interests of the capital markets (and society as a whole) that those investing do so in the knowledge that they will be provided with 'true and fair' information about the enterprise. This should result in the efficient allocation of capital as investors are able to make rational decisions on the basis of transparent financial information.

(v) The requirement for an audit can help prevent investors from being defrauded, although there is no guarantee of this because the external audit has inherent limitations. Reducing the possibility of false information being provided by managers to owners is achieved by the requirement for external auditors to be independent of the managers upon whose financial statements they are reporting.

(vi) The purpose of the external audit under International Standards on Auditing is for the auditor to obtain sufficient appropriate audit evidence on which to base the audit opinion. This opinion is on whether the financial statements give a 'true and fair view' (or 'present fairly in all material respects') of the position, performance (and cash flows) of the entity. This opinion is prepared for the benefit of shareholders.

(b) **Main audit procedures and processes: interim and final audit**

(i) The interim audit generally involves risk assessment, the testing of internal controls, and certain analytical and other substantive procedures. Many of these procedures are often performed concurrently.

(ii) Risk assessment involves gathering information about the business, inquiries, analytical procedures and determining the response to assessed risk. In practice it also involves the determination of materiality and tolerable error.

(iii) Risk assessment also involves evaluating the design of internal controls and determining whether they have been implemented.

(iv) Final audit procedures also involve a review of the financial statements as a whole to ensure that they are internally consistent, and in accordance with the relevant financial reporting framework and the auditor's knowledge of the business.

(v) Substantive procedures, which include analytical procedures, are designed to provide evidence that the figures and disclosures in the financial statements are complete, relevant, and accurate. Arriving at the final conclusions often involves the performance of further analytical procedures on the financial statements as a whole.

(vi) It is common for auditors to provide management with lists of control weaknesses (both structural and operational) together with recommendations for improvement both after the interim and final audits.

(vii) Auditors are also required to communicate with those charged with governance.

NB: Mention could also be made of management representations, third party confirmations, the review of working papers, and a number of other matters.

2 BILLINGTON TRAVEL

Key answer tips

In part (a) make sure you say why auditors have to be perceived as independent as well as be independent.

In part (b) plan your answer before you start so that you don't repeat the same issues for (i) and (ii); some issues are indeed relevant to both, but you won't get marks for repeating yourself.

Parts (c) and (d) are unusual in that they consider ethics from an internal audit perspective. There are no specific ethical rules to apply here, so apply your common sense and think about what you would do in real life.

(a) Independence

(i) It is important for external auditors to be independent of their audit clients because external auditors act on behalf of the owners of the business (normally the shareholders) and report on the financial statements prepared by the management for the benefit of shareholders.

(ii) If external auditors are not independent of their clients, for example if they hold shares in the companies that they audit, their ability to form an objective opinion on the financial statements is impaired.

(iii) External auditors must also be seen to be independent because if they are not, the owners of the business will not have confidence in the audit reports that the auditors issue.

(iv) The ACCA's Rules of Professional Conduct require that auditors are independent, and that they are seen to be independent. The Rules cover a number of areas in which the auditors' independence may be, or be seen to be, impaired.

(v) National legislation also normally requires external auditors to be independent.

(b) Billington Travel

(i) The statutory audit

- The Rules of Professional Conduct state that it is important that the firm is competent to undertake the audit; it must have adequate resources in terms of staff with sufficient experience in this sector. The fact that the services to be provided would constitute a substantial amount of fee income indicates that the firm might not, at present, have those resources.
- It may be appropriate to consider whether experience in this sector can be brought in, by the recruitment of additional staff.
- The firm should consider whether staff are available at the right time of year and whether the work fits in with the firm's existing obligations.
- The Rules of Professional Conduct also state that the firm must be independent of its clients; in particular, this means that it must not take too much of its fee income from one client (or group of clients).
- Generally, for non-public interest clients, the fee income (including income from additional services) should not exceed 15% of the gross practice income. If that figure is exceeded, it may be possible to consider providing some, but not all, of the services requested.

(ii) The provision of other services

- Preparation of financial statements: it is generally acceptable under the Rules of Professional Conduct for auditors to provide assistance with the preparation of financial statements for private company clients, provided that the client takes full responsibility for the accounting records and financial statements.
- It is important to know why the company needs assistance in this area and it would be preferable in the long run for the company to be able to prepare its own financial statements.
- It is important that those preparing the financial statements are independent of those performing the audit as far as possible, in order that the firm is seen to remain independent.
- Systems review: the external auditor is often well placed to provide assistance with such reviews as the firm obtains a working knowledge of systems during the course of the audit.

– However, there is always the danger that the firm finds itself in the position of having to report on a system that it has helped to improve, and it may be difficult in such circumstances to be critical of the system. This detracts from the firm's ability to remain independent, and in this case, given that it is the first year of audit and that assistance is also needed with the preparation of financial statements, it seems preferable not to tender for the systems review, this year.

(c) Actions to be taken

(i) It may be appropriate to discuss the matter, discreetly, with other staff members to establish whether or not it is of concern to them, as well as to you. It would be preferable to discuss the matter with persons who are known to be reliable.

(ii) If the concerns are shared, or if the other staff have no knowledge of the matter, or if you are still concerned about the matter, it may be appropriate to discuss the matter with the chief internal auditor to try and establish why the matter has not been reported, as there may be a good reason. If other staff support you in your view, it may be appropriate to take another member of staff along to the discussion.

(iii) If the chief internal auditor is able to reassure you (either that it is not necessary to report the matter, or that the matter will be reported), no further action will be necessary, although it may be useful to make a brief note of the discussion.

(iv) If you are not satisfied, or if the chief internal auditor undertakes to report the matter but does not do so within a reasonable time, the situation may be more serious and it is more important in such circumstances to make notes of any discussions. It may be appropriate to have further discussions with the chief internal auditor.

(v) If you are still not satisfied, and you consider that the matter is sufficiently serious, it may be appropriate to approach a more senior member of management to voice your concerns. You may wish to avoid this situation but it may be necessary in order to protect yourself.

(vi) On the assumption that the matter is one of internal concern to the company and there is no question of illegality, the question of reporting the matters to third parties outside the organisation does not arise.

(d) Doing nothing

(i) The principal danger in doing nothing lies in the possibility that you may be accused of not bringing attention to the matter or even of being actively involved in a 'cover-up'.

(ii) Professional ethics do not permit chartered certified accountants to take no action at all where serious matters are concerned and to do nothing might, in extreme circumstances, involve you in disciplinary proceedings by the ACCA, even as a student.

(iii) To do nothing might also mean that the business of the company you work for is damaged, and therefore your own employment prospects.

3 TOUREX AND PUDCO

Key answer tips

This is a well structured question which tests professional conduct matters relating to conflicts of interest, the requirements of IAS 37 together with their application to a given set of circumstances and related aspects of the audit report. The marks on this question are evenly spread over the three part requirement – it is therefore important you give a reasonable amount of attention to each of the requirements.

In dealing with part (a) you must make sure you focus on the area of managing possible conflicts of interest.

In part (b) approximately half the available marks are awarded for explaining the accounting rules of IAS 37 – the remaining marks will only be given for relevant application of those principles to the facts given about the companies referred to in the question – make sure you cover all aspects of the question!

Part (c) requires you to exercise judgement based on your knowledge of the audit report categories under the auditing standard. There may be no clear cut answer to this part of the question – you may require more information before you can reach a conclusion. In this type of question, you should make your thinking clear to the examiner by explaining the approach you are taking.

(a) **Managing conflicts of interest**

(i) ACCA's Rules of Professional Conduct state that auditors should avoid conflicts of interest (both conflicts between the firm and clients, and conflicts between clients) wherever possible. In some cases, such as these, they are unavoidable.

(ii) Full disclosure is important – both companies should be fully aware that the firm is acting for the other party.

(iii) One or both companies may object to the firm acting for the other company and the auditor may be forced to make a decision as to which company to resign from. However, this is not an attractive course of action because the audits may already have commenced and it may be difficult for one of the companies to find a new auditor, quickly.

(iv) The auditor should probably not, therefore, resign unless forced to do so – this might be prejudicial to the interests of one of the clients.

(v) It is important in such cases that different teams of staff, and different engagement partners work on the respective audits.

(vi) Internal procedures within the firm should be set up to prevent confidential information from one client being transferred to the other and the interests of one firm damaging the interests of the other. Such procedures are sometimes known as 'Chinese Walls'.

(vii) If two completely separate offices could work on the two engagements, so much the better.

(b) **Main requirements of IAS 37**

IAS 37	**Application**
IAS 37 states that a provision is a liability of uncertain timing or amount. It should only be recognised when there is a present obligation (legal or constructive) arising from past events and it is probable that a transfer of economic benefits will be required to settle the obligation and a reliable estimate of the amount can be made.	If the firm can obtain sufficient appropriate audit evidence to show that Tourex and/or Pudco are likely to have to make a payment, and that the amount can be reliably estimated, a constructive obligation seems to exist and provision should be made.
IAS 37 states that a contingent liability is either a possible obligation arising from past events whose existence will be confirmed by uncertain future events outside the control of the entity or, a present obligation arising from past events that is not recognised because a transfer of economic benefits is not probable, or because the amount of the obligation cannot be measured with sufficient certainty.	If Tourex and/or Pudco are uncertain as to whether a payment will have to be made, or if they are certain but the amount cannot be estimated, a contingent liability should be disclosed in the accounts.
IAS 37 states that a contingent asset is a possible asset arising from past events whose existence will be confirmed by uncertain future events outside the control of the entity. Contingent assets should only be disclosed where an inflow of economic benefits is probable. If they are virtually certain, a contingency does not exist at all and the income may be accrued.	This might apply to Tourex in its claim against the food company. It seems unlikely that there is sufficient certainty relating to the claim and therefore no disclosure should be made.
It also states that expected re-imbursements (such as those arising from insurance contracts) should be recognised only where they are virtually certain, and treated as separate assets. The net expense may be recognised in the income statement.	If either Tourex or Pudco hold insurance against such events, and it is probable that the insurance claim will be met, a contingent asset may need to be disclosed. If there is any uncertainty, there should be no disclosure. If it is virtually certain that the claim will be met, a separate asset should be recognised.
A brief description of the nature of each class of contingent liability should be made unless the possibility of the transfer of benefits is remote. Where practical, an estimate of the financial effect, an indication of the relevant uncertainties, and the possibility of any reimbursement should be disclosed. Similar rules apply to contingent assets.	

(c) **Sufficient audit evidence and audit reports**

(i) The main problem for the auditors will be gaining sufficient evidence to determine whether any amounts should be provided for and/or disclosed in the financial statements of the two companies.

(ii) The lawyers refuse to provide anything other than informal evidence and this will almost certainly not be sufficient to form an audit opinion.

(iii) Unless audit evidence can be obtained elsewhere – a qualified opinion, 'except for', on the basis of a limitation in the scope of the audit may be needed for both companies as the amounts involved are material.

(iv) However, it may be possible to take the view that there is a significant uncertainty, and that an explanatory paragraph referring to this significant uncertainty is therefore appropriate, rather than a qualification to the auditors' opinion, provided that the matter is adequately disclosed in the financial statements.

(v) It may be possible for the auditors to suggest to the companies that it would be very helpful for the lawyers to provide some indication as to their view of the likely outcome and the amounts involved, in order to avoid a qualified opinion.

(vi) The auditors should also take note of the progress of any legal proceedings and any proceedings that may be instigated by the public health authorities as such authorities might impose significant fines, and they might even close the businesses down, which has implications for the going concern status of both.

4 CLIENT CONFIDENTIALITY

Key answer tips

This question is testing your knowledge of ACCA's professional rules, and if you are familiar with these this question will not cause you any problems. Part (a) relates to auditors disclosure of information and when this is permitted; essentially it is only requiring you to detail those circumstances, which are very limited. Part (b) provides a scenario and asks you to explain how the auditor should respond to requests for information from various public bodies. You should ensure you explain how you have come to your conclusion(s) and give reasons why the auditor responds in a certain way, in order to gain maximum marks.

(a) **Disclosure of information relating to clients to third parties**

(i) Auditors are permitted or required to disclose information about their clients to third parties without their knowledge or consent in very limited circumstances.

(ii) Generally, auditors can be required to, or are permitted to, disclose information to certain regulatory bodies, including certain specialist units within police forces under legislation. Such legislation in many countries includes financial services legislation, legislation concerning banks and insurance companies, legislation concerning money laundering and legislation concerning the investigation of serious fraud or tax evasion.

(iii) Auditors are also permitted or required to disclose information where they are personally involved in litigation, including litigation that involves the recovery of fees from clients, or where they are subject to disciplinary proceedings brought by ACCA or other, similar professional bodies.

(iv) Auditors are also permitted to disclose information where they consider it to be in the 'public interest' or in the interests of national security. Factors to take into account include the seriousness of the matter, the likelihood of repetition and the extent to which the public is involved. This right is rarely used in practice.

(b) **Response to requests**

(i) It is not unusual in practice for various bodies to request information from auditors 'informally' because it relieves them of the obligation to obtain the necessary statutory authorities which may be time consuming or difficult.

(ii) Auditors must not disclose information without the consent of the client or unless the necessary statutory documentation is provided by the person(s) requesting the information.

(iii) Unless the auditor has reason to believe that there is a statutory duty not to inform the client that an approach has been made, the client should first be approached to see if consent can be obtained, and to see if the client is aware of the investigations, as should normally be the case. The auditor should ensure that the client is aware of the fact the voluntary disclosure may work in the client's favour, in the long run, but if the client refuses, the auditor should inform the client if the auditor has a statutory duty of disclosure.

(iv) Auditors should take legal advice in all of the cases described.

(v) Where the auditor is made aware of potential actions against the client that may have an effect on the financial statements, the auditor must consider the effect on the audit report. If the client is aware of the investigation, the auditor will be able to seek audit evidence to support any necessary provisions or disclosures in the financial statements.

(vi) The auditors should consider whether the suspected fraud relating to the managing director relates to the company and affects the financial statements.

(vii) Auditors will be in a very difficult situation if they become aware of an action that may materially affect the financial statements, but where the client is not, and where auditors are under a statutory duty not to inform the client. This situation will not be improved by the resignation of auditors as they may be obliged to make a statement on resignation. This puts auditors in a very difficult position and legal advice is essential in such circumstances.

(viii) Tax authorities normally have powers to ask clients to disclose information voluntarily. Such voluntary disclosure is often looked on favourably by the tax authorities and the courts. Tax authorities normally also have statutory powers to demand information from both clients and auditors. The same is generally true of environmental and health and safety inspectors.

(ix) The power of the police to demand information is sometimes less clear and auditors and clients should take care to ensure that the appropriate authorities are in place. Those sections of the police investigating serious frauds usually have more powers than the general police. It is unlikely that trade union representatives have any statutory powers to demand information.

5 TELA & CO

Key answer tips

Corporate governance has become an established exam topic due to its significance for listed companies as they attempt to shake off the shadow of high profile frauds such as Enron. The issues are easy to identify as the volume of information provided is modest, but ensure your answer contains specific recommendations and explanations as it is easy to waffle without providing clear mark scoring points!

Memo

From: A Manager, Tela & Co

To: Jumper & Co

Subject: Corporate Governance in the SGCC Company

Date: 13 June 2006

As requested, I write to explain where your client SGCC does not appear to be following appropriate corporate governance codes and to recommend changes to ensure that the principles of good corporate governance are being followed.

Chief Executive Officer (CEO) and Chairman

Mr Sheppard is both CEO and chairman of SGCC. Corporate governance indicates that the person responsible for running the company (the CEO) and the person responsible for controlling the board (the chairman) should be different people. This is to ensure that no one individual has unrestricted powers of decision.

I recommend that Mr Sheppard is either the CEO or the chairman and that a second individual is appointed to the other post to ensure that Mr Sheppard does not have too much power in SGCC.

Composition of board

The current board ratio of executive to non-executive directors is 5:2. This means that the executive directors can dominate the board proceedings. Corporate governance codes suggest that there should be a balance of executive and non-executive directors so this cannot happen. A minimum of three non-executive directors are also normally recommended, although reports such as Cadbury note this may be difficult to achieve.

I recommend that the number of executive and non-executive directors is equal to help ensure no one group dominates the board. This will mean appointing more non-executive directors to SGCC.

Director appointment

At present, Mr Sheppard appoints directors to the board, giving him absolute authority over who is appointed. This makes the appointment procedure and qualities directors are being appointed against difficult to determine. Corporate governance suggests that appointment procedures should be transparent so that the suitability of directors for board positions can be clearly seen.

I recommend that an appointments committee is established comprising three non-executive directors to ensure there is no bias in board appointments. Formal job descriptions should also be published making the appointment process more transparent.

Review of board performance

It is correct that the performance of senior managers is reviewed, but this principle should also be applied to the board. While Mr Sheppard may undertake some review, this is not transparent and it is not clear what targets the board either met or did not meet.

I recommend that performance targets are set for each director and actual performance assessed against these on a regular basis. Reasons for underperformance should also be ascertained and where appropriate, changes made to the composition of the board.

Board pay

At present, board members' pay is set by Mr Sheppard. This process breaches principles of good governance because the remuneration structure is not transparent and Mr Sheppard sets his own pay. Mr Sheppard could easily be setting remuneration levels based on his own judgements without any objective criteria.

I recommend that a remuneration committee is established comprising three non-executive directors. They will set remuneration levels for the board, taking into account current salary levels and the performance of board members. Remuneration should also be linked to performance, to encourage a high standard of work.

Internal control

The system of internal control in SGCC does not appear to be reviewed correctly. While external auditors will review the control system, this review is based on their audit requirement and cannot be relied on to test the overall effectiveness of the system.

I recommend that some more formal review of internal control is carried out, perhaps by establishing an internal audit department, as noted below. The relationship with the company's auditors must also be reviewed so that the work of the board and the auditors regarding internal control is understood by both parties.

Internal audit

SGCC does not have an internal audit department. Given the lack of formal review of internal control in the company, this is surprising. Good corporate governance implies that the control system is monitored and that an internal audit department is established to carry out this task.

I recommend that an internal audit department is established, reporting initially to the audit committee who will monitor internal control and then summarise reports for the board.

Financial statements

There appears to be acceptable disclosure in the financial statements regarding the past results of the company. However, the board should also provide an indication of how the company will perform in the future, by a forecast review of operations or similar statement. This is partly to enable investors to assess the value of their investment in the company.

I therefore recommend that the annual accounts of SGCC include some indication of the future operations of the company.

Audit committee

There is no mention in the report of an audit committee. Good corporate governance implies that there is some formal method of monitoring external auditors as well as checking that the reports from the external auditors are given appropriate attention in the company.

I recommend that an audit committee is established – made up from non-executive directors. The committee will receive reports from the external and internal auditors (as mentioned above) and ensure that the board takes appropriate action on these reports.

I hope this information is useful. Please contact me again if you require any further assistance.

Sincerely
Ann C. Outent

6 MCKAY

Key answer tips

Part (a) is theoretical and requires that you have learned the key ethical aspects of the syllabus. The mark allocation is quite high, but this often implies that the marking guide will be generous so do not be intimidated. Make sure you adhere to the principles of good presentation with each mark-scoring point being clearly separated.

Part (b) provides a wide range of ethical issues to identify, but do not overlook that you are also specifically asked to suggest mitigating factors and this will be worth at least one third of the marks on offer in this section.

(a) Confidential information

General rules

Information obtained during an audit is normally held to be confidential; that is it will not be disclosed to a third party. However, client information may be disclosed where:

- consent has been obtained from the client
- there is a public duty to disclose
- there is a legal or professional right or duty to disclose.

However, these rules are general principles only; more detailed guidance is also available to accountants, as explained below.

ACCA's Code of ethics – obligatory disclosure

As noted above, ACCA's Code of ethics confirms that when a member agrees to work for a client in a professional capacity, it is an implied term of that agreement that the member will not disclose a client's affairs to any other person.

The recognised exceptions to this rule are where a member knows or suspects that his client has committed treason, or is involved in drug trafficking or terrorist offences. In this situation, information must be disclosed to a competent authority. The actual disclosure will depend on the laws of the jurisdiction where the auditor is located.

The auditor may also be obliged to provide information where a court demands disclosure. Refusal to provide information is likely to be considered contempt of court with the auditor being liable for this offence.

ACCA Code of ethics – voluntary disclosure

A member may also disclose client confidential information voluntarily, that is without client permission, in a limited number of situations. Examples include:

- To protect a member's interest, e.g. to allow a member to sue a client for unpaid fees or defend an action for negligence.
- Where there is a public duty to disclose, e.g. the client has committed an action against the public interest such as unauthorised release of toxic chemicals.

(b) Independence risks

Audit partner – time in office

Mr Grace has been the audit partner of Ancients for eight years. His objectivity for the audit may be threatened by the ongoing close relationship with the client. In other words, he may be too friendly with the directors of Ancients. This means he may not be willing or able to take difficult decisions such as issuing a modified audit report for fear of prejudicing his friendship with the directors. Rotating the audit partner would remove this threat.

Unpaid taxation fees

Ancients has not paid the taxation fees for work that took place nearly six months ago. The non-payment of fees can be a threat to objectivity similar to that of an unpaid loan. In effect, McKay is providing Ancients with an interest free loan. The audit partner in McKay may not wish to issue a modified report for fear that the client leaves and the 'loan' is not repaid. The unpaid fee must be discussed with the directors in Ancients and reasons for non-payment obtained. McKay may wish to delay starting the audit work for this year until the fee is paid to remove the potential independence problem. If the fee is not paid at all then McKay may decline to carry out the audit.

Fee income

No details are provided regarding fee income obtained from Ancients. However, the company is growing rapidly and McKay does provide other services besides audit. As a limited liability company, McKay should ensure that no more than 10% of its recurring practice income (including auditing, accountancy and other work combined) is derived from this client. Obtaining more than 10% could indicate undue financial reliance on one client, and impair objectivity regarding the audit report (again fear of issuing a modified report and losing the fee income from the audit client). If the 10% limit is close, McKay may have to limit other services provided so that independence is not impaired. An annual review will be required on clients where the fee is between 5 and 10% to ensure that the fee income rules will not be breached.

Allyson Grace

Allyson Grace is not deemed to be connected to Mr Grace because she is presumably over the age of 18. If she was still a minor, then there would be a connection and it would be inappropriate for Mr Grace to be the audit partner as he could in theory influence Allyson's decisions. However, there may still appear to be an independence problem as Mr Grace may not be objective in making audit decisions. He may not wish to annoy his daughter by having to qualify the financial statements. Appointing another audit partner would remove the perceived independence problem.

Meal

The offer of a meal by Allyson may appear to be a threat to independence; having received an expensive meal, the audit staff may be favourably disposed towards Ancients and be less inclined to investigate potential errors. Audit staff are allowed to receive modest benefits on commercial terms; whether there is a benefit depends on how expensive the meal is. To ensure no independence issues it would appear that the invitation should be declined. One possible option would be for Mr Grace and Allyson to pay personally as a purely social event even though this may be unlikely. However, this does not remove the implied independence issue.

INTERNAL AUDIT

7 FRAUD AND ERROR

Key answer tips

This question comprises three sections with an even split of marks between them. All three sections are testing your knowledge of fraud and error, but from different angles.

Part (a) examines how the internal audit function can assist an organisation in the detection and prevention of fraud and error. Clearly you should consider corporate governance and stewardship and discuss internal control systems in order to obtain full marks.

Part (b) focuses on the responsibilities of the external auditors in relation to fraud and error. A knowledge of ISA 240 is necessary to fully answer this question and you must consider the external auditor's responsibility in respect of the risk of fraud, as well as if actual fraud is detected.

In part (c) you are given a scenario and asked to describe the nature of the risks which might arise from fraud and error. You do not need an in depth awareness of holiday companies, you just need to apply your general audit knowledge of risk assessment, including specific computer systems risks, and risks related to monetary transactions.

(a) **Internal audit function: risk of fraud and error**

(i) The internal audit function in any entity is part of the overall corporate governance function of the entity. Corporate governance objectives include the management of the risks to which the entity is subject that would prevent it achieving its overall objectives such as profitability. Corporate governance objectives also include the overarching need for the management of an entity to exercise a stewardship function over the entity's assets.

(ii) A large part of the management of risks, and the proper exercise of stewardship, involves the maintenance of proper controls over the business. Controls over the business as a whole, and in relation to specific areas, include the effective operation of an internal audit function.

(iii) Internal audit can help management manage risks in relation to fraud and error, and exercise proper stewardship by:

1 commenting on the process used by management to identify and classify the specific fraud and error risks to which the entity is subject (and in some cases helping management develop and implement that process);

2 commenting on the appropriateness and effectiveness of actions taken by management to manage the risks identified (and in some cases helping management develop appropriate actions by making recommendations);

3 periodically auditing or reviewing systems or operations to determine whether the risks of fraud and error are being effectively managed;

4 monitoring the incidence of fraud and error, investigating serious cases and making recommendations for appropriate management responses.

(iv) In practice, the work of internal audit often focuses on the adequacy and effectiveness of internal control procedures for the prevention, detection and reporting of fraud and error. Routine internal controls (such as the controls over computer systems and the production of routine financial information) and non-routine controls (such as controls over year-end adjustments to the financial statements) are relevant.

(v) It should be recognised however that many significant frauds bypass normal internal control systems and that in the case of management fraud in particular, much higher level controls (those relating to the high level governance of the entity) need to be reviewed by internal audit in order to establish the nature of the risks, and to manage them effectively.

(b) **External auditors: fraud and error in an audit of financial statements**

(i) External auditors are required by ISA 240 The Auditor's Responsibility to Consider Fraud in an Audit of Financial Statements to consider the risks of material misstatements in the financial statements due to fraud. Their audit procedures will then be based on a risk assessment. Regardless of the risk assessment, auditors are required to be alert to the possibility of fraud throughout the audit and maintain an attitude of professional scepticism, notwithstanding the auditors' past experience of the honesty and integrity of management and those charged with governance. Members of the engagement team should discuss the susceptibility of the entity's financial statements to material misstatements due to fraud.

(ii) Auditors should make enquiries of management regarding management's assessment of fraud risk, its process for dealing with risk, and its communications with those charged with governance and employees. They should enquire of those charged with governance about the oversight process.

(iii) Auditors should also enquire of management and those charged with governance about any suspected or actual instance of fraud.

(iv) Auditors should consider fraud risk factors, unusual or unexpected relationships, and assess the risk of misstatements due to fraud, identifying any significant risks. Auditors should evaluate the design of relevant internal controls, and determine whether they have been implemented.

(v) Auditors should determine an overall response to the assessed risk of material misstatements due to fraud and develop appropriate audit procedures, including testing certain journal entries, reviewing estimates for bias, and obtaining an understanding of the business rationale of significant transactions outside the normal course of business. Appropriate management representations should be obtained.

(vi) External auditors are only concerned with risks that might cause material error in the financial statements. External auditors might therefore pay less attention than internal auditors to small frauds (and errors), although they must always consider whether evidence of single instances of fraud (or error) are indicative of more systematic problems.

(vii) It is accepted that because of the hidden nature of fraud, an audit properly conducted in accordance with ISAs might not detect a material misstatement in the financial statements arising from fraud. In practice, routine errors are much easier to detect than frauds.

(viii) Where auditors encounter suspicions or actual instances of fraud (or error), they must consider the effect on the financial statements, which will usually involve further investigations. They should also consider the need to report to management and those charged with governance.

(ix) Where serious frauds (or errors) are encountered, auditors need also to consider the effect on the going concern status of the entity, and the possible need to report externally to third parties, either in the public interest, for national security reasons, or for regulatory reasons. Many entities in the financial services sector are subject to this type of regulatory reporting and many countries have legislation relating to the reporting of money laundering activities, for example.

(c) **Nature of risks arising from fraud and error: Stone Holidays**

(i) Stone Holidays is subject to all of the risks of error arising from the use of computer systems. If programmed controls do not operate properly, for example, the information produced may be incomplete or incorrect. Inadequate controls also give rise to the risk of fraud by those who understand the system and are able to manipulate it in order to hide the misappropriation of assets such as receipts from customers.

(ii) All networked systems are also subject to the risk of error because of the possibility of the loss or corruption of data in transit. They are also subject to the risk of fraud where the transmission of data is not securely encrypted.

(iii) All entities that employ staff who handle company assets (such as receipts from customers) are subject to the risk that staff may make mistakes (error) or that they may misappropriate those assets (fraud) and then seek to hide the error or fraud by falsifying the records.

(iv) Stone Holidays is subject to problems arising from the risk of fraud perpetrated by customers using stolen credit or debit cards or even cash. Whilst credit card companies may be liable for such frauds, attempts to use stolen cards can cause considerable inconvenience.

(v) There is a risk of fraud perpetrated by senior management who might seek to lower the amount of money payable to the central fund (and the company's tax liability) by falsifying the company's sales figures, particularly if a large proportion of holidays are paid for in cash.

(vi) There is a risk that staff may seek to maximise the commission they are paid by entering false transactions into the computer system that are then reversed after the commission has been paid.

8 CLEANCO

Key answer tips

This question provides you with a lot of information about Cleanco so you must ensure that your answer addresses the issues raised. Always remember to use the information provided. It states at the end of the question 'you may present your answer in tabular format', so it is guiding you to do this – do not ignore such advice. This answer lends itself to a table as you can see below; it will also make it easier for you and help you focus on the relevant control and tests of control for the different risks. Remember to segregate your answer into the three different functions. As long as you are logical and methodical in your approach you will not find this a difficult question. This was set as question 1 of the exam paper but remember that you can do the questions in any order. By answering your best question first you can boost your morale and leave yourself feeling calmer to approach the more difficult questions.

	Risks	*Controls*	*Tests of control*
(a)	**Human resources**		
	There is a risk that staff without proper experience or training are employed (and might cause damage to client property).	All staff should be required to fill in proper application forms and submit references with them. References should be checked for all new staff employed. To the extent permitted by law, staff should be asked to provide details of criminal convictions. All staff, particularly those without experience, should receive proper training.	The auditor should: – take a representative sample of staff from the payroll and inspect the relevant application forms to ensure that they have been properly completed. References should also be inspected.
	Inappropriate staff, such as those with criminal convictions, perhaps, might be employed in high security environments.	Systems for allocating staff to assignments should ensure that only appropriate staff are allocated to high risk clients – by means of a staff classification system.	– for a sample of high risk clients, ensure that only appropriately classified staff have been utilised.
	Staff might misappropriate company or client property.	There should be documentary controls over the movement of cleaning materials and reviews of the usage of cleaning materials. The company should ask clients regularly about the levels of satisfaction with the service provided (and have investigation and disciplinary procedures in place where allegations of misappropriation are made).	– take a sample of entries in the documentation showing movements of materials and ensure that appropriate entries in systems have been made. – review the overall usage of cleaning materials and investigate any unusual variations. – review the result of client satisfaction surveys and establish if appropriate management responses have been made.

Risks	*Controls*	*Tests of control*
There is a risk that staff are paid for hours not worked or that incorrect payroll deductions are made.	All normal payroll controls such as the use of timesheets, reconciliations and regular reviews of payroll costs should be in place. Personnel controls should ensure that new staff can only be entered onto the payroll system with appropriate authorisation from an independent official.	– for a representative sample of entries in the payroll, re-perform calculations to ensure that they are made correctly, ensure that appropriate authorisation has been made and review the overall level of payroll cost, investigating variations.
A high turnover of staff increases all of the risks noted above.	Staff should receive feedback on their performance and be rewarded for good performance and long service.	– inspect the documentary evidence of staff reviews and assess the processes by which good performance and long service are rewarded, and for a sample of staff with good reviews and/or long service records, determine whether rewards have been forthcoming.

(b)

Procurement		
There is a risk of fictitious or excessive payment to suppliers (i.e. fraudulent payments).	Authorisation controls should ensure that an appropriate independent official authorises the acceptance of new suppliers onto the system and that only authorised suppliers can be used.	The auditor should: – review a representative sample of suppliers on the system and inspect written evidence of authorisation for them.
There is a risk of inaccurate, delayed or incorrect payments.	Authorisation checks on invoices should ensure that only goods that have been received are paid for and that agreed prices are being paid.	– analytically review the level of payments for, and utilisation of, goods on a periodic basis and investigate any significant variations.
There is a risk that the company does not obtain the best value for money by using existing suppliers.	Controls over the accounts payable ledger such as reconciliations with an accounts payable ledger control account and the matching of documents should be in place to ensure that discounts are obtained for timely payment and that good relations with suppliers are maintained.	– review a representative sample of invoices, credit notes and other documentation (hard copy or electronic) for evidence of matching to appropriate goods received documentation and price lists.
	There should be regular documented negotiations with existing suppliers and discussions with alternative suppliers to ensure that value for money is being obtained.	– review and critically assess the documentation and regularity of negotiations and discussions.

(c)

Marketing		
The third party advertiser may be in breach of advertising regulations. The type of aggressive direct mail advertising may actually damage the reputation of Cleanco which might result in a decrease in market share.	The contract between Cleanco and the advertising company should require that all advertising is in accordance with regulations and any best practice guidance (Cleanco wishes to retain its high reputation). There should be clauses in the contract requiring the company to indemnify Cleanco against any costs arising from such breaches. Cleanco should take legal advice on the wording of such clauses.	The auditor should: – review the contract with the company, and the advertising material to ensure that it is in accordance with regulations and any best practice guidance. The auditor should ensure that appropriate legal advice was taken with regard to indemnities and other important elements in the contract.
	The third party should be required to submit all advertising material to Cleanco for approval, and control over the design and content of the advertising material.	– obtain documentary evidence to show that the advertising material has been approved at an appropriate level within Cleanco.
There is a risk of expensive marketing expenditure not resulting in new business.	There should be proper budgeting for advertising costs, and regular review of such costs by comparison with new business obtained.	– review budgets and management accounts to ensure that advertising costs have been controlled and are resulting in an appropriate level of increased business at appropriate prices.
	Cost controls should ensure that discounts offered are not so great as to make contracts unprofitable, after marketing costs have been taken into account.	

Note: There are several other issues that might be dealt with in the answer to this question, for example risks, controls and tests relating to health and safety procedures.

9 ZX COMPANY

Key answer tips

The role of internal audit in risk management and corporate governance is an important area of the syllabus, so you must be fully prepared for a question such as part (a) here.

Part (b) is standard bookwork. You should aim to explain at least five advantages and five disadvantages to earn the 10 marks available.

From: Chief Internal Auditor

To: Board of ZX

Subject: Role of Audit Committee

Date: June 20X5

(a) Areas where the internal audit department can assist the directors with the implementation of good corporate governance in an organisation include:

Board reports

Reviewing reports to the board and reports produced by the board to ensure that they do present a balanced and understandable assessment of the company's position and prospects. The internal audit department will have good knowledge of the operations of the company as well as access to accounting information. The department can effectively 'audit' board reports to ensure they are accurate and understandable.

Internal controls

The board need to maintain a sound system of internal control. The internal audit department will be able to review existing controls and recommend improvements to ensure this objective is met.

Application of ISAs and IASs

The board need to have a policy for applying appropriate International Standards on Auditing (ISA) and International Accounting Standards (IAS) to the organisation. Internal audit will certainly be aware of new auditing standards and will have the technical expertise (especially where internal auditors are professionally qualified) to identify changes required by accounting standards. Amendments to control systems for new auditing standards and financial accounting systems for new accounting standards can therefore be recommended.

Communication with external auditors

Under corporate governance regulations, communications with external auditors will normally be via the audit committee, although the board must maintain an appropriate relationship with the external auditors. However, internal and external auditors can also work together to ensure that the internal control system is sufficient; possibly by external audit delegating work to internal audit, and each auditor reviewing the work of the other auditor. The board will therefore receive reports from both sets of auditors which will be accurate because they have been properly checked.

Communication to the board

The internal auditor can also check that appropriate information is provided to the board from the external auditor. ISA 260 Communication of audit matters with those charged with governance provides a list of matters which should be communicated to the board and the internal auditor can work with the external auditor to ensure that this information is provided.

(b) The advantages of an audit committee include:

Public confidence

Providing increased public confidence in the credibility and objectivity of published financial information. This will be particularly important for ZX if listing arrangements go ahead. While an internal audit department is not normally necessary for incorporated companies, the provision of that department will provide additional confidence in the accuracy of the financial statements and hopefully make ZX an attractive investment.

Financial reporting

Supports the directors in fulfilling their financial reporting obligations. The directors have to prepare financial statements for ZX. The committee can assist by checking the financial statements to ensure that they comply with appropriate reporting requirements. This is especially important where the board do not have detailed knowledge of accounting requirements.

Communication

Enhancing the role of ZX's external auditors by providing an appropriate channel of communication. Use of the audit committee will enable the external auditor to discuss issues with the financial statements with the internal auditor, prior to providing a final summary of key points to the board.

'Friend' of the Board

The audit committee may also act as a 'critical friend' to the board by monitoring the work of the board and providing helpful guidance, where corporate governance requirements do not appear to be being met. The audit committee should have detailed knowledge of corporate governance as part of its monitoring function of the company and can share this with the board who may not have the time to obtain detailed information.

The disadvantages of an audit committee include:

Lack of understanding of function

As the directors in ZX do not have much knowledge of corporate governance, they may see the additional involvement of the audit committee as a threat to their authority or taking away some of their responsibilities. This memo has hopefully outlined the advantages of an audit committee in supporting the work of the directors, removing this as a problem.

Role of non-executive directors

As the audit committee will be made up mainly from non-executive directors, the board may see this as a means of decreasing their power and possibly letting other people run the company. Again, the audit committee must be seen as fulfilling a supporting role for the main board. It will utilise the special knowledge of accounts production and internal controls from the external auditor and business non-executives to provide appropriate review of information being given to the board.

Cost

The audit committee will increase the expenditure of the company as the non-executive directors will require some remuneration due to their additional responsibilities. While this cannot be avoided, the benefits of the committee in terms of providing assistance to the board and raising the profile of ZX ready for possible listing must not be forgotten.

10 OCTBALL

Key answer tips

There are no tricks in this question, but you do have to make sure you read the requirements carefully, as the question is not quite what you'd expect. In particular you must ensure that in part (a) you don't discuss the advantages and disadvantages of outsourcing, as that's not what's being asked. In part (c) ensure that the controls you mention are those that may be operated by the client.

(a) **Benefits of outsourcing to NFA**

Expertise available

The NFA partnership will be able to provide the necessary expertise for internal audit work. They may be able to provide a broader range of expertise as they serve many different clients therefore staff may be available for specialist work that Octball could not afford to employ.

Buy-in skills as necessary

If internal audit is only required for specific functions or particular jobs each year then the expertise can be purchased as required. Taking this approach will minimise in-house costs.

Independence/Qualifications

No information is provided on the qualification of staff in NFA, although as an independent firm it is likely that care will be taken that staff do remain independent and have the appropriate qualifications in order that they can provide an appropriate high level of service.

Audit techniques – training

Outsourcing will remove the need for training internal staff. Effectively training will be provided for 'free' as the outsourcing firm will be responsible for keeping staff up-to-date with new auditing techniques and processes.

Problems with outsourcing to NFA

Fee pressure

NFA may experience some fee pressure, but only in respect of maintaining cost effectiveness of the internal audit department. The relationship needs to be managed carefully to ensure that NFA do not decrease the quality of their work due to insufficient fees.

Knowledge

The NFA partnership will not have any prior knowledge of Octball. This will be a disadvantage as this will mean the partnership will need time to ascertain the accounting systems and controls etc in Octball before commencing work. However, provision of an independent view may identify control weaknesses etc that the current internal audit department have missed.

Location

The NFA partnership may not be able to provide this service to Octball as they are a local firm and therefore the issue of travel and working away from home would remain.

Continuity of service – staffing

As provision of audit services is the NFA partnership's main activity, they should also be able to budget for client requirements although this cannot be guaranteed as staff may still leave. However, as a larger internal auditing firm, they will be able to offer staff better career progression which should assist staff retention.

(b) **Items to be considered by T&M**

Independence

T&M need to ensure that independence can be maintained in a number of areas:

- Independence regarding recommending systems or preparing working papers and subsequent checking of those systems or working papers. While the internal audit department may need to carry out these functions, T&M must ensure that separate staff are used to provide the internal and external audit functions.
- Staff from T&M will be expected to follow the ethical guidance of ACCA which means that steps will be taken to avoid conflicts of interest or other independence issues such as close personal relationships building up with staff in Octball. Any real or perceived threats to independence will lower the overall trust that can be placed on internal audit reports produced by T&M.

Training

As a firm of auditors, T&M will automatically provide training for its staff as part of the in-house compliance with association regulations (e.g. compulsory CPD was introduced from January 2005). T&M will need to ensure that staff providing the internal audit function to Octball are aware of relevant guidance for internal auditors.

Skills

T&M must ensure that they have staff with the necessary skills and sufficient time to undertake the internal audit work in Octball. Skills may not be an issue because staff in T&M will already understand audit procedures.

Fee pressure

There may be fee pressure on T&M, either to maintain the cost effectiveness of the internal audit department, or to maintain the competitiveness of the audit fee itself in order to keep the internal audit work.

Knowledge

As external auditors, T&M will already have knowledge of Octball. This will assist in establishing the internal audit department as systems documentation will already be available and the audit firm will already be aware of potential weaknesses in the control systems.

(c) **Controls to maintain the standard of the internal audit department**

- If T&M are appointed, ensure that the internal and external audit is managed by different departments in the firm.
- Setting and review of performance measures such as cost, areas reviewed, etc with explanations obtained for any significant variances.
- Use of appropriate audit methodology, including clear documentation of audit work carried out, adequate review, and appropriate conclusions drawn.
- Review of working papers by myself, ensuring adherence to International Standards on Auditing where appropriate and any in-house standards on auditing.
- The work plan for internal audit is agreed prior to work commencing and this is followed by the outsourcing company.

11 INTERNAL AUDIT AND CORPORATE GOVERNANCE

Key answer tips

Note that part (a) actually has 6 requirements: you need to consider prevention, detection, reporting of fraud for each of internal and external auditors.

In part (b), don't forget to give relevant examples.

In part (c), the question is not asking whether internal audit should be outsourced but the issues that should be considered after the decision has already been made.

(a) Fraud and error

(i) The duties of internal auditors are generally determined by the organisation that has set up the internal audit department and employs the internal auditors. Internal auditors normally have a general responsibility to perform their work and their reviews of systems with the possibility of fraud and error in mind. This means that when they review the structure and operation of systems they have regard to strengths in the system that will prevent or detect fraud and error and weaknesses that will facilitate fraud and error.

(ii) When internal auditors discover structural or operational weaknesses that facilitate or fail to prevent or detect fraud and error, they generally have a duty to report such matters internally. The precise method of reporting varies from organisation to organisation. If internal auditors discover actual instances of fraud or error, they also have a duty to report it.

(iii) It can be difficult in practice for internal auditors to deal with actual or suspected management fraud. The 'Rules of Professional Conduct' do not permit auditors to remain silent on the subject. There is no general duty to report fraud or error outside the organisation and internal auditors, like other employees, have a duty of confidentiality to the organisation they work for. In extreme circumstances however, it may be necessary for internal auditors to report matters to persons outside the organisation (where money laundering is discovered, for example).

(iv) External auditors plan and perform their work with an attitude of professional scepticism. ISA 240 'Fraud and error' states that the audit is designed to detect material errors, which may be due to fraud or error, but this does not mean that the audit can be guaranteed to detect material fraud or error. Fraud or error should only be reported in the financial statements to shareholders if it is material. Like internal auditors, external auditors are bound by a duty of confidentiality to their clients. In most countries, external auditors do have a number of legal rights and duties to report certain types of suspected fraud, such as money laundering, to certain bodies. Confidential advice is available to external auditors from their professional bodies.

(b) Internal audit's role

(i) **Corporate governance**

(1) The objectives of good corporate governance include: the proper constitution of the board, proper arrangements for the remuneration of directors, proper mechanisms for shareholder relations, and proper accountability and audit.

(2) Accountability and audit includes the maintenance of a proper system of internal control. A proper system of internal control includes appropriate risk management systems and overall organisational control.

(3) Internal audit's role in the context of these objectives includes assisting management by suggesting ways in which these objectives can be achieved, and by monitoring progress.

Example for manufacturing company

The internal auditors can recommend to the board those areas in which structural changes need to be made in order to comply with codes of corporate governance, such as those issued by the OECD and the World Bank. They could recommend processes for setting objectives and targets, and for measuring their achievement.

(ii) **Risk management**

Internal audit has a particular interest in investigating and evaluating the company's risk management structures. Internal audit can manage the provision of the basic data which management can use in order to identify, prioritise and manage the risks facing the company. Internal audit can also help by developing models and techniques for identifying, prioritising and managing risk.

Example for manufacturing company

(1) In a manufacturing company, risk management issues to be addressed include operational, financial, health and safety and other regulatory issues. Internal audit can help in identifying the issues, evaluating their importance and suggesting mechanisms for managing or transferring the risk.

(2) The management of risk depends on the business objectives, short and long term, strategic and operational, and conflicts between objectives. These objectives include, for example, the need to provide a return to investors, the need for long-term investment, and the need to produce a quality product. Internal audit can help classify those risks.

(iii) **Organisational control**

The simple existence of an internal audit function is an example of organisational control. Internal audit can investigate and document existing control systems, and recommend improvements.

Example for manufacturing company

Areas of control to be addressed include the overall control environment, operational control and other areas designed to manage the risks as identified above. Internal audit can help in providing cost-benefit analyses in respect of the implementation of control procedures, as well as making recommendations on structural control.

(c) Out-sourced internal audit issues

The issues to be considered include:

(i) The costs of out-sourcing the function, including the internal administrative costs and the costs of managing the function. These may be more or less than internal costs, and a cost-benefit analysis will help establish the likely financial implications.

(ii) An out-sourced internal audit function will be more independent than an internal function, but this has to be set off against the (probably) superior knowledge of the business of the existing function.

(iii) Out-sourcing the internal audit function probably means a loss of control, whilst the responsibility for the function will remain with the company.

(iv) Change management issues have to be addressed (which can be time consuming and expensive). Existing staff have to be re-deployed (perhaps to the company to which the function is out-sourced) and there may be resentment of the new internal auditors and deliberate attempts to frustrate them.

(v) The choice of the out-sourcing company is important – it must have sufficient resources and experience and there is always a risk associated with this; the contract with the out-sourcing company will have to be carefully worded and the initial contract should only be for a limited period of time.

12 ROXY HOTELS

Key answer tips

Part (a) is examining you on the context in which an internal audit department is set up.

Part (b) is 'book' knowledge, and a reasonably prepared student will have no problem.

Parts (c) and (d) require you to apply your knowledge of the kinds of work internal auditors do. Use the information in the question to help you generate ideas for your answer.

(a) Role of internal audit

(i) Internal audit is part of the organisational control of a business; it is one of the methods used by the management to ensure the orderly and efficient running of the business as a whole and is part of the overall control environment.

(ii) A properly functioning internal audit department is part of good corporate governance, as recognised by national and international codes on corporate governance.

(iii) One of the objects of good corporate governance is to ensure that the needs of all stakeholders are met as far as possible and internal audit procedures meet the needs of the owners of the business, its employees, and the business community at large, as well as the needs of management.

(iv) The main way in which internal audit exercises its functions is by enabling management to perform proper risk assessments in relation to corporate objectives by means of properly understanding the strengths and weaknesses in all of the control systems in the business.

(v) The role of internal audit has expanded considerably in recent years and the scope of internal audit work is no longer routine or low level; internal audit is involved at all levels of management and internal audit work includes non-routine matters such as assisting in setting corporate objectives and assessing performance against them.

(b) Types of activities

(i) The review of management, organisational, operational, accounting, internal control, and other business systems.

(ii) Making recommendations in relation to the improvement of systems and monitoring the performance of systems against targets.

(iii) Performing value-for-money (economy, efficiency and effectiveness), best value and similar audits.

(iv) Compliance work involving the review of compliance with legislation, regulations and codes of practice.

(v) The detailed examination of financial and operating data.

(vi) Special investigations, such as fraud investigations.

(c) Checking transactions and balances

(i) The internal audit department might trace representative samples of room bookings and the booking of conference facilities from source documentation through the system, to ensure that the correct amounts are billed, that the facilities are paid for within the time limits agreed and that the correct amounts have been recorded in the correct accounting period.

(ii) The department might trace representative samples of orders for food and other consumables through the system to ensure that authorised suppliers are used where necessary, that the correct prices have been billed by suppliers, that payment has been made on the agreed terms, and that the correct amounts have been recorded in the correct accounting period.

(iii) The department might trace representative samples of additions to and disposals of assets through the system from the physical assets themselves, through the daybooks and ledgers to the original authorisation for purchase, to ensure that all assets acquired are properly authorised.

(iv) The department might trace representative samples of additions to and disposals of assets in the opposite direction, i.e. From authorisations to assets to ensure that they are in good condition and still in the hotels.

(v) The department might select representative samples of receivables and payables for direct confirmation.

(vi) The department might check on the existence of certain employees and on the accuracy of the payroll calculations with reference to records of hours worked kept at the hotels.

(d) Reviews of systems

(i) The internal audit department might review the documentation of the centralised booking systems and evaluate it. They might then review the actual operation of the system in practice and make recommendations for improvements or change.

(ii) The department might review the integrity of the systems by the use of computer assisted audit and other techniques to ensure that access to the system is restricted to those who should have access and to ensure that the system is producing exception reports as it should. The use of dummy data and false passwords might be used in such an assessment.

(iii) Analytical procedures could be performed to evaluate the relative financial and operational performance of individual hotels, hotels in certain regions and the performance of the various classes of business (tourist and business accommodation, conference and leisure facilities, restaurants and bars etc.). Performance could be also evaluated against budgets, on a seasonal basis and by comparison with prior years and periods.

(iv) Analytical procedures could be performed on relationships such as those between drinks and meals consumed, and those between occupancy rates and other facilities used.

PLANNING AND RISK ASSESSMENT

13 RELIANCE ON INTERNAL AUDIT

Key answer tips

This question focuses on the relationship between the internal and external audit functions. This is a standard area which should have been covered thoroughly in your studies – however, as always, the exam question as set gives the topic a specific emphasis which must be fully reflected in your answer.

In dealing with part (a) it is important to appreciate that the objectives of the external auditors are more concerned with the true and fair view presented by the financial statements than are the internal auditors. Consider the situations given in the question in this context.

Much of your answer to part (b) can be based on standard material – but note that a good answer must make some specific reference to the cyclical aspect of the work of the internal auditors.

Parts (c) and (d) are dealing with reasonably standard aspects of the relationship between the internal and external audit functions – these should not produce major difficulties in answering the question.

(a) Reliance on work of internal auditors

(i) As requested, the external auditors will seek to rely on the work of internal audit to the maximum extent possible. This might cover planning, risk assessment, tests of controls and substantive testing.

(ii) In all cases, the external auditor should be aware that the purpose of internal audit's work will not be primarily directed towards the financial statements.

(iii) In relation to the cyclical audit of internal controls, it may be possible to rely on the work of internal audit in relation to all of the areas noted, but only if the internal controls audited affect the financial statements. It may be that internal audit's work on operations and customer support is less relevant than its work in other areas.

(iv) In relation to the four-year review of internal controls – the extent of reliance will depend on how long ago the last review was conducted. If it was conducted recently, it will provide help in relation to the external auditors' assessment of the accounting and internal control systems.

(v) In relation to risk management – the relevance of internal audit work depends on the extent to which risks in relation to reporting in general, and the financial statements in particular, have been addressed separately by management. This work will be relevant to the external auditors' risk assessment and planning.

(b) Information required

(i) The information required to determine the extent of external audit reliance on internal audit's cyclical audit will be:

- internal audit's systems documentation (the work on information systems and finance may include documentation of the company's accounting and internal control systems);
- internal audit's planning documentation which may cover a risk analysis, tests of controls and substantive procedures;
- the results of tests of control and substantive procedures;
- documentation on the four-year review of internal controls, particularly in relation to the finance and information services functions.

(ii) The external auditors should ask to see all documentation relating to the work performed by internal audit on information services restructuring during the year because the external auditors' assessment and testing of systems will be split into two parts, pre- and post-restructuring.

(iii) Other documentation requested will include internal audit's operating procedures manuals and documentation relating to the recruitment, training and development of internal audit staff, and management responses to internal audit recommendations. This information is required to enable the external auditor to form an opinion on the competence and effectiveness of the internal audit function.

(c) Circumstances in which it would not be possible to rely on the work of internal audit

(i) It may not be possible to rely on the work of internal auditors if they:

- are not competent (this relates to experience as well as qualifications);
- lack integrity;
- do not properly plan or document their work, or if management does not act on (or at least respond to) recommendations made;
- do not perform work relevant to the external auditor.

(ii) It will also not be possible to rely on internal audit if internal audit is insufficiently independent within the organisation, i.e. where internal auditors have insufficient operational freedom, where they are reporting to those who control the functions that they work on, or where they are reporting on their own work.

(d) External auditor work

(i) External auditors will wish to perform work independently, regardless of internal audit work, in all areas that are material to the financial statements. For immaterial areas in which internal audit work can be shown by testing and review to be adequate, it may be possible to rely on the work of internal audit without performing any other work.

(ii) Areas material to the financial statements are likely to be long and short-term leasing receivables and inventory. Leases may be complex and the auditors will wish to ensure that accounting policies are appropriate and that they have been properly applied. The valuation of inventory will have a direct effect on the profit for the period. This is an area that is easy to manipulate and external auditors will wish to ensure that this has not happened.

(iii) External auditors will also wish to perform their own risk analysis and final review of financial statements in order to ensure that no high risk areas have been overlooked.

14 FLYLO

Key answer tips

This question provides you with a basic scenario about an airline company and is testing your knowledge of internal audit and how this relates to the external auditor. It is vital that you are clear as to their different purpose(s). In part (a) you need to explain why the work of the internal auditor is of use to the external auditor, remember to relate this to the question and split your answer into the three functions given. It is important not to panic if you know nothing about airlines – the question is not testing your knowledge of airlines but of key functions such as sales, accounts receivable, non-current assets, accounts payable and long term loans (borrowings).

Part (b) focuses on the quality of the internal audit function and how this affects the extent of the external audit's reliance; this is very straightforward and shouldn't cause you any problems if you have revised sufficiently. There are 5 marks to be gained, so essentially you are looking to provide a minimum of 5 key points in your answer.

Part (c) is worth 6 marks and is examining your knowledge of audit evidence and the different types available to the auditor. You are being asked to concentrate on the areas of payroll and catering; clearly with payroll there are key security issues and with catering there are health and safety issues. Again, you must remember to tailor your answer to the question and not just provide general details about audit evidence.

(a) Use of the work of the internal auditors by external auditors

Sales and ticketing

(i) The sales function is likely to be integrated with the accounting and internal control system used to produce the figure in the financial statements for revenue, on which the external auditor reports.

(ii) The internal auditors' work on the ticketing system is less likely to be useful because it relates to an operational area which does not have a direct impact on the financial statements. There are, however, regulatory matters that may need to be considered by the external auditor. Ticketing may also have an indirect effect because it is likely to be integrated with the sales system and there is likely to be some crossover between the controls over ticketing and controls over sales generally. The work of the internal auditors is therefore likely to be of some use to the external auditor.

Fleet acquisition and maintenance

(iii) The internal auditors' work on the fleet acquisition system is likely to be very relevant to the external auditors because owned aircraft and leased aircraft will constitute a substantial element of balance sheet assets and liabilities, and depreciation and finance charges in the income statement.

(iv) Much of the internal auditors' work is likely to relate to ensuring that company policy has been complied with. Policy will relate to the authorisation for and acquisition of aircraft, and accounting for aircraft in terms of the correct classification of leases (operating or financing) and depreciation policy, for example. Company policy is likely to be extensive and detailed for such material items and external auditors will be concerned to ensure that it is both appropriate and has been complied with.

(v) It is also possible that the internal auditors' work may involve some verification of the income statement and balance sheet entries at the year-end. Given the likely materiality of the amounts involved, this work will also be of interest to the external auditors.

(vi) It is possible that the internal auditors' work may also relate to the quality of aircraft, and other operational aspects of fleet management. These issues may also be relevant to the external auditors, at least insofar as they relate to compliance with laws and regulations.

(vii) In relation to maintenance, the internal auditors' work is likely to relate to the authorisation and correct accounting for maintenance expenditure (capitalisation or expensing), and on the operational side, to the quality thereof, as for fleet acquisition (above). Maintenance expenditure in the income statement may well be material and the work of the internal auditors is therefore of interest to external auditors.

Trade payables and long term debt financing

(viii) The extent of the external auditor's interest in the internal auditors' work on trade payables and long term financing will depend on the materiality of the amounts involved. Trade payables (for certain types of routine maintenance, and payables due to the service organisations, for example) may be material. Long term debt financing is very likely to be material as many airlines have substantial debt financing.

(ix) Internal audit work on trade payables is likely to involve ensuring that routine internal controls are properly designed and are operating. The external auditors may well be interested in the internal auditors' work in this area.

(x) There are substantial financial statement disclosures required for debt financing. The internal auditors' assistance with ensuring that disclosures are properly made, as well as with ensuring that any covenants have been complied with and that the accounting for the financing is appropriate, may also be helpful to the external auditors.

(b) Quality of internal audit function: extent of reliance

(i) The quality of the internal audit function will have a significant effect on the extent of the external auditor's reliance. If the quality of work is not adequate, reliance will not be possible, regardless of the extent and relevance of the work performed.

(ii) The firm will seek to ensure that there is an appropriate structure within the department itself, with appropriate reporting lines outside the department, preferably reporting to the audit committee.

(iii) The internal audit function has recently been expanded and there are likely to be changes in the way that it is organised. The function should have operational independence within the organisation and formal terms of reference that encompass the recent changes made.

(iv) The function should have a clearly defined set of operating procedures, as well as a work program. Proper documentation of all work performed is essential.

(v) Staff should be appropriately trained, experienced and qualified. The head of such an important department should preferably be professionally qualified.

(c) Audit evidence: outsourced functions

(i) Internal controls exercised by the company over in-flight catering and payroll must be properly designed and operated. The firm will seek to review documentation of controls and internal audit reports. It will seek to obtain evidence that controls have been applied.

(ii) A breach of regulations or a deterioration in the quality of catering could both have a significant effect on the financial statements, particularly if fines were payable or adverse publicity was likely. Enquiries into both areas and a review of relevant documentation provided by, for example, food licensing authorities to the company or the service organisation, and company lawyers (in relation to passenger complaints, perhaps), will be necessary.

(iii) Evidence of controls sought by the firm will include:

- controls over the selection of the service organisations selected (by competitive tendering, for example);
- evidence relating to the completeness, accuracy and timeliness of information provided to, and received from, the payroll organisation (batch summaries and exception reports, for example);
- evidence relating to the security measures taken by the payroll organisation to ensure that confidential information is kept confidential;
- evidence relating to the security measures taken by the catering organisation to ensure that health and safety standards are maintained and that no 'sabotage' of the food can take place.

15 EWHEELS

Key answer tips

Part (a) is book knowledge, but part (b) requires application of your knowledge of risk to the scenario. This type of question is very common.

Part (c) is following on from part (b) in that risks have been identified relating to going concern and you now have to say how you would investigate to see if they're serious.

Make sure you understand the impact of going concern status on the audit report; it's examined frequently and often answered badly.

(a) Audit risk

(i) Audit risk is the product of inherent risk, control risk and detection risk. Audit risk is often 'set' by the audit firm at a certain level (say 3% to 5%), and the nature and extent of testing in a particular audit are determined by an assessment of the other elements of risk.

(ii) Inherent risk is the risk that material errors will occur both at the entity level, and at the level of individual transactions and balances. Certain account balances and certain entities are more inherently risky than others. For example, inventory is more inherently risky than cash, volatile businesses are more inherently risky than stable businesses.

(iii) Control risk is the risk that internal controls will not prevent or detect material errors, both at the entity level, and at the level of individual transactions and balances.

(iv) Detection risk is the risk that auditors will fail to detect material errors (due to human error or sampling risk, for example).

(b) Risks associated with the audit

(i) In the case of EWheels, the level of inherent risk, control risk and detection risk all appear to be higher than normal.

(ii) EWheels is in a volatile sector of the economy. It has grown rapidly and is planning further expansion which will require additional resources. There is a real risk of 'over-trading', i.e. that the business will exhaust its cash resources too soon as a result of rapid growth. In such circumstances, there is a risk that creditors will go unpaid and that the business will be forced into liquidation. This is risky for both the directors and for the auditors.

(iii) In a highly competitive sector, there is a possibility that the company itself will be vulnerable to take-over, particularly if it is in a weak financial position which it appears to be with net liabilities. The dispute between the ex-director and the current directors means that the current directors do not have overall control of the company. It is particularly important in take-over situations for auditors to be cautious in the audit opinion they give.

(iv) The overall control environment at EWheels is weak. There has been no proper control of the accounting function for six months and errors are appearing as a result. This may mean that the accounting records are unreliable and the financial statements may be materially misstated.

(v) The attitude of the directors (which is relevant to the overall control environment) is suspect, they have indicated that they would prefer an unmodified opinion in circumstances which may warrant a modified opinion. They also appear to be overly ambitious in their expansion plans.

(vi) EWheels is suffering from financial pressures; it wishes to expand but additional resources are needed and they are becoming scarcer, loan finance may become more expensive. The ex-director is claiming a substantial amount of money from the company. It may be preferable for the company to seek further equity finance or to delay the expansion plans.

(vii) The audit is also risky for the firm because this is the first year of audit (and mistakes are therefore more likely to be made) and because there is pressure to issue an unmodified opinion. It will be important for the firm to ensure that adequate time and resources are allocated to what is likely to be a difficult audit. Any pressure by the directors to complete the audit quickly should be resisted.

(c) Reference to going concern status

(i) It will be necessary to review the overall financing position of the company in detail. This will involve examining budgets and cash flow forecasts, and performance against budgets and cash flow forecasts. If this information is not available for whatever reason, it will probably be necessary for the directors to produce it.

(ii) The relationship between the company and its bankers should be investigated thoroughly, because if the relationship is poor, additional finance is unlikely to be forthcoming.

(iii) It is likely that financial information will be sent to the bank on a regular basis and this should be inspected. It will be necessary to inspect correspondence with the bank and possibly for the auditors to make their own enquiries of the bank, although banks do not normally provide much information to auditors in this context.

(iv) Enquiries should be made of directors about that availability of additional equity and other finance which will be necessary for the planned expansion. All statements in this respect should be corroborated and supported by documentation.

(v) Enquiries should be made of the company's lawyers as to the nature and likely outcome of the dispute with the ex-director. It will be necessary to make either a provision or disclosure in the financial statements unless it is very unlikely that any amount will be payable to him.

(d) Audit reports

(i) The audit report would probably be modified by means of the inclusion of an 'emphasis of matter' paragraph, highlighting the problem. This would only be possible however, if the matter were adequately disclosed in the financial statements.

(ii) If the matter were not adequately disclosed in the financial statements, it might be necessary to issue an 'except for' opinion, disagreeing with the lack of disclosure in the financial statements.

(iii) An 'adverse' opinion stating that the financial statements do not fairly present the position at all because of the lack of disclosure might be necessary if the auditors considered the matter to be fundamental to the view given by the financial statements as a whole.

(iv) In extreme circumstances, where it was clear that the company was not a going concern, and the financial statements were still prepared on a going concern basis, it would probably be necessary to issue an 'adverse' opinion.

16 BONDI

Key answer tips

This question is about risk, but doesn't ask you to identify risks as such. Part (a) is about how the identified risks should affect your decision to accept the audit. Part (b) is about the work you will do to get more information in response to these risks.

(a) Arguments against acceptance of nomination

- Rapid growth is often accompanied by inadequate accounting systems and weak internal controls. Of itself this is not sufficient reason to decline an audit but it increases inherent risk.
- Rapid growth through aggressive take-overs implies a management philosophy that is willing to accept risks and this is likely to apply to controls as well. Again this increases inherent risk.
- Failure to take action against employee fraud brought to their notice by the auditors is more serious. This fosters a visible culture of unethical behaviour that is likely to permeate the company and to be shared by all employees. This will result in a weak control environment.
- Introduction of a new computer system must be undertaken very carefully. In addition, an unnecessarily complicated system is one of the warning signs of fraud. Such a computer system may be difficult to audit.
- Aggression against audit failure through fear of the audit staff to query management explanations.
- The complexity of contractual arrangements between car manufacturers and dealers provides powerful incentives to management to manipulate the records to secure short term gains.

- The impending public listing means that the company is under pressure to show an improving performance but also means that the work of the auditor will come under increasing scrutiny. There are always significant risks in accepting an audit under such terms.

Arguments for accepting nomination

As a larger firm your firm is likely to have the capability of influencing the directors of Bondi and persuading them of the benefits of a more ethical style of business. This will benefit the company's shareholders. If your firm rejects the audit they are likely to appoint a less reputable firm. This will not be in the shareholders' interest and may discredit the profession.

(b) Audit planning

Employee frauds

- I would be anxious to obtain information about the alleged employee frauds. I would need to identify the control weaknesses that were exploited and whether any changes had been made to the accounting and internal control systems.
- I would also want to know the current positions held by the guilty employees.

Computer system

- I would pay particular attention to the control environment relating to computer systems and to evaluation of general and application controls.
- I would need to ensure the audit team included sufficient computer audit specialists.
- My tests of controls would almost certainly include the use of computer assisted audit techniques.

Contracts with manufacturers

I would enquire closely into such contracts and the strategies adopted by the company for securing maximum benefit from the contracts. I would need assistance from an industry specialist as to problems encountered by manufacturers and dealers in confirming compliance with the contracts.

(c) Misstatement

- This appears to be a fraud against the government through falsification of accounting records. I would need to be satisfied that the falsification of the records is deliberate and not an accidental consequence of a poorly designed computer system.
- I would raise the matter with management and request that they correct the fictitious records, make full provisions for all taxes including any penalties for which they are potentially liable and make a full disclosure to the taxation authorities.
- If management refuse, I would qualify my opinion as to the amount of taxes not provided for, if material. I would not spell out my detailed reasons nor accuse the directors of impropriety.
- I would need to consult with solicitors as to any further action I should take. Unless there is a statutory duty of disclosure of such matters, the matter is hardly one of public interest. I am probably constrained by my duty of confidentiality from raising the matter with the taxation authorities.
- If I am not statutorily required to make disclosure and the directors refuse to make a voluntary disclosure, I should consider resigning from the audit.

17 NEPCO

Key answer tips

One of the main characteristics of modern auditing is the 'risk based' approach. Some marks can be gained on this question for explaining the risk concepts involved, but more marks are available for application of the principles to the facts in the question.

In part (a) you could briefly explain the concept of inherent risk, but you must spend most of your time identifying the key risk elements which affect the company. You are concerned here with the concept of 'entity risk', which revolves around the general environment in which the company operates – a lot of information on this is given in the question. There appears to be little to say about control risk – but note that the type of incentive schemes operated by the company may promote manipulation of accounting data in order to boost perceived performance. As far as detection risk – you should have noticed that the audit firm is new to this client and this industry – there also seems to be pressure on the audit fee.

Your answer to part (b) should lead to relevant points to mention in part (b) – for example the audit consequences of the reward systems in place. You can also add comments on such standard areas as materiality.

(a) Risks

(i) **Inherent risks include**:

(1) The competition from Asian and Far Eastern companies, and rising raw material prices. This means that there is pressure on profits and the ability to reward employees and pay dividends to institutional shareholders which increases the pressure to manipulate the financial statements to show good returns.

(2) The potentially volatile market (computer components) in which new technology can render hardware obsolete in a very short time. This means that there is an ongoing risk to the business as a whole (a potential going concern risk) – the company must be adaptable.

(3) The risk that regulators may reject a product which has taken many months or years to develop.

(4) The pressures for returns from institutional investors which means that there may be a temptation to manipulate the financial statements.

(5) The possible sale of shares, increasing the pressure for returns in order to get the best possible price, which increases the pressure to manipulate the financial statements.

(6) The inherent risks in diversification into unknown areas (the supply of other customers) –but these are not current risks.

(ii) **Control risks**: there are apparently very few except for the performance-related payment, including share options, which provides an incentive to produce 'acceptable' figures.

(iii) **Detection risk**: this is the firm's first year as auditors and there are tight controls on audit costs, which may lead to inadequate audit evidence unless the audit is properly directed, supervised and reviewed. This is compounded by the firm's lack of experience in this area. It is important that those with experience are employed on this audit, at least in a review capacity.

(b) Matters to which attention should be paid and work to be performed

(i) The good accounting records and internal control combined with the need to keep audit costs down means that a compliance approach, rather than a substantive approach will be necessary wherever possible.

(ii) Audit work will need to be directed towards inventory (despite the fact that it is well controlled) because it is material to the accounts. There is no year-end inventory count, and inventory is relatively easy to manipulate. It is likely that there will be a substantial amount of work-in-progress and its valuation will need to be reviewed carefully. It may be possible to rely on any interim or cyclical inventory counting.

(iii) The projects on which compliance problems have arisen should be examined carefully as the costs may be significant and there may be a temptation to understate them.

(iv) Overall profits and any unadjusted errors should be examined carefully because of the inherent risks noted above and the performance-related pay.

(v) The company's going concern status should be reviewed by examining its financial status, financial support and likely future developments in high risk areas.

18 RISKS

Key answer tips

Part (a) of this question may appear to be difficult or even obscure at first sight – it is however based on straightforward principles: identifying and managing business risk, which is seen to be one of the key functions of the internal auditor and of the internal review concept. The examiner asks you to consider the possibilities of transferring, reducing or accepting each of the risks outlined in the question. It is important to appreciate that it may not be necessary to deal with each of these possibilities in respect of each risk identified – think what techniques may (and may not) be appropriate in each situation. A good, practical, business approach is more important than technical auditing knowledge in tackling a question of this type!

Part (b) is more textbook based, dealing with the extent to which the external auditor may rely on work performed by the internal auditors. Here, you must make sure that your answer relates specifically to the area of risk assessment – a generalised answer would not score well here.

(a) Transfer, reduce or accept

(i) **Contaminated foodstuffs – market share and profit margins**

The business would reduce the risk relating to contaminated foodstuffs by having good quality control procedures in place, by adhering to quality control standards such as ISO 9000, and by commissioning independent audits of the production process. The business might also try and transfer the risk by means of insurance against the consequential losses.

The business would reduce the risk of the loss of market share or profit margins by monitoring the activities of competitors carefully, by monitoring production costs and techniques, and by maintaining an appropriate level of advertising expenditure and other methods of promoting brand loyalty.

(ii) **Non-availability of a basic element of production – injuries to employees or damage to property**

It may be necessary to accept these risks as some insurance policies exclude liability caused by events such as 'acts of God' and there is likely to be little cover for a significant world shortage of basic commodities such as sugar.

The business would reduce the risk relating to sugar by maintaining a variety of suppliers. In relation to earthquake, it would implement normal health and safety procedures to prevent injuries to employees and would maintain the buildings properly. It would attempt to transfer the risk of any damages payable to employees and the costs of repairing property by means of insurance.

(iii) **Minor damage to property**

The business is likely to accept this risk or to transfer it by means of insurance.

Low impact, low likelihood risks are sometimes not viewed as risks at all. They are included for the sake of completeness in the analysis to ensure that risks have not been ignored as a result of misclassification.

(iv) **Drivers involved in vehicle accidents – production employees may be ill**

The business is likely to reduce the risk by maintaining its vehicles and training its drivers, and to transfer it by insuring against the cost of repairs and lost time. Alternatively, it might require drivers to buy their own vehicles and maintain them, but permit drivers to claim expenses. Another possibility is a fleet management programme dealing with all matters relating to vehicles, including providing alternative vehicles whilst others are being repaired.

The risk of production employees being ill is likely to be accepted as the cost of transferring it by insurance may not be worthwhile. The business may reduce it by providing a good working environment, free or subsidised health insurance, and incentives for good attendance records. It would also plan for a certain level of absences by production employees.

(b) External auditor use of internal auditor work

(i) The external auditor may review the work performed by internal auditors because financial statement risk may be viewed as just one part of the overall risk to the business.

(ii) The performance of the risk assessment itself is indicative of good overall management controls.

(iii) The external auditor, with the permission of management and the co-operation of the chief internal auditor, would review the work performed by the department with a view to ensuring that it appears to be complete, and that classifications are appropriate.

(iv) It is important to bear in mind that what is low risk or low impact to one entity may be high risk and high impact to another.

(v) The external auditor will pay particular attention to those risks identified that are either high risk, or high impact. Such risks may have a material impact on the financial statements.

(vi) The external auditor will then assess how the business has dealt with those risks (by transferring, reducing or accepting them) and include that risk assessment in his or her own assessment of risk for the financial statements as a whole, and for particular account areas. This will then affect the nature and extent of audit testing.

(vii) For example, if the risk of contamination to foodstuffs in the production process is not properly managed, there is more likelihood that a provision may be required at the period-end and there may even be a risk that the business may not be a going concern if the business is in breach of health and safety regulations.

19 HIVEX

Key answer tips

Part (a) requires you to comment on the performance indicated by the figures presented to you. Analytical procedures are the key technique required here. A sound approach would be to identify the main features as revealed by a comparison between the two years' figures and by identifying key relationships within each year's figures. Note that this part carries only 8 marks – do not spend too much time on it.

Part (b) follows on from your performance evaluation in part (a). You are asked to identify high risk areas and related audit procedures. Use the information gained in part (a), supplemented if necessary by other points. Try to take a logical and systematic approach to your answer – an answer plan structured under appropriate headings will help you in this respect. It is also important, as always, to answer the question fully – risks and audit procedures are both required!

(a) Performance

(i) The company has increased its sales by 12% and its gross profit by 16% which in a competitive market is very good (if not entirely credible) however, increased operating expenses have resulted in a reduction in operating profits of 20%.

(ii) The gross margin is very high; this is not abnormal in this sector, especially for software (although the margin is high for hardware), but it may also be the result of errors, because the information has been produced very quickly. This is also true of the other figures.

(iii) Total expenses as a percentage of sales have increased substantially with the result that operating profit as a percentage of sales has reduced by around a third.

(iv) The increase in the selling expenses as a percentage of sales may reflect the need for the company to spend more on advertising.

(v) The increase in the distribution costs as a percentage of sales may reflect inefficiencies in the method of distribution in an industry that separates these functions.

(vi) The administrative expenses as a percentage of sales have halved although they do not represent a significant amount in absolute terms.

(vii) The reduction in operating profits has been partially offset by increased net interest receivable but profit before tax is still down 10%.

(viii) The reduction in profit before tax and the increased tax charge have resulted in a reduction in profit after tax of over 40%.

(ix) Total dividends have been increased, despite the lower profits, which has meant an overall reduction in retained profits of almost 60%.

(x) The reduction in earnings per share is partly due to the reduction in profits but there is insufficient information to state whether it is also attributable to an increase in the number of shares, although this seems likely.

(b) Higher risk areas and audit procedures

Gross margin and operating expenses

(i) I would obtain a detailed schedule of revenue and cost of sales showing the opening and closing inventory figures for both software and hardware and I would perform a detailed review of changes on, say, a monthly, quarterly and half-yearly basis.

(ii) I would ascertain the accounting policies for revenue recognition for both software and hardware and ensure that they were in accordance with relevant International Accounting Standards. I would then test the application of these policies to individual transactions. IAS 38 Intangible assets requires certain development costs to be capitalised in the balance sheet and requires that research costs and costs that do not meet the criteria for capitalisation be expensed.

(iii) I would seek to establish why all three categories of operating expenses have changed so dramatically, by enquiry and by obtaining a schedule of operating expenses and a breakdown of the cost of sales figure.

(iv) I would perform detailed analytical procedures on operating expenses and cost of sales/gross margins, on a quarterly and monthly basis and I would also perform detailed testing of transactions in these areas in order to ensure that misclassifications have not occurred.

(v) Audit evidence provided by balance sheet work on the inventory figures (such as analytical procedures performed on the inventory levels and attendance at the inventory count) will provide evidence in relation to cost of sales.

(vi) It is possible that some reclassifications or even errors have been made – some costs appearing as operating expenses might properly belong in cost of sales. It certainly seems odd that while sales have increased by 12%, the cost of sales figure has hardly increased at all. The reduction in administrative expenses should also be investigated.

(vii) I would obtain schedules relating to non-current assets and establish the extent to which these had contributed to an increase in depreciation costs. I would enquire as to the nature of the additions and their purpose. Additional non-current assets would also be expected to contribute to revenues. If the change in the earnings per share figure is (partly) a result of a new issue of shares, it may be that the cash generated has been used for investment in non-current assets.

(viii) Because of the possibility of errors, I would increase my sample sizes during tests of controls over the recording, processing and posting of transactions that are posted to revenue, cost of sales and operating expense accounts.

(ix) I would perform detailed substantive testing on samples of transactions in these areas from source documentation (such as licensing documentation, payroll records, purchase invoices for components, etc.) through to the daybooks, ledgers, and schedules supporting the income statement (for completeness), and vice versa.

(x) The extent of substantive procedures will depend on the extent to which controls are shown to be effective and I would be particularly careful to follow up any errors discovered in both tests of controls and substantive testing. I would also pay particular attention to any unauthorised, substantial or late adjustments.

Interest receivable

(xi) I would ask for a breakdown of, and explanation for, the increase in net interest receivable. I would perform further analytical procedures on the interest costs and income and ensure that these are in line with current interest rates and the types of investments held by the company.

Taxation

(xii) It seems strange that the tax figure has increased so dramatically. I would ask for copies of the tax calculations for detailed review, and to corroborate explanations provided by management.

Dividends and earnings per share

(xiii) I would enquire as to why dividends had increased, despite the lower profits, and establish whether this trend can be maintained in the face of falling profits. I would also enquire as to whether the company has any plans to restructure in line with trends in the industry, what the company intends to do about the competition, and whether there is any possibility of a take-over.

(xiv) I would establish whether there had been any share issue during the year that had affected the calculation of the earnings per share and, if there had been, what was the purpose of the share issue.

20 ROCK

Key answer tips

This question is split into two equal sections and both relate to the scenario about the audit of Rock. It concentrates on the planning/audit approach and review elements of the audit. Part (a) is relatively straightforward and is testing your knowledge of the procedures you would perform during the planning/risk assessment stage of the audit, methods you would use to decide your audit approach and the information you would obtain and from whom. Part (b) focuses on the review stage and tests your knowledge of audit working papers and their completion. Clearly, you should include details of the different types of audit working papers and their purpose. With this type of question it can often help to put yourself in the position of the reviewer and consider your expectations of a junior.

(a) Information and procedures: understanding the entity and its environment and risk assessment for Rock

(i) Understanding the entity and risk assessment is likely to involve a review of prior year risk assessments as a starting point and the identification of changes during the year from the information gathered that may alter that assessment.

(ii) Risk assessment procedures involve enquiries of management and others, analytical procedures and observation and inspection. Members of the engagement team should discuss the susceptibility of the financial statements to material misstatements.

(iii) Risk assessment also involves obtaining an understanding of the relevant industry, regulatory and other matters including the financial reporting framework, the nature of the entity, the application of accounting policies, the entity's objectives and related business risks, and its financial performance. This may involve:

1 a review of prior year working papers noting any particular issues that arose warranting attention in the current year;

2 discussions with the audit senior or manager working on Rock in prior years to establish any particular problem areas;

3 discussions with Rock (and their other advisors such as banks and lawyers) to establish any particular problem areas;

4 review of any third party information on the client such as press reports;

5 a review of management accounts, any financial information provided to the stock exchange or draft financial statements that may be available to establish trends in the business;

6 a review of any changes in stock exchange requirements;

7 a review of systems documentation (either generated by Rock or held by the firm) to see if it needs updating.

(iv) Auditors should obtain an understanding of the control environment, the entity's process for identifying and dealing with business risk, information systems, control activities and monitoring of contents.

(v) Risks should be assessed at the financial statements level, and at the assertion level, and identify significant risks that require special audit consideration, and risks for which substantive procedures alone do not provide sufficient, appropriate audit evidence.

(vi) Analytical procedures are often used to highlight areas warranting particular audit attention. In the case of Rock, they are likely to focus on inventory which is likely to have a significant effect on profit (there may be slow moving or obsolete inventory that needs to be written down) and on property, plant and equipment which (as a manufacturer and distributor) is likely to be a significant item on the balance sheet.

(vii) Risk assessment will facilitate the determination of materiality and tolerable error (calculations are normally based on sales, profit and assets) that will be used in determining the sample sizes and in the evaluation of errors.

(b) Types and features of audit working papers

(i) *Types of audit working papers include*:

1 systems documentation (flowcharts, systems manuals, narrative notes, checklists and questionnaires, etc.);

2 constitutional documents;

3 agreements with banks and other providers of finance;

4 details of other advisors used by the entity such as lawyers;

5 regulatory documentation relating to the stock exchange listing;

6 audit planning documentation;

7 audit work programs;

8 working papers showing the work performed;

9 lead schedules showing summaries of work performed and conclusions on individual account areas and the amounts to be included in the financial statements;

10 trial balances, management accounts and financial statements;

11 standard working papers relating to the calculation of sample sizes, for example;

12 schedules of unadjusted differences;

13 schedules of review points;

14 letters of weakness and management representation letters.

(ii) *Features of audit working papers*:

1 All working papers (without exception) should show by whom they were prepared and when, and when they were reviewed and/or updated, and by whom, by means of signatures and dates – these may be electronic in the case of electronic working papers;

2 audit planning documentation should include the risk assessment which should be cross referenced to the audit program, and the audit program should be cross referenced to the audit working papers and vice versa;

3 working papers showing the work performed should be cross referenced to the audit program and the lead schedule on that particular section of the audit file, and should describe the nature of the work performed, the evidence obtained, and the conclusions reached;

4 each section of the audit file should have a lead schedule which should be cross referenced back to the relevant working papers;

5 trial balances should be cross referenced back to the relevant section of the audit file, and cross referenced forward to the financial statements;

6 the financial statements should be cross referenced to the trial balance;

7 schedules of unadjusted differences should be cross referenced to the sections of the file to which they relate;

8 schedules of review points should all be 'cleared' to show that all outstanding matters have been dealt with.

21 ANALYTICAL PROCEDURES

Key answer tips

Students tend to be good at calculating ratios but less good at commenting on them. This question asks you ONLY to suggest possible reasons for the changes, so there are no marks for calculations. You MUST understand how changes in numbers in the financial statements affect ratios.

An understanding of materiality is fundamental. Ensure you understand the concept of qualitative as well as quantitative materiality.

(a) Possible reasons for changes

All of the changes noted below may also be due to simple accounting errors or, in some cases, misappropriation of inventory or cash.

(i) *Increase in current ratio*

An increase in the current ratio may indicate increased inventory, cash or receivables levels. The implications of this may be that the company is expanding, or alternatively that it is experiencing trading difficulties and is unable to sell its inventory or to collect its receivables. An increase may also be due to a decrease in trade payables or other current liabilities.

(ii) *Decrease in gross profit margin*

A decrease in the gross profit margin may indicate that the cost of raw materials or bought in goods has increased, or that discounts or selling prices have decreased. This may not be a bad thing if the reason for this is an overall increase in sales revenue.

(iii) *Increase in inventory holding period*

The inventory holding period indicates the number of days the company could continue to trade if supplies were to cease. The longer the period, the higher the level of inventory held. Inventory holding involves expenditure. Generally, the lower the figure the better provided that the company does not run out of inventory. An increase can indicate that the company is unable to sell its inventory. An increase can also indicate that the company is expecting additional sales, or simply that the business is expanding. Many businesses are cyclical and increases and decreases are to be expected.

(iv) *Increase in dividend cover*

Dividend cover shows how many times a company could pay the dividends it has decided to pay to shareholders. If a company's dividend cover is increasing, it may simply mean that it is making greater profits in relation to the dividends it pays out. It may also mean that the company could pay out more dividends in future, or that the company is paying out a reduced dividend and is investing more in the business.

(v) *An increase in capital gearing (leverage)*

Gearing is the relationship between equity and borrowings. A high level of gearing generally indicates that the company must service (pay the interest on) fixed interest borrowings. This means that there is less available for shareholders but it may also mean that the company is expanding, which means greater returns for shareholders in the future. A high gearing ratio may mean that the company is at risk of going concern problems.

(b) Materiality

(i) *Concept*

Information is material if its omission or misstatement could influence the economic decisions of users taken on the basis of financial statements. Materiality depends on the size of the item or error judged in the particular circumstances of its omission or misstatement. So what might be material in one year might not be material the next, and what might be material to one company might not be to another.

(ii) *Audit work*

1 The quantitative aspects of materiality are often, in practice, calculated as a percentage of revenue, profit before tax or assets, or a particular class thereof. Auditors calculate materiality for individual account areas, and for the financial statements as a whole. They look at the aggregate (net) effects of misstatements and omissions for the financial statements as a whole. Companies sometimes adjust the accounting records and financial statements for immaterial items, sometimes they do not.

2 Materiality is related to risk and is used in the calculation of sample sizes and tolerable error, and in the performance of analytical procedures. Less work is performed in immaterial areas than in material areas, although some work is always performed because an area that may appear to be immaterial may, when tested, prove to be material.

(iii) *Qualitative example*

1 The disclosure of accounting policies is a qualitative aspect of materiality – if accounting policies are not adequately described in the financial statements, the financial statements will not fairly present the position in all material respects, even though the figures are 'correct'.

2 The description of an operation as discontinued when it is not is another example of a matter that is material.

22 WORKING PAPERS

Key answer tips

For Part (a) remember to ensure that your answer explains the purpose of each of the four matters selected. Assume that each item identified and explained is worth 2 marks.

In Part (b), remember to focus on the need for audit programmes and how they should be designed, as well as covering the benefits of both types of programmes. Standardised programs are pre-printed programs, the same document being used on all clients. Tailored programs may follow a standard model but are modified to suit each audit.

Part (c) asks you to explain the importance and content of audit evidence. Ensure you cover the two main requirements. First, the importance of capturing evidence of what has been reviewed during an audit in order to draw conclusions. Second, the explanation should include details to be recorded in the working papers and the type of audit trail required.

(a) Matters to be recorded in the permanent audit file

Matter	*Purpose*
Summary of accounting policies	Consistency is an important requirement in the adoption and application of accounting policies. It is useful for the auditor to keep a record of major accounting policies adopted as a means of ensuring consistency during the technical check of the financial statements in the closing stages of the audit.
Key ratios and other significant performance data over the past five years	The use of analytical procedures is facilitated if the auditor has a record of key ratios and other data developed in prior years. This enables the auditor to identify trends that enable better prediction of expected ratios etc in the current year.
Copies of long-term contracts such as leases and loan agreements	It is convenient for the auditor to have a record of such agreements that have a continuing effect on entity performance. Not only does it save time that would otherwise be incurred in obtaining access to the original documents kept by the entity, it protects against the risk that the originals may be tampered with to conceal an irregularity. Having a permanent record of such agreements also provides the auditor with a check that the financial implications continue to be reflected in the financial statements. If the entity accidentally or deliberately failed to make provision for expenses and liabilities arising under the terms of such an agreement, the omission would be readily apparent to the auditor.

Matter	*Purpose*
Description of the entity's business including its products, markets, production facilities etc	This information facilitates continuity of the audit process. It enables audit staff to remind themselves of such matters on commencing a new audit of an existing client to ensure they evaluate the reasonableness of transactions in the context of the nature of the business. It is particularly important as a means of safeguarding such knowledge against the risk that it may be overlooked through the ongoing process of staff turnover.

Other contents that may be mentioned include:

(i) Continuing analysis of accounts particularly those relating to shareholders' funds, long-term debt and property, plant and equipment.

(ii) Extracts from minutes of continuing importance.

(iii) Matters relevant to audit planning such as the location of branches and subsidiaries and, particularly, procedures performed and locations visited on a rotational basis.

(iv) Copies of significant correspondence with the entity of continuing relevance such as the engagement letter and management letters.

(v) Chart of accounts, flowcharts or narrative descriptions of the accounting system, organisational charts, etc.

(vi) The legal and organisational structure of the entity such as its memorandum and articles of association.

(b) Audit programs

Design and use

Audit programs are lists of audit procedures to be performed by audit staff in order to obtain sufficient appropriate audit evidence. The individual procedures are determined after obtaining the understanding of the accounting system and determining the audit strategy to be followed. The procedures reflect the understanding of the system and will incorporate the mix of tests of control and substantive procedures based on the planned audit approach for each material financial statement assertion.

The program also serves as a means of monitoring and co-ordinating the progress of the audit. The program should be designed with columns alongside each procedure for staff members to enter their initials and date on completing the performance of each procedure and to note the reference of the working paper detailing the results of the tests performed and the conclusions drawn.

Standardised or tailored

It used to be common for audit firms to pre-print standardised audit programs; usually one set for larger entities and another set for smaller entities. The advantages were:

(i) A consistent approach to all audits.

(ii) Reduced risk of procedures being omitted.

(iii) Reviewers could quickly check the progress of the audit being familiar with the contents of the program.

Although most firms continue to provide model audit programs, these are designed to be tailored to the specific circumstances of each engagement. The benefits of this approach are:

(i) The design of procedures and the names of the documents and records detailed in the program match the actual accounting system of the entity.

(ii) The balance between tests of control and substantive procedures can be varied to match the preliminary assessment of inherent and control risk separately for each major financial statement assertion.

(iii) It provides engagement staff with greater control over the audit based on their knowledge of the entity and of the specific audit risks. This, in turn, results in a better understanding of the purpose of each procedure since the staff member performing the procedure will have been involved in designing the program being followed.

(c) Audit trail

Recording details of evidence examined and leaving a trail that could enable the evidence procedure to be replicated serves a number of purposes.

(i) It facilitates the progress of the audit on a day-by-day basis where a procedure is performed over several days or by different staff members. By maintaining detailed records, procedures completed, partially completed and as yet unperformed can be readily identified. For example, a variety of tests may be carried out on a sample of purchase invoices. Each of the sample of invoices is listed, as a row, on a working paper with columns for the separate tests to be performed on each invoice. Progress is indicated by recording the results of the test in the appropriate cell.

(ii) As in any control procedure, requiring staff to evidence the work performed provides assurance that the task is likely to be properly performed. If staff members know that their work could be checked, they are likely to perform it more conscientiously.

One of the risks of auditing, especially where staff are required to work to a time budget is that of premature sign-off – claiming to have performed tests that were not properly completed. The temptation for audit staff to skimp the proper performance of each procedure is also reduced by requiring them to leave a visible trail on entity records. In the above example, the invoices selected for sampling would be initialled by the staff member and where procedures require it, other documents examined and entries in the records would also be 'ticked' by the staff member.

(iii) Marking documents and records provides evidence, to management of the entity that a thorough audit has been performed. It also serves to alert entity staff that their work is subject to audit and adds to the incentives to perform their work carefully.

(iv) Not least is the need to demonstrate proper performance of the audit in the event of a claim for negligence. Reliance on sample evidence means that it may be necessary for the audit firm to prove that a properly designed and selected sample was examined and that failure to detect an error or misstatement was not due to negligence in the performance of the audit.

Although the level of detail recorded is a matter of judgement, it is usually desirable to include:

(i) Results of all tests performed.

(ii) Details of individual items selected for sampling including an indication of how the sample was selected.

(iii) A tick or some other mark on entity records and documents vouched, traced or otherwise inspected during the course of specific tests of details of transactions or balances.

23 SPECS4YOU

Key answer tips

Parts (a) and (b) are book knowledge. Part (c) expects you to apply that knowledge to identify weaknesses in a working paper, illustrating that memorising without understanding is insufficient.

(a) The purposes of audit working papers include:

– To assist with the planning and performance of the audit.

– To assist in the supervision and review of audit work.

– To record the audit evidence resulting from the audit work performed to support the auditor's opinion.

(b)

Documentation	Information obtained
Memorandum and articles of association	Details of the objectives of Specs4You, its permitted capital structure and the internal constitution of the company.
Most recent published financial statements	Provide detail on the size of the company, profitability, etc as well as any unusual factors such as loans due for repayment.
Most recent management accounts/budgets/cash flow information	Determine the current status of the company including ongoing profitability, ability to meet budget, etc as well as identifying any potential going concern problems.
Organisation chart of Specs4You	To identify the key managers and employees in the company and other people to contact during the audit.
Industry data on spectacle sales	To find out how Specs4You is performing compared to the industry standards. This will help to highlight any areas of concern, for example higher than expected cost of sales, for investigation on the audit.
Financial statements of similar entities	To compare the accounting policies of Specs4You and obtain additional information on industry standards.
Prior year audit file	To establish what problems were encountered in last year's audit, how those problems were resolved and identify any areas of concern for this year's audit.
Search of Internet news sites	To find out whether the company has any significant news stories (good or bad) which may affect the audit approach.

(c) The audit working paper does not meet the standards normally expected in a working paper because:

- The page reference is unclear making it very difficult to either file the working paper in the audit file or locate the working paper should there be queries on it.
- It is not clear what the client year-end date is – the year is missing. The working paper could easily be filed in the wrong year's audit file.
- There is no signature of the person who prepared the working paper. This means it is unclear who to address queries to regarding the preparation or contents of the working paper.
- There is evidence of a reviewer's signature. However, given that the reviewer did not query the lack of preparer's signature or other omissions noted below, the effectiveness of the review must be put in question.
- The test 'objective' is vague – it is not clear what 'correct' means for example, it would be better to state the objective in terms of assertions such as completeness or accuracy.
- The test objective is also stated as an audit assertion. This is not the case as no audit assertions are actually listed here.
- It is not clear how the number for testing was determined. This means it will be very difficult to determine whether sufficient audit evidence was obtained for this test.
- Stating that details of testing can be found on another working paper is insufficient – time will be wasted finding the working paper, if it has, in fact, been included in the audit working paper file.
- Information on the results of the test is unclear – the working paper should clearly state the results of the test without bias. The preparer appears to have used personal judgement which is not appropriate as the opinion should be based on the facts available, not speculation.
- The conclusion provided does not appear to be consistent with the results of the test. Five errors were found therefore it is likely that there are some systems weaknesses.

24 TEMPEST

Key answer tips

Book knowledge is required in both parts of this question. In part (a) the answer is entirely knowledge based. In (b) you should use your knowledge of the auditing standard to help you structure the headings for your answer.

(a) Importance of audit planning

According to International Standard on Auditing 300 (Revised), the auditor should plan the audit work so that the engagement will be performed in an effective manner. Specifically, planning is required for the following reasons:

- To develop a general strategy and detailed approach for the specific nature, timing and extent of the audit work. This will help to ensure that the audit is carried out in an efficient and timely manner.
- So that attention is devoted to the important areas of the audit. Planning will also help to identify problem areas so they can be addressed in a timely fashion.

- To determine the amount of work to be carried out and therefore assist in determining the number of staff required to perform the audit work.
- To provide a document as a reference for an initial discussion of the approach to the audit with the company's audit committee. The plan will also help ensure that audit work is co-ordinated with client staff, e.g. for production of specific documentation to assist the auditor.
- To act as a basis for the production of the audit program.

(b) Tempest

Year-end 31 December 2005

Prepared by: A Manager

Audit Strategy – Tempest Ltd 31.12.05

Characteristics of entity

Tempest requires a normal statutory audit – there are no audit or filing exemptions available.

The financial reporting framework is the International Accounting Standards and there are no industry specific reporting requirements.

Tempest buys and then resells all types of fixtures and fittings for ships from yachts through to large cruise ships. The company has ten warehouses, seven of which are located near to branches of our audit firm.

Key dates

Key dates in the audit timetable are:

- Interim audit.
- Final audit.
- Meeting with Audit committee.
- Financial statements approved by management.

Specific dates are to be confirmed.

Overview of audit approach

The shipping supply industry has grown by 7% during the last year. Tempest's sales increase is 12% indicating that the company continues to perform well with the industry.

There have been no changes to the accounting policies of Tempest during the year.

This is the first year that International Standards on Auditing (ISAs) are relevant to this company. A detailed check will be required to ensure that no changes are required to the audit plan.

The overall audit approach will be to use tests of control where possible. However, the fall in gross profit indicates that sales may be understated or Cost of Sales (COS) overstated, so additional substantive procedures may be required in this area.

Materiality determination

Materiality will initially be set at 0.5% to 1% of revenue as this figure appears to be more accurate than gross profit.

Materiality on the balance sheet will be based on net asset values.

Identification of risk areas with a higher risk of mis-statement

A review of the draft financial statements for the company shows the following risks:

- Sales have increased by 12% but COS by 19%. There is a risk of COS being overstated.
- Inventory on the balance sheet is down significantly on last year indicating that there may be valuation or quantity errors.
- Trade receivables have increased by about 50%, significantly more than the increase in sales. This indicates that the company may have debt collection problems. Additional testing may be required on after date cash collections to check for bad debts.
- Non-current assets have fallen by $900k, which is significant given that most non-current assets are land and buildings. The reason for sale must be ascertained.
- Non-current liabilities have also fallen by $1 million. While not necessarily linked to the fall in non-current assets, there is a possibility that non-current assets have been sold to pay off the liabilities.

Audit approach – extent of control testing

Audit testing will focus on the use of compliance testing where possible. However, changes have been made to the inventory system limiting the extent of compliance testing. Client systems have changed in the year with a new computerised inventory control system. Unfortunately, the change was not identified until audit planning started. Three actions are necessary in respect of this system:

- Audit initial installation of the system including transfer of balances. One of the reasons for the low inventory value could be omission of inventory balances on transfer.
- Test count inventory at the year-end and agree to the computerised inventory records (and vice versa) to test their accuracy. Note that the client will not be counting inventory at the year-end but relying on the computerised system.
- Test check bookings into and out of inventory from the purchases and sales systems.

Other risk areas

- The client appears to be a going concern, although the fall in gross profit must be investigated. Cash and profit forecasts for the next 12 months must also be obtained to confirm ongoing profitability and that the fall in cash balances will not continue.
- There is the possibility of related party transactions. One of the directors purchased a yacht during the year. Checks must be made to determine whether company products were purchased, and if so whether these were in the normal course of business.
- A new engagement letter is required in ISA format.
- Assistance may be required on the inventory count; three warehouses are located away from our offices.

25 ZPM

Key answer tips

Part (a) is a 'bread and butter', i.e. standard, requirement. Remember that internal audit questions are now a regular feature of the exam.

Part (b) focuses on the differing roles of internal and external audit, and the interaction between them. The internal audit department is fundamentally an internal control established by management, and will have to be assessed if reliance is to be placed upon them.

(a) Factors to consider when evaluating and testing the work of the internal auditor include:

- A check that the work is performed by persons having adequate technical training and proficiency as internal auditors, by ensuring appropriate training programmes are in place and the auditor has appropriate qualifications.
- Ensuring that the work of assistants is properly supervised, reviewed and documented by reviewing the procedure manuals of the internal audit and the audit working papers produced.
- Determining that sufficient and appropriate audit evidence is obtained to afford a reasonable basis for the conclusions reached, again by reviewing the internal auditor's working papers.
- Checking that the conclusions reached are appropriate in the circumstances and that any reports prepared are consistent with the results of the work performed by reviewing the work performed and the reports produced.
- Ensuring any exceptions or unusual matters disclosed by internal audit are properly resolved by the external auditor and management.

(b) (i) **Objectives of internal audit**

Year-end inventory count

The main aim of the year-end inventory count is to ensure that the figure for inventory in the financial statements is accurate. The objective of the internal audit department is to check the accuracy of the inventory count to ensure that the physical goods inventory is correctly stated on the inventory sheets. This objective is achieved by checking the control system over counting inventory. Internal audit work will involve ensuring that all inventory is counted, teams of two people are counting inventory, and then performing test counts to determine the accuracy of the test counts.

Internal controls over procurement systems

The internal auditor will be ensuring that the procurement system is achieving its key objectives and operating according to company guidelines. Specific aims will include:

- Ensuring purchases are authorised.
- Quantity discounts are obtained.
- Inventory received is recorded on goods received notes or similar.

Reviewing operations of the marketing department

The internal auditor will review the work of the marketing department with aims such as ensuring that the process is being managed effectively and information is available to the marketing manager as required. Where deficiencies in the information provided are noted, then an internal audit report will highlight those deficiencies and make recommendations for improvement to the information systems. The objectives of internal audit in this case are more to ensuring the efficiency of operations rather than any specific financial objective.

(ii) **Objectives of the external auditor**

Year-end inventory count

The external auditor also needs to ensure that the figure for inventory is materially correct in the financial statements. Part of the work of the external auditor is to attend the physical inventory count to ensure that the quantities and condition of inventory is correctly recorded. Given that ZPM does not appear to have any perishable inventory, the main objective will be to ensure correct recording of inventory quantity.

Internal controls over procurement systems

The external auditor will test the procurement system with the overall objective of determining that the purchases and payables figures in the financial statements are correct. The objectives of testing will be to ensure that the control system over procurement is operating efficiently, and ensure complete and accurate recording of purchases and payables liabilities. If errors are found then this implies that the financial statements could also contain errors.

Reviewing operations of the marketing department

As the operations of the marketing department do not normally impact on the financial statements, the external auditor may not actually review this function.

(iii) **Reliance by the external auditor**

Year-end inventory count

ZPM has 103 stores – which is likely to mean that the external auditor will not be able to attend the inventory count in all stores, simply due to lack of staff. However, if inventory count procedures are the same at all stores, then reliance can be placed on the internal auditor to attend some stores and check that the internal control systems are being correctly applied in those stores. This reliance does not mean that the external auditor does not carry out any work; the external auditor will compare results from stores tested with those of the internal auditor. Results should be about the same; any differences in terms of errors found will be investigated, and reasons for those differences obtained.

Internal controls over procurement systems

The external auditor may rely on the work of the internal auditor regarding the procurement systems, where the work of the internal auditor is relevant to the financial statements. Some areas such as ensuring quantity discounts are obtained are less important than ensuring completeness of recording of liabilities. Again, the external auditor must perform some work on the procurement systems; the presence of an internal auditor simply means that the work can be reduced.

Reviewing operations of the marketing department

Given that the external auditor does not need to review the operations of the marketing department then no formal reliance is needed on the work of the internal auditor. However, internal audit reports may be reviewed to determine, for example, the effectiveness of advertising spend etc to help determine the going concern situation of the company. In the case of ZPM, the effectiveness of advertising new stores could be reviewed.

26 SMALLER ENTITIES

Key answer tips

This question examines your knowledge of auditing small entities and lists the five key characteristics which apply to them. You have to then relate these to a typical audit and the auditor/client relationship. If you approach this question logically, consider each characteristic in turn and take account of the factors detailed in the question in respect of audit approach, audit risk and conduct of the audit then this is a fairly straightforward question.

(a) Common ownership and management

(i) The existence of an owner-manager who is actively involved in the day-to-day running of the business is a common feature of smaller entities.

(ii) This characteristic can be seen as increasing audit risk because such an owner-manager is easily able to override any internal controls that have been set up (although the management override of internal controls is not restricted to smaller entities and has been a feature of many large corporate scandals).

(iii) On the other hand, this characteristic can also be seen as decreasing audit risk because the presence of the owner manager on a day-to-day basis can be seen as an effective substitute for formal internal controls.

(iv) Risk assessment will depend on the auditor's knowledge of the integrity and competencies of the owner-manager (or any single manager to whom the owner has delegated his management duties).

(v) The owner-manager may not understand why an audit is necessary and may fail to co-operate with the auditor. The owner-manager may also be buying a suite of services from the auditor, including tax, accounting and systems advice which may give rise to problems of independence for the auditor, particularly if the auditor is a sole practitioner (see below).

(b) A control framework that is different to the control framework for larger entities

(i) International Standards on Auditing need to accommodate the needs of auditors of larger and smaller entities and always make reference to a full range of internal formal controls. Many smaller entities lack formal internal controls; a lack of staff among whom to segregate duties for example and a lack of authorisation controls.

(ii) As noted above, the presence of the owner-manager can compensate for this lack of control in the auditor's risk assessment. Auditors should not assume that because formal internal controls do not exist, there is no internal control framework to be assessed.

(iii) High-level general or environmental controls, such as those relating to entity requirements for integrity in those in whom trust is placed, and controls involving the overall review of day to day accounting records (such as invoices, the bank statement and management accounts) may or may not be formally documented, but such controls can be evidenced in other ways and can therefore be tested.

(iv) It is always efficient for auditors to rely on internal controls wherever possible. However, where no such controls exist, auditors may decide that a wholly substantive approach is more appropriate.

(c) The use of standardised computer packages

(i) Well-established standardised computer packages are generally more reliable and 'auditor-friendly' than they used to be. Computer Assisted Audit Techniques (CAATs) have been developed for use with some such packages, for example, and many small firms of auditors advise their clients on the selection of such packages, although this can create independence problems (see below).

(ii) Such packages may not be easily adaptable to the particular needs of very small entities and some such packages still fail to provide an adequate audit trail.

(iii) The common use of well-established computer packages enables auditors to become familiar with their advantages and disadvantages, which makes planning audits more efficient and enables auditors to provide useful recommendations to clients where problems are encountered.

(iv) The proper use of computer packages by adequately trained staff means that, to an extent, there is less scope for a certain type of human error; this may have an effect on the auditor's risk assessment. However, systematic errors resulting from inadequate programming or from the inappropriate use of such packages can give rise to significant risks such as large volumes of data that lack integrity.

(v) Teething problems are always encountered where such packages are introduced which also has to be factored into the risk assessment and time budget for the audit.

(d) Reliance on the auditor for accounting expertise

(i) The packages referred to above mean that staff at many smaller entities are able to produce a trial balance, which might not have been possible with a manual system. However, many smaller entities still rely on auditors for the preparation of the final statutory financial statements. ACCA's Rules of Professional Conduct permit this.

(ii) The Rules do not permit the auditor to prepare the basic accounting records, to initiate transactions or to prepare journal entries, for example. This is because auditors must not perform the function of management, otherwise they will be reporting on their own work.

(iii) In practice, the dividing line between what constitutes 'advice' to the client, and what constitutes doing the client's job for the client, can be difficult to draw, and clients often want their auditors to do their jobs for them. For example, a client might wish the auditor to help 'sort out' a difficult reconciliation. It is therefore important for auditors to explain clearly to their clients their responsibilities as directors for the accounting records and to ensure that properly drafted engagement letters are in place.

(iv) It is important that where auditors are involved in the preparation of the financial statements in any way, that other audit staff review their work.

(v) Where auditors are providing a suite of services (accounting expertise, tax advice and advice on computer packages, for example), they may wish to consider whether they can be seen to be independent (as required by the Rules) and whether appropriate safeguards can be put into place to maintain the auditor's independence and objectivity.

(e) A lack of sufficient appropriate audit evidence to support financial statement assertions relating to income from cash transactions

(i) Where auditors are unable to obtain sufficient appropriate audit evidence on any material area in the financial statements, they must qualify their audit report on the grounds of a limitation in the scope of the audit ('except for').

(ii) If the effect of the lack of evidence is pervasive and affects the view given by the financial statements as a whole, the auditor may need to disclaim an opinion (the auditor cannot form a view as to whether the financial statements give a true and fair view).

(iii) Qualifications and disclaimers of opinion may be regarded as problematic if they are attached to financial statements that are presented to banks or other providers of finance. If they are attached to financial statements supporting tax computations they may raise the possibility of a tax investigation. This may harm the relationship between auditor and client and the client may seek to persuade the auditor to issue an unmodified opinion where it is not appropriate.

(iv) Auditors should consider carefully whether they wish to accept audit engagements where they know at the outset that the client is unable or unwilling to provide them with sufficient appropriate audit evidence (auditors do not wish to be associated with fraud).

(v) Owner-managers may seek to persuade auditors, either verbally, or by written management representations, that cash transactions are complete, despite the lack of written evidence. Management representations are no substitute for audit evidence that should be present.

INTERNAL CONTROL

27 BESTWOOD ENGINEERING

Key answer tips

This is a fairly standard question dealing with the purchases function of a manufacturing company.

Part (a) uses the word 'procedures' – this can safely be interpreted as 'controls'. You must focus your answer on the work of the purchasing department – not any other department.

Your answer to part (b) must focus on the work of the accounts department and on the control procedure of 'authorisation'. Ensuring that a trail of appropriate documentation is in place is a key point here.

Part (c) asks you to draw a contrast between controls operating on the purchase of goods and those relating to the purchase of services. One key point here is that these services are used continuously – so the use of requisitions and purchase orders is not possible.

(a) Purchasing department – procedures to control the purchase and receipt of goods

The controls the purchasing department should exercise over ordering and control over receipt of goods and services should include:

(i) For all goods ordered, there should be a purchase requisition from a user department. The purchasing department should not be permitted to raise purchase requisitions, as this would create a weakness in the division of duties. For goods required by the purchasing department, they should request another department (e.g. the accounts department) to raise a purchase requisition.

Before raising the purchase requisition, the accounts department should ensure it is for goods the purchasing department require and are authorised to order.

(ii) The purchasing department should check the purchase requisition is for goods the user department is authorised to buy or consume. If the value of the order is substantial, the purchasing department should ensure there is a need for such a large order, by checking current inventory levels and future orders to determine whether so large a quantity or value is required.

(iii) The purchase requisition should use a standard form and be signed by an authorised signatory.

(iv) The purchasing department should order the goods from an authorised supplier. Where there is a choice of supplier or a new supplier is required, the purchasing department should obtain the product from the supplier who provides the product or service at the best price, quality and delivery. For audit purposes, it is desirable for staff in the purchasing department to record details of the suppliers contacted, the price, delivery date and perceived quality, and the decision on which supplier was finally chosen.

(v) The purchasing department should raise the purchase order which should be signed by the purchasing manager. For large value purchases, a director may be required to sign the purchase order. The purchase order should be sent to the supplier, the goods received department, the user department and the accounts department.

(vi) The purchasing department should ensure the goods are received on time. This may require them to contact the supplier a week before the expected delivery date to ensure they are received on time, and allow action to be taken if the delivery date is later than specified on the purchase order.

(vii) When the goods are received, the purchasing department should receive a copy of the goods received note (GRN) from the goods received department. They should record the goods received against the order. From this information, they will be able to take action when there are short deliveries or the goods are received late. Frequently purchasing departments file purchase orders in three types of file:

- where none of the goods have been received
- where some of the goods ordered have been received
- where all the goods ordered have been received (i.e. 'dead' purchase orders).

(viii) The purchasing department may be part of the system which authorises purchase invoices. They should check the goods on the invoice are consistent with the purchase order and the price per unit is correct.

(ix) The purchasing department should be informed about short deliveries (i.e. the quantity of goods received is less than on the purchase order or advice note) and when there are quality problems. From this information, they can contact the supplier so that corrective action is taken. Also, such details may be helpful in determining whether the supplier should be used for future orders.

(x) The purchasing department should be informed of situations when goods or services are received but no purchase order has been raised. With this information, the purchasing department should contact the 'offending' department and ensure that in future a purchase order is raised for all the goods they order. The supplier should be contacted and informed that an authorised purchase order must be received by them (the supplier) before any goods or services are provided by the supplier.

(b) Controls over obtaining authorisation of purchase invoices

The procedures the accounts department should undertake before the purchase invoice is input into the computer and posted to the accounts payable ledger and general ledger should include:

(i) The accounts department will receive the purchase invoice, which they should record in a register.

(ii) The invoice expense will be included on the invoice (for posting to the general ledger). The expense analysis will be checked by an independent department (e.g. the purchasing or user department).

(iii) The accounts department will either match the purchase invoice to the goods received note and delivery note or ask the goods received department to check and authorise the purchase invoice.

(iv) The purchasing department will be asked to confirm the goods are as described on the purchase order and the price per unit is correct.

(v) The user department may be asked to authorise the purchase invoice.

(vi) An appropriate responsible official will be asked to authorise the purchase invoice.

(vii) Provided these checks are satisfactory, the accounts department should input the invoice details into the computer which will post it to the accounts payable ledger and the general ledger.

Where there is a problem with the invoice (e.g. concerning the quantity, quality or price of the goods received) the accounts department should put the invoice in a 'hold' file. They should contact the supplier (sometimes with the help of the purchasing or user department) and try to resolve the problem. When either a credit note is received or the correct quantity and quality of goods have been received, the accounts department will get authorisation (e.g. from the purchasing department) that the situation is resolved and they should input the purchase invoice into the computer (and credit note if this is required).

Periodically, an independent person should check suppliers' statements against the balances on the accounts payable ledger. Differences between these two balances should be recorded. If the transaction which created the difference is close to the date of the check, it is probable that no action will be taken. However, older items should be investigated to ensure that action is being taken to resolve the problem.

(c) Controls over the purchase of services

Frequently, procedures over receiving services are less strong and less effective than those over receiving goods.

For some types of service, such as receipt of electricity, gas, water and telephone charges there may be no system for raising purchase orders. However there should be a system for reviewing these costs, by comparing them with the previous year (or period), with budget and with amounts charged by alternative suppliers. In this way, the company can ensure these services are received at the most economical cost. For some of these services it may be possible to suggest ways in which these costs can be reduced (e.g. by turning off lights and reducing the temperature settings in winter).

Costs of gas, electricity and water can be monitored by checking the meter readings monthly and determining whether the consumption is reasonable. For telephone expenses, the system should provide information on the cost for each department, and each department manager should review his/her department's costs. A risk with telephone systems is that they can be abused by staff, who make personal telephone calls using the company's telephone system. The department managers should be made responsible for checking this abuse is kept to a minimum.

For receipt of all other services, before the service is obtained, a purchase requisition should be raised by the user department, and the purchasing department should raise a purchase order. In emergency situations, it may be acceptable to raise a purchase requisition and order after the service has been received (e.g. the repair of a vehicle which has broken down). There should be a system whereby action is taken when no purchase order has been raised for a service which has been received. In many situations when a service has been received, it is probably appropriate that the department receiving the service should issue a goods received note and send it to the purchases accounts and the purchasing departments. In this way, the same system can be used for processing receipt of services as for receipt of goods.

28 AUDIT RISK

Key answer tips

Part (a) is essentially testing your knowledge of the concept of inherent risk – but focused at the entity, rather than account or transaction, level. This can be thought of as risk that results from the nature of the organisation, its business environment and its management.

Part (b)(i) is looking for an explanation of a basic principle of modern auditing – where inherent risk and control risk are high, the overall level of audit risk is managed by carrying out a high level of detailed substantive audit testing. More emphasis can be placed on tests of controls where inherent and control risk is lower.

In answering part (b)(ii) it is important to pay attention to the phrase 'other factors' – presumably those not related to the risk and control environment. The cost/benefit approach to audit testing could be relevant here, as could the quality of evidence available to the auditor.

Note that part (c) is testing your knowledge of the control environment, not of any particular control mechanisms in operation.

(a) **Inherent risk at the entity level**

At this level inherent risk relates to factors affecting the susceptibility to misstatement of all account balances or transactions classes. In assessing inherent risk at the entity level the auditors will consider factors such as:

- the integrity of management that might predispose them to misstate the financial statements or creates a culture within which misstatement is likely to occur
- management experience and knowledge such as in making necessary estimates and judgements affecting the financial statements
- pressure on management that might predispose them to misstate the financial statements such as a failure to achieve announced profit targets
- the nature of the entity, such as the technology of its products or processes, its capital structure or its geographical spread that complicates the process of identifying truth and fairness in financial reporting
- factors affecting the industry within which the entity operates that, in turn, could magnify the effect of the above factors such as increased competitiveness, regulatory requirements, etc.

Inherent risk at the account balance and class of transactions level

Inherent risk at this level relates to factors peculiar to that account balance or transaction class that affect its risk of misstatement relative to other account balances and transactions classes. The auditors will consider factors such as:

- account balances susceptible to misstatement such as those requiring adjustment in the past or involving a high degree of estimation
- complexity of underlying transactions which might require using the work of an expert
- degree of judgement involved
- susceptibility of assets to loss or misappropriation, notably cash and attractive assets which are highly desirable
- completion of unusual or complex transactions particularly at or near period-end
- transactions not subject to ordinary processing.

(b) (i) **Effect of assessment of accounting system and control environment on the mix of tests of control and substantive procedures**

The auditor uses the understanding of the accounting and internal control system together with other information to form a preliminary assessment of inherent and control risk. If these are assessed as high then all of the evidence needed to reduce audit risk to the level required for the expression of an opinion on the financial statements must be derived through substantive procedures.

Where the assessed level is less than high the auditor may tolerate a higher level of detection risk in performing substantive procedures. In order to substantiate the assessment of control risk as less than high, however, the auditor will need to perform tests of the controls to confirm that they are operating satisfactorily. Since tests of controls are generally less costly to perform than substantive procedures, this is normally a preferred strategy.

The assessment is made for each account balance or transaction class assertion and only applies to substantive procedures relevant to that assertion. For example, control risk as to the occurrence of purchase transactions is usually low. This also means that control risk over the existence of accounts payable is low. Control risk as to completeness of purchase transactions and thus over the accounts payable balance is often high. In testing cut-off of purchases at the year-end, auditors usually perform more extensive substantive tests of details in verifying that all goods delivered before the year-end are recorded than verifying that recorded transactions relate to deliveries received before the year-end.

Effect of assessment of accounting system on the design of substantive procedures

In tolerating a higher level of detection risk the auditor may alter the nature, timing or extent of substantive procedures.

In altering their nature the auditor concentrates on less expensive procedures. Typically this involves more reliance on analytical procedures and less on tests of details.

In altering the timing it can involve performing procedures other than at the year-end when the auditor is under less time pressure. For example, the auditor could observe a physical inventory count other than at period-end and rely on controls over perpetual records in verifying inventory on hand at period-end.

The most obvious reduction, however, is in reducing the extent of testing such as circularising fewer accounts receivable.

(ii) **Other factors affecting the mix**

Preliminary assessment of inherent and control risks as less than high does not require the auditor to perform tests of controls. The auditor may still decide to rely predominantly on substantive procedures where they are more cost effective. This applies where there are few transactions, such as verifying property, plant and equipment purchases, or where the balance at the year-end can be verified with an independent custodian, such as share capital records maintained by a registrar and transfer agent.

(c) **Control environment**

The control environment can be defined as the attitude adopted by management as to the importance of controls and the existence of procedures that reinforce their importance such as the establishment of an internal audit department and the operation of budgetary controls. Control procedures are more likely to be effective in an environment in which it is known that they are held to be important.

Factors reflected in the control environment are those of:

- the function of the board of directors and its committees
- management's philosophy and operating style
- the organisational structure and methods of assigning authority and responsibility to ensure that it is only given to those capable of exercising it effectively and with due regard to segregation of duties
- methods of imposing control such as the establishment of an internal audit function and in establishing proper procedures for investigating new employees.

The control environment provides the background against which control procedures are operated and has the potential to affect the effectiveness of all control procedures. A strong control environment supports the auditors' assessment of control risk as less than high while a weak control environment reduces control effectiveness and increases the assessed level of control risk.

29 XY CO

Key answer tips

You should be well aware of the general structure of the contents of a management letter. For each weakness covered by your answer you should:

- identify and explain the weakness
- comment on the possible consequences of the weakness
- recommend action to eliminate the weakness.

Note that the examiner defines the meaning of the three types of problems on which the question is based in the text of the question. Your job is to identify the weaknesses which exist in each of the three areas. Try to set out your answer under appropriate headings in order to give it a logical structure.

(a) **Occurrence**

Ordering

Weaknesses. At the moment there is no control over ordering. Managers may not be ordering goods and services at the most advantageous terms and conditions. They may be ordering goods already held by another department. They could even be ordering goods for their own personal use.

Consequences. The company may be paying too much for its goods and services and may even be being defrauded by its managers.

Recommendations. We suggest that the following procedures be instituted.

(i) A separate purchasing department should be established under the newly appointed purchasing officer.

(ii) Managers should requisition the purchase of goods and services through the purchasing department.

(iii) The requisitioning authority of each manager should be laid down and the purchasing officer required to check each manager's requisitioning authority before placing orders.

(iv) Only the purchasing department may issue orders, which should be made on official pre-numbered forms. Copies of the orders should be sent to the goods received department and the accounts department

Receiving

Weaknesses. At the moment, reliance is placed entirely on managers to ensure that goods and services are received before invoices are approved for payment.

Consequences. In the absence of a formal system, managers may not always be sure whether or not goods have been received and may even accept delivery of goods that have not been ordered. Lack of segregation of duties makes it easier for managers to order goods for their private use.

Recommendations. We suggest that the following procedures should be instituted.

(i) Purchase orders should require suppliers to deliver goods to a centralised receiving area.

(ii) The receiver should be responsible for checking that the goods are in agreement with the order and are in a satisfactory condition.

(iii) The receiver should issue a prenumbered goods received note with copies to the requisitioning department, purchasing department and accounts department.

Recording

Weaknesses. At the moment reliance is placed on managers to approve invoices for payment.

Consequences. In the absence of a formal system managers may not always ensure that invoices they approve relate to goods and services properly ordered and received. Lack of segregation of duties makes it easier for managers to approve payment for goods for their private use.

Recommendations. We suggest that the following procedures should be instituted.

(i) Purchase orders should require suppliers to send invoices directly to the accounts department The post room should also be instructed to deliver all invoices to the accounts department.

(ii) Before recording invoices the accounts department should check them against copies of the order and goods received notes. For the supply of services it may continue to be necessary to forward invoices to managers for approval.

Payment

Weaknesses. At the moment payments are based on amounts recorded on suppliers' statements.

Consequences. Payment could be made for invoices incorrectly entered on the statement due to error by suppliers.

Recommendations. We suggest that the following procedure be instituted.

(i) Suppliers' statements should be checked against invoices recorded before being paid and any differences other than for goods in transit be queried with the supplier.

(ii) If all of the above procedures are adopted, the risk of paying invoices for goods or services improperly ordered or that have not been ordered and received will be significantly reduced.

(b) **Completeness**

Recording

Weaknesses. At the moment there is no certainty that all invoices are recorded in the purchase journal.

Consequences. Managers may lose or misplace invoices or delay their transmission to the accounts department so that they are recorded in the wrong accounting period. Managers may deliberately fail to pass on invoices for goods for private use especially if they know that payment is based on suppliers' statements. The debit balance in accounts payable probably arises from unrecorded invoices. The difference between the balance of accounts payable in the ledger and the true amount owed to suppliers represents an understatement of liabilities and expenses and an overstatement of profit.

Recommendations. We suggest that the following procedures be instituted.

(i) All invoices should be numbered on receipt and, after approval, recorded in the purchase journal in numerical sequence.

(ii) A record should be maintained of invoices for services sent to department managers for approval and such invoices chased to ensure their prompt return.

(iii) The purchase journal should be independently scrutinised to confirm the numerical continuity of recorded invoices.

(iv) The accounts department should check the numerical continuity of copies of orders and goods received notes. Any that are not matched with invoices within a reasonable period of time should be investigated as they may represent invoices that have been lost.

(v) Unpaid invoices should be agreed with invoices listed on the suppliers' statements. Invoices on suppliers' statements not recorded in the accounts payable ledger should be investigated as possibly representing unrecorded purchases.

If the above procedures are adopted, the risk that purchase records might not record all purchase transactions will be significantly reduced.

(c) **Measurement**

Recording

Weaknesses. At present there is no internal check on the accuracy of recording of purchase invoices.

Consequences. This could mean that the financial statements are incorrect due to undetected errors in the books.

Recommendations. We suggest that the following procedures be instituted.

(i) A separate accounts payable ledger should be established with an account for each supplier. This should be entered directly from invoices by an employee other than the one responsible for entering the purchase journal.

(ii) A total should be recorded of the total of invoices in each batch entered separately in the purchase journal and accounts payable ledger. The totals should be independently compared, any difference representing an error in recording invoices in one of the two records.

(iii) Each month there should be an independent comparison of the general ledger accounts payable balance which has been posted from the purchase journal and the total of the list of balances in the accounts payable ledger. Any difference probably represents an error in totalling columns or balances or in posting and needs to be investigated.

(iv) The balance for each supplier in the accounts payable ledger should be reconciled with the balance on the supplier's statement. Any difference may be due to an error in the amount recorded in the accounts payable ledger.

Used this way, subsidiary ledgers, such as the accounts payable ledger represent the use of double entry in ensuring that no mistakes have been made.

If these procedures are adopted, the risk of errors in recording the invoice amounts will be significantly reduced.

30 INTERNAL CONTROL AND CASH

Key answer tips

This question deals with a number of aspects of the audit of cash balances – a standard area that you should be well prepared for in the exam.

Part (a) deals with internal controls relating to cash – but focused specifically on the areas of errors and misappropriations.

Part (b) requires an application of the principles of ISA 500. This part of the question can be answered effectively by listing the relevant 'assertions' and identifying, for each one, examples of the audit verification work which you would perform.

Part (c) gives you scope for scoring marks on a standard audit evidence area – the use of bank confirmation letters (as a source of written, external evidence) and the contents of such a letter.

(a) **Errors and misappropriations – cash**

(i) *Receipts*

1 Money paid into the bank may be stolen. If cash is not properly controlled it is possible to falsify documentation in relation to receivables, and to pay company receipts into private bank accounts. This is sometimes known as 'teeming and lading'.

2 Money paid into the bank may be incorrectly accounted for, either by the bank or by the company, if there are no controls to check the accuracy of the company's records or the bank statements. This could mean that the internal records and the financial statements are incorrect.

(ii) *Payments*

1 Money paid out of the bank may be paid to incorrect suppliers, or may be paid for incorrect amounts resulting in operational difficulties with cash and supplier management.

2 Money paid out of bank accounts may also be misappropriated by payments for goods and services that are not received, or simply by payments into private bank accounts if there are no controls to prevent this.

(iii) *Interest and charges*

1 Banks make errors in calculating interest and charges. If the company does not check these, it may lose money and the amounts appearing in the financial statements may be incorrect. This is particularly important for companies that hold high levels of cash.

(b) **Principal audit objectives of cash audit and related audit evidence**

Audit objectives are dealt with in ISA 500 *Audit Evidence*

(i) Existence: to ensure that the cash actually exists at a given date. The related evidence will include cash counts. Cash counts need not necessarily be conducted at each location (unless the amounts are material), the firm might consider conducting counts on a rotational basis, year on year. If it is necessary to conduct counts at all locations, it may be possible to use the offices of another firm of auditors (with the permission of the client). The decision as to which sites to visit might be determined on the basis of materiality and analytical procedures. Cash balances should be reconciled to records held at the shop and records held at head office. Any shortfalls in cash, or 'IOUs' should be thoroughly investigated.

(ii) Completeness: to ensure that there is no unrecorded cash. This means reconciling cash balances to records held at the shop and records held at head office, as above, ensuring that proper sales cut-off has been achieved.

(iii) Rights and obligations: to ensure that the company has a right to the cash. This means checking to ensure that credit card vouchers are correctly made payable to the company, and not to third parties.

(iv) Occurrence: to ensure that the cash belongs to the company at the year-end date. This means checking to ensure that no credit card vouchers are post-dated.

(v) Cut off: to ensure that amounts are correctly recorded in the proper period. This means ensuring that cut-off is correct and consistent between the records held at shops, the returns to head office, and the records held at head office.

(vi) Classification and understandability: to ensure that the cash balance and related income statement entries are correctly disclosed in the financial statements in accordance with legislation and accounting standards.

(c) **Why auditors seek bank confirmations – matters confirmed**

This matter is noted in ISA 505 External Confirmations.

Auditors seek bank confirmations in order to provide third party, written evidence in relation to the balance sheet disclosure of cash, liabilities and related items.

The matters typically confirmed by the bank include:

(i) Details of all bank balances, overdrafts and loans held at all branches.

(ii) The charges or restrictions over any such accounts.

(iii) The terms and repayment conditions of loans and overdrafts.

(iv) Any right of set-off between accounts in credit and other balances.

(v) Any securities held by the bank (such as mortgage documentation).

(vi) Any relationships with other banks the bank is aware of.

(vii) Additional information such as details of trade finance and derivative instruments (such as foreign exchange contracts, options, futures and swaps).

31 DINKO

Key answer tips

A knowledge of the principles contained within ISA 315 and ISA 500 is essential to provide a good answer to this question. It is a fairly standard question testing your knowledge of auditing a payroll system and your understanding of internal controls, control environment, testing procedures and audit objectives. The marks are split equally between parts (a) and (b). In part (a) using the mnemonic SOAPMAPS (or you may have another mnemonic you use) can help you remember the different internal controls that may exist in any system. Part (b) lends itself to a tabular layout, i.e. a column showing the audit objective and a column showing the corresponding tests of control and substantive procedures. Using a table for this type of question/answer often helps to focus your mind on the different objectives and controls and ensures you don't get too descriptive and lose sight of what the question is asking you.

(a) ***Note***: Using the mnemonic SOAPMAPS (or other similar mnemonic) can help you to remember the different internal controls and use the relevant information in answering the question, i.e. Segregation of duties, Organisation, Authorisation, Personnel, Management, Accounting, Physical, Supervision.

(i) **Internal control objectives**

Control objectives include policies and procedures designed by management to:

(1) Achieve the orderly and efficient running of the business including adherence to internal policies – this would include the regular, accurate processing and recording of payroll payments.

(2) Safeguard assets – this would include the physical safeguarding of cash and safeguarding money held in bank accounts by means of other controls.

(3) Prevent and detect fraud and error – fraud and error would include incorrect payments or deductions from payroll and payments of incorrect amounts for tax and social insurance, payments for work not performed and payments to dummy employees, for example.

(4) Achieve accuracy and completeness of accounting records and timely preparation of reliable financial information; this would include making correct payments and deductions from payroll, correct payments for tax and social insurance, and making payments for work performed only (not to dummy employees, for example), in order that quarterly or half-yearly accounts can be prepared (possibly), but in any case in order that annual accounts can be prepared within the time limits for small companies.

(ii) **Internal control environment and control procedures**

The control environment relates to:

(1) Management's overall style in encouraging awareness of the need for good controls, for example.

(2) The existence of organisational controls such as review of the payroll by an independent person such as the managing director, and the rotation of payroll duties amongst staff responsible for processing it – this helps achieve all of the objectives set out above.

(3) Segregation of duties and supervisory controls to avoid the misappropriation of cash (or allegations thereof) and to avoid fraudulent collusion to create, for example, dummy employees or to make inflated payments – this prevents the loss of assets and/or inaccurate records.

Internal control procedures include:

(4) Limiting direct physical access to the cash, such as the use of a security firm to deliver cash, locking doors to areas where cash is held, keeping cash in a fire-proof safe and the protection of the computer by password controls – this will help safeguard assets and ensure the completeness and accuracy of the records and financial statements.

(5) Controls over computerised applications, checking the arithmetical accuracy of documents and the maintenance of control accounts – this can be achieved by, for example, the use of timesheets or clockcards, the use of reliable software with programmed controls for the calculation of deductions, and the use of batch and hash totals for information that is input into the computer system – this helps achieve the orderly and efficient running of the business and the accuracy and completeness of records and financial statements.

(6) Approval and control of documents, such as the authorisation of the payroll itself, and authorisation for the bank to make transfers and to deliver cash.

(b)

Objectives	**Tests of control and substantive procedures**
Existence of assets and liabilities such as cash on hand and in the bank, and of the liability to pay staff and the associated tax and social insurance liabilities.	Testing controls over the security of cash to ensure that they are operating effectively throughout the relevant period. Performing cash counts, with reconciliations to the records and observing cash payments to staff, ensuring that appropriate signatures are obtained and that unclaimed cash is promptly re-banked, for example. Making checks on the physical existence of staff to ensure that the related expenses and liabilities are genuine. Checking after date payments to staff and for tax and social insurance contributions.
Occurrence: payroll transactions occurred during the relevant accounting period.	Performing cut-off test to ensure that payroll costs incurred during the period have been recorded during the period by examining entries in the payroll records just before and just after the period-end and checking back to source documentation, such as time sheets or clock cards.

Objectives	Tests of control and substantive procedures
Completeness: there are no unrecorded assets or liabilities (such as those noted under 'existence' above) or transactions (such as payroll payments or undisclosed items such as unrecorded payroll liabilities).	Performing starters and leavers tests to ensure that staff are not paid before they join the company and are not paid after they leave – this involves checking the payroll for two separate periods and examining entries relating to starters and leavers in the intervening period. Manually checking the accuracy of payroll calculations to ensure that correct payments and deductions are being made in accordance with approved pay rates and approved deduction rates for tax and social insurance. Reviewing evidence of authorisation controls to ensure that the payroll has already been checked.
Accuracy: transactions such as payroll payments are recorded at the correct amounts and are recorded in the correct period.	As for completeness, above, and checking to ensure that the payroll has been properly authorised and reviewed. Checking entries relating to hours of time worked in the payroll to source documentation.
Classification and understandability: an item is disclosed and described in accordance with accounting standards and company law.	Reviewing the financial statements with the aid of a disclosure checklist to ensure that disclosure requirements have been met. Reviewing the overall presentation of payroll transactions and balances to ensure that they give a true and fair view.

32 FLOWERS ANYTIME

Key answer tips

In part (a) be careful not to write too much. You only get 2 marks for each explanation and it's easy to write too much and spend too long on this question. In part (b) be careful to only talk about controls in the specific areas required, and make your answers to (i) and (ii) different.

(a) **Key procedures**

(i) *Documentation of accounting and internal control systems*

Auditors document accounting and internal control systems in order to evaluate them for their adequacy as a basis for the preparation of the financial statements and to make a preliminary risk assessment of internal controls.

In very simple systems with few internal controls where auditors do not intend to perform tests of internal controls, it is not necessary to document the internal control system in detail. It is always necessary, however, to have sufficient knowledge of the business to perform an effective audit.

For large entities, where the client has already documented the system, it is not necessary for the auditors to repeat the process if they can satisfy themselves that the client's documentation is adequate.

(ii) *Walk through tests*

The purpose of walk-through tests is for the auditors to establish that their recording of the accounting and internal control system is adequate.

Auditors trace a number of transactions from source to destination in the system, and vice versa. For example, customer orders can be traced from the initial documentation recording the order, through to the related entries in the daybooks and ledgers.

It is common for walk-through tests to be performed at the same time as tests of controls, where auditors are reasonably confident that systems are recorded adequately.

(iii) *Audit sampling*

Auditors perform tests of controls and substantive testing on a sample basis in order to form conclusions on the populations from which the samples are drawn.

It is not possible in anything but the very smallest of entities to take any other approach, as testing 100% of a population may be impractical, not cost effective and not accurate because populations are too large and because of human error.

Samples can be selected in a number of ways – either statistically or on the basis of auditor judgement. In all cases, the sample selected must be representative of the population as a whole.

(iv) *Testing internal controls*

Auditors test internal controls in order to establish whether they are operating effectively throughout the period under review. If controls are operating effectively, auditors can reduce the level of substantive testing on transactions and balances that would otherwise be required.

In testing internal controls, auditors are checking to ensure that the stated control has been applied. For example, auditors may check that there is a grid stamp on a sales invoice with various signatures inside it that show that the invoice has been approved by the credit controller, that it has been checked for arithmetical accuracy, that the price has been checked, and that it has been posted to the sales ledger. The signatures provide audit evidence that the control has been applied.

Auditors are not checking to ensure that the invoice is, in fact, correct. This would be a substantive test. Nevertheless, it is possible to perform tests of control and substantive tests on the same document at the same time.

(v) *Dealing with deviations from the application of control procedures*

Where it appears that an internal control procedure has not been applied, it is necessary to form an opinion as to whether the deviation from the application of the procedure is an isolated incident, or whether the deviation represents a systematic breakdown in the application of the control procedure. This is usually achieved by selecting a further sample for testing.

If it cannot be shown that the non-application of the procedure is isolated (i.e. there are no further instances in which the control has failed), it is necessary either to find a compensating control that can be tested, or to abandon testing of controls and to take a wholly substantive approach. Where there is a breakdown in internal controls it is also necessary to reassess the auditor's preliminary risk assessment. Abandoning tests of control may place strains on the budget for the audit and auditors should always consider the possibility of compensating controls before abandoning tests of controls.

(b) **Internal controls**

(i) *Receipt, processing and recording*

1. All orders taken should be recorded on a pre-numbered multi-part document generated by the computer. One part might be a copy for the customer, one might form the invoice, one might be for the despatch department and one might be retained for accounts receivable ledger purposes. Manual or computer systems should perform checks on the completeness of the sequence of pre-numbered documents at various stages. Any documents unaccounted for should be traced and investigated.
2. The computer system should apply the credit limits set by the credit controller and the system should reject any orders that exceed customer credit limits at the point at which the order is taken, so that the customer can be advised. Any override of credit limits should be authorised by the credit controller.
3. From time to time, there should be an independent check to ensure that the credit limits within the system are being properly calculated and properly applied to individual transactions. Similar considerations apply to prices maintained within the system.
4. The computer system should also reject any order for which there are no flowers available so that orders cannot be taken for flowers that cannot be delivered.
5. All invoices should be posted to the sales daybook, the accounts receivable ledger and the accounts receivable control account automatically by the system and the accounts receivable ledger and the accounts receivable control account should be reconciled each month in order for sales and receivables records to be kept up to date.
6. There should be controls in place to deal with credit notes and other discrepancies involving the price, type or quality of flowers delivered in order to maintain the accuracy of records and customer goodwill.

(ii) *Collection of cash*

1. At the end of each period, the system should produce a list of overdue receivables. There should be procedures for chasing these customers and for putting a 'stop' on accounts where amounts are significant in order to control bad debts.
2. When bank transfers are received from customers, they should be input into the system and matched with individual transactions and controls should ensure that the correct amounts are allocated to the correct customers and transactions.
3. An exception report should be produced for any unallocated bank transfers. Exceptions should be promptly investigated. This will ensure that receivables information is accurate and up to date and that customers are not chased for amounts that have been paid.
4. A bank reconciliation should be performed on a monthly basis in order to ensure that the company's cash records are complete, accurate and up to date.

33 TWINKLETOES

Key answer tips

Questions on risk assessment are becoming increasingly popular with the way the audit profession is currently progressing, so you should ensure that you have a good knowledge of this subject area. Part (a) is only worth 4 marks and is very straightforward. Parts (b) and (c) require you to provide an answer relating the detail to the information provided in the question. Ensure that you use the headings provided for each part otherwise you could lose easy marks. Remember, you do not need to have an in-depth knowledge of how shoe shops operate, you just need to have a good knowledge of audit principles and procedures.

(a) **Risk classification**

(i) Risk classification is part of the overall risk management process that can be applied to individual account areas as well as to the financial statements and to the business as a whole.

(ii) Risk *classification* is part of risk *assessment*, which in turn is part of the overall risk *management* process whereby the risks to the business of not achieving its objectives are analysed, and split down into risks associated with the various business or operational units according to the way the business is managed.

(iii) The classification of risk as high, medium or low, together with classification as to whether a risk is, for example, 'probable', 'possible' or 'remote' (or high, medium or low likelihood) permits the entity to allocate its resources to optimum effect.

(iv) Risks, once properly understood, can then be managed by means of, for example, reduction, transference or acceptance. For example, a high risk of non-payment in a receivables ledger can be reduced by implementing controls that reduce the risk (such as performing credit checks and by regularly chasing overdue debts). The risk might instead be transferred by factoring the debt. For low risks (such as the risk of non-payment by a long-standing customer who always pays promptly) the risks may be accepted.

(b) **Classification of risks for receivables**

(i) *Small retail shoe shops*

Despite the fact that individual accounts in this category have small balances, the category as a whole is significant to Twinkletoes because of the total amounts owed (one third of total receivables), the rising level of bad debts and the adverse effect of slow payers on cash flow. It is likely that most of these accounts individually are low risk because customers pay promptly and the amounts are small. Accounts that are significantly overdue may be classified as medium risk, but probably only if they are substantial accounts because all entities must expect to experience a small number of small bad debts. If however, a large number of accounts are significantly overdue, they may be classified as high risk.

(ii) *Large retail shoe shops*

Some of these accounts are large and overdue and may therefore be classified as medium or high risk. However, as the total value of such accounts is around 22% of total receivables and the total value of the overdue accounts may be small in relation to total receivables, the classification should probably only be medium risk. The classification for accounts that are not overdue may be low risk.

Overseas accounts. Whilst these might at first appear to be at risk because the accounts are being lost, they represent a small proportion of accounts by both number and value (customers currently pay in advance). This means that they may be viewed as low risk.

(iii) *Chains of shoe shops*

As with the large shoe shops, large and overdue accounts might be classified as medium or high risk. However, 'high street' chains of well-established shops are less likely to become insolvent than less well-established entities and therefore represent a lower risk. This means that the classification may be low risk, even for accounts that are large and overdue.

(iv) *Mail order companies*

New accounts generally represent an increased risk of bad debts and a large number of new accounts increases this risk. However, there is no history of bad debts in this category at all so the new accounts may therefore be classified as medium risk. Existing accounts within this category may be classified as low risk because there is no history of bad debts.

(c) **Internal controls**

(i) *All customers*

I would recommend that:

- credit checks be performed when new customers seek credit, and that cash in advance or on delivery is required where large orders are placed by new customers;
- credit limits be set for all customers based on the length of the relationship with the customer, the volume of sales and their payment history;
- payment terms be set (say, 30 days for local customers, 45 days for overseas customers);
- insurance be taken out against the risk of bad debts.

These controls will help ensure that accounts do not become overdue, damaging the company's cash flow and increasing the risk of bad debts.

(ii) *Slow paying customers*

I would recommend that:

- dedicated staff are assigned to chase slow payers regularly for outstanding amounts and to ensure that a 'stop' is put on accounts that are significantly overdue;
- legal action is taken against those customers owing large amounts for long periods for which there are no good reasons.

(iii) *Larger accounts – large shops, chains of shops and mail order companies*

- I would recommend that dedicated staff are assigned to manage the relationship with larger customers, particularly the mail order companies.

(iv) *Overseas customers*

I would recommend that:

- overseas customers be allowed a credit period of say, 45 days in order to permit the required bank transfers to take place;

– overseas customers be required to pay in the currency used by Twinkletoes (except perhaps for large orders which may be backed by government guarantees) or in a stable currency which does not fluctuate significantly against the currency used by Twinkletoes.

34 CLIFF

Key answer tips

This question focuses on internal controls and provides you with a scenario of a small company running a chain of supermarkets. As with all questions of this type you must ensure that you read the data in the question and relate your answer to it – it often helps if you re-read the question at least once while answering it to ensure that your answer does not lose focus! Part (a) asks you to outline problems that you may find as a result of poor internal controls; ensure that your answer is specific and clearly explain the reason why you have listed a particular problem (e.g. poor inventory control results in...). Part (b) asks you to make recommendations to improve internal controls and explain the advantages and disadvantages of each one. You must give all these considerations for each recommendation or you will not gain full marks; be careful not to give a detailed recommendation without advantages and disadvantages.

(a) **Problems expected at Cliff: poor internal control**

(i) I would expect the company to experience some level of over-ordering, leading to reduced profitability as a result of inventory going past its 'best before' date.

(ii) Inventory that is not well-controlled in a supermarket may result in a breach of health and safety regulations which may result in fines or even closure of the supermarkets.

(iii) I would expect there to be stock-outs leading to the potential loss of business to other supermarkets.

(iv) I would expect there to be inefficiencies as a result of a lack of central ordering system resulting from quantity discounts not being obtained.

(v) All of the problems noted above are likely to be exacerbated where local managers or staff are either inexperienced or possibly dishonest – the question states that poorer quality staff have been recruited recently.

(vi) Supermarket inventory is very easily pilfered either by staff or customers even where it is well-controlled. The lack of regular inventory counts in particular means that pilferage is very easy to hide.

(vii) I would expect there to be a lack of understanding in the business as a whole as to the availability of new products, products with high margins or other areas in which profitability might be improved.

(b) **Four recommendations, explanation of advantages and disadvantages: improvements to internal control**

1 **Recommendation 1**: that an integrated system be introduced across all supermarkets that links sales, purchases and inventory records.

Advantages

This would provide the company with an overall view of what inventory is held at any particular time, enable it to order centrally and reduce the scope for pilferage. It would result in reduced stock-outs and reduced inventory obsolescence.

Disadvantages

This would require considerable capital investment in hardware, software and training. It would also take control away from local managers which would almost certainly cause resentment.

2 **Recommendation 2**: the imposition of regular, or continuous inventory counting procedures together with the prompt update of inventory records for discrepancies found and investigation of the reason for the discrepancies.

Advantages

This would further reduce the possibility of stock-outs and provide evidence of over-ordering, which would enable purchasing patterns to be refined.

Disadvantages

There are costs in terms of staff time and, again, a certain level of resentment among staff who may feel that they are being 'spied on', or that they are no longer trusted. Training would also be required and additional administrative work would need to be undertaken by local managers.

3 **Recommendation 3**: that management accounts are produced on at least a quarterly basis, that figures relating to each supermarket are provided to head office on a monthly basis, and that an analysis is undertaken by head office on the performance of individual supermarkets and inventory lines.

Advantages

This would enable the company to determine which supermarkets are performing better than others. It would also enable the company to identify those inventory lines that sell well and those that are profitable.

Disadvantages

The production of more regular and detailed information will be time-consuming. Local managers may feel that they are unable to service the particular needs of their customers if decisions are made on a global basis; customers may feel the same way.

4 **Recommendation 4**: that sales price decisions are made by head office.

Advantages

This would enable the company to experiment with the use of 'loss leaders', for example, and to impose a degree of consistency across supermarkets to prevent inappropriate pricing decisions being taken by local managers.

Disadvantages

Again, loss of control at a local level is likely to result in resentment and the possible loss of good staff. What sells well in one supermarket may not do so in another. To the extent that head office have less experience of local conditions than local staff, it is possible that inappropriate pricing decisions may be made by head office.

AUDIT EVIDENCE

35 WALSH

Key answer tips

Your answer to Part (a) should use the question data and give precisely the information which the examiner requires. Note that the answer below is presented in a tabular form. This part is worth half the marks of the question and clearly requires at least five weaknesses and corresponding improvements.

You must expect questions on the paper to be set in a computer environment – this becomes relevant in Part (b) here. The question covers points on both main aspects of computer auditing – controls and computer assisted audit techniques (test data here). As far as access controls are concerned, remember that you are dealing with payroll – these controls are very important here because of the sensitive nature of the data.

Note that in Part (b) the second requirement to recommend test data is worth more marks than the first which requires recommendations on access and program controls.

(a) **Use of Computer-Assisted Audit Techniques (CAATs)**

Testing programmed controls

– Reliance on CAATs will force the auditor to rely on programmed controls during an audit; in fact using CAATs may be the only way to test controls within a computer system. Use of the CAAT enables the auditor to meet the auditing standard requirement of obtaining appropriate audit evidence.

– For example, in Walsh Co, an overtime report is generated by the computer, although this can also be overridden by the accountant. Test data can be used to check that the overtime report is being created correctly and audit software can monitor that only the accountant's password can be used to override the overtime payment.

Test larger number of items

– Using CAATs enables the auditor to test a larger number of items quickly and accurately, meeting the auditing standard requirement of obtaining sufficient audit evidence.

Using audit software, the auditor can check the deduction and net pay calculations of a significant proportion of wages calculations – or all of them if necessary. Checking each calculation manually would take a long time.

Test actual accounting records

– Using CAATs enables the auditor to test the actual accounting records (the electronic version) rather than relying on printouts or other copies of the data. It is always appropriate for the auditor to test original documentation where possible.

– In the case of Walsh, the actual wages will be tested rather than any paper copies.

Cost

– After initial set up costs, using CAATs is likely to be cost effective; the same audit software programs can be run each year as long as the client does not change the accounting systems.

- In Walsh Co, the system has just been implemented. Hopefully the wages system will be used for a number of years, making the use of CAATs cost-effective for the audit firm.

(b) **Examples of the use of audit software**

- Calculation checks. For example, re-calculation of net pay for a number of employees to ensure the mathematical calculation is correct.
- Reviewing the list of employees paid each week/month and printing a list of employees, who have not be been paid, for further investigation.
- Detecting unreasonable items. Reviewing the list of net wages for large or negative payments.
- Detecting violation of system rules. For example, where other people besides the accountant have been overriding overtime payments or employees amending their own gross wages.
- Conducting new analysis as part of the analytical review of wages. For example, calculating total wages for the year from the number of employees and average wages paid.
- Completeness checks – ensuring there is an electronic record of all employees who 'clocked in' for a day's work and 'clocked out' again.

(c) **Audit test data consists of data submitted by the auditor for processing on the client's computer-based accounting systems.**

The data can be processed during a normal processing run (a 'live' testing situation) or in a special run outside of the normal processing cycle (a 'dead' testing situation).

In Walsh, the auditor can create a 'dummy employee' record on the wages master file, and then use a magnetic card to mimic that employee working a certain number of hours in the company over the course of, for example, one week.

Knowing how many hours has been input into the wages system; the auditor can calculate the expected net pay and then compare this to the actual net pay produced by the computer system.

If the amounts agree then this provides appropriate audit evidence of the accuracy of recording and processing of the wages software.

The problems of using this audit technique include:

- The possibility that the client's computer system will be damaged by the testing being undertaken by the auditor. For example, by errors being caused by entering data that the client's software cannot process.
- The need to reverse or remove any transactions input by the auditor. The transactions may be incorrectly or incompletely removed leaving dummy data in the client's live computer system.
- Use of test data can be expensive – the auditor needs to ensure that the benefit gained from the test outweighs the expense.
- In this situation, it will take a long time to input employee details and there may be more efficient audit tests available.

36 PORTHOS

Key answer tips

This question follows a common format in that (a) is knowledge based and then (b) and (c) ask you to apply this knowledge in a given scenario. Most questions on CAATs seem to be set in a sales system, so make sure you can answer a question in this context.

(a) The advantages of Computer-Assisted Audit Techniques (CAATs) are that they:

- Enable the auditor to test program controls – if CAATs were not used then those controls would not be testable.
- Enable the auditor to test a greater number of items quickly and accurately. This will also increase the overall confidence for the audit opinion.
- Allow the auditor to test the actual accounting system and records rather than printouts which are only a copy of those records and could be incorrect.
- Are cost effective after they have been set up as long as the company does not change its systems.
- Allow the results from using CAATs to be compared with 'traditional' testing – if the two sources of evidence agree then this will increase overall audit confidence.

(b)

Test Data	**Reason for test**
Input of an order for a negative number of tennis racquets	Ensures that only positive quantities are accepted – tennis racquets although the company cannot despatch negative quantities anyway.
Input of an order for ten tennis racquets	There are reasonableness checks in the system to identify possible input errors. A warning message should appear on screen asking the customer to confirm any order for more than say two racquets.
Input of an order without payment details	Ensures that orders are paid for prior to despatch – being completed this also limits the number of bad debts.
Input of invalid inventory code	Ensures that the computer detects the invalid code and presents an error message rather than taking the nearest code and accepting that.
Input of invalid customer credit card details	Online checking of credit card details to the credit card company ensures that goods cannot be despatched without payment.
	This will also limit the number of bad debts.
Input of invalid address	Ensures that the address and post code are valid, possibly by accessing a database of valid codes. If the code is not valid an error message should be displayed. This ensures that goods are only despatched to valid addresses.

(c) **Audit software**

(i) *Difficulties of using audit software*

- Substantial setup costs because the client's procedures and files must be understood in detail before the audit software can be used to access and interrogate those files.
- Audit software may not be available for the specific systems set up by the client, especially if those systems are bespoke. The cost of writing audit software to test those systems may be difficult to justify against the possible benefits on the audit.
- The software may produce too much output either due to poor design of the software or using inappropriate parameters on a test. The auditor may waste considerable time checking what appear to be transactions with errors in them when the fault is actually in the audit software.
- Checking the client's files in a live situation. There is the danger that the client's systems are disrupted by the audit program. The data files can be used offline, but this will mean ensuring that the files are true copies of the live files.

(ii) *Audit tests*

Audit software	**Reason for test**
Calculation check of the sales day book	Ensures that the computerised sales day book has been cast correctly and helps to verify the sales balance in the financial statements.
Analysis of the aging of items in the inventory ledger	Help to detect inventory items which are relatively old which may need valuing at net realisable value rather than cost.
Selecting a sample of inventory at the end of the year as part of the physical verification	Removes bias from sample selection as well as being quicker than selecting the items manually.
Selecting a sample of sales invoices for checking to despatch documentation	Removes bias from sample selection as well as being quicker than selecting the items manually.
Checking completeness of sales invoice numbers	Ensures that all sales invoices are recorded in the sales day book.
Check that all sales invoices have been paid for	All sales are paid for on ordering, unpaid sales would be a violation of systems rules and would need to be investigated by the auditor.
List large credit notes (perhaps more than five racquets) for investigation by the auditor	The auditor will find reasons for the return – this is also a check on the accuracy of the ordering system – ordering errors may result in customers returning goods later.

37 TAM

Key answer tips

Questions based on audit sampling ((part a) here) are rarely 'popular' with students. This is perceived to be one of the more technically advanced aspects of auditing and tends to be associated with 'maths' in the mind of students.

However, you should take the question at its face value. Very often, as is the case here, the examiner makes it very clear what you are expected to do and almost 'leads you through the answer'.

Part (a) is testing your knowledge of the main determinants of sample size in the context both of tests of controls and of substantive testing procedures. This is where a knowledge of the technical language of statistical sampling will score you marks here.

Part (b) is dealing with an area that most students may find more to their liking – general controls in a computer based accounting system. This topic should be part of your basic bank of knowledge on the computer auditing area.

(a) **Sampling risk**

Sampling risk is the possibility that the auditor's conclusion, based on a sample, may be different from the conclusion reached if the entire population were subjected to the audit procedure.

The auditor may conclude from the results of testing that either material misstatements exist, when they do not, or that material misstatements do not exist when in fact they do.

Sampling risk is controlled by the audit firm ensuring that it is using a valid method of selecting items from a population and/or increasing the sample size.

Non-sampling risk

Non-sampling risk arises from any factor that causes an auditor to reach an incorrect conclusion that is not related to the size of the sample.

Examples of non-sampling risk include the use of inappropriate procedures, misinterpretation of evidence or the auditor simply 'missing' an error.

Non-sampling risk is controlled by providing appropriate training for staff so they know which audit techniques to use and will recognise an error when one occurs.

(b) The audit manager suggests checking all invoices, effectively ignoring any statistical sampling; in other words this is not statistical sampling. Audit tests will be applied to all of the sales invoices. This approach may be appropriate for the audit of Tam because:

- The population is relatively small and it is likely to be quicker to test all the items than spend time constructing a sample.
- All the transactions are not large but could be considered material in their own right, e.g. compared to project. As all the transactions are material, then they all need to be tested.

The audit senior suggests using statistical sampling. This will mean selecting a limited number of sales invoices from the population using probability theory ensuring a random selection of the sample and then applying audit tests to those invoices only. This approach may be appropriate because:

- The population consists of similar items (i.e. it is homogeneous) and there are no indications of the control system failing or changing during the year. There is the query about how long it will take to determine and produce a sample, which may make statistical sampling inappropriate in this situation.

The audit junior suggests using 'random' sampling, which the junior auditor appears to understand as manually choosing which invoices to look at. The approach therefore involves an element of bias and is not statistical or true 'random' sampling.

While this approach appears to save time, it is not appropriate because:

- The sample selected will not be chosen 'randomly' but on the whim of the auditor. Human nature will tend to avoid difficult items for testing.
- Also, as invoices will not have been chosen using statistical sampling, no valid conclusion can be drawn from the results of the test. If an error is found it will be difficult extrapolating that error on to the population.

(c) Information is material if its omission or misstatement could influence the economic decisions of users taken on the basis of the financial statements.

Materiality depends on the size of the item or error judged in the particular circumstances of its omission or misstatement.

It is important that the auditors of Tam ensure that the financial statements are free from material error for the following reasons:

- There is a legal requirement to audit financial statements and present an opinion on those financial statements. If the auditors do not detect a material error then their opinion on the financial statements could be incorrect.
- There are only two owner/directors who will be the initial users of the financial statements. While the owners/directors maintain the accounting records, the directors will want to know if there are material errors resulting from any mistakes they may have made; the auditor has a responsibility to the members to ensure that the financial statements are materially correct.
- There are also other users of the financial statements who will include the taxation authorities and the bank who have made a loan to the company. They will want to see 'true and fair' accounts. The auditors must therefore ensure that the financial statements are free from material misstatement to avoid any legal liability to third parties if they audit the financial statements negligently.

38 STRATHFIELD

Key answer tips

The wording of the requirement to this question should be analysed carefully and understood before you attempt your answer.

In dealing with part (a)(i) it is important to remember that the objective of sampling is to be able to draw a conclusion relevant to the entire population based on the results of a sample. To this end, the sample selected needs to be representative of the population. The method of selection used in the question is unlikely to produce a representative sample – for example no government accounts are included.

Monetary unit sampling is the recommended method for selection for receivables circularisation – primarily because it should produce a representative sample. The process of population stratification can also be useful here. These techniques can be referred to in answering part (a)(ii).

Part (a)(iii) is testing your knowledge of three items of terminology which are often confused – it emphasises the importance of learning technical terms which are widely used in auditing.

When preparing your answer to part (b) you will need to think about the meaning of the term 'qualitative aspects'. This can be seen to relate to the possible audit significance of the items as far as the total population of receivables is concerned.

Part (c) is asking you to evaluate the likely error in the total receivable population based on the results of the circularisation. A fairly simple calculation is required, based on the percentage 'error' in the sample.

(a) (i) **Inconsistencies with sampling**

To be a sample, each item must have an equal chance of selection. Sarah's approach does not meet that requirement in that:

- all large accounts are selected
- no accounts under $100 are selected
- no government accounts are selected.

Selecting all large accounts for testing is quite common but the basis for defining 'large' needs explanation. The population being sampled is then defined as all receivables balances below the threshold for items selected as large.

Ignoring very small balances is irregular but, in a test primarily concerned with testing for overstatement and valuation, unlikely to affect the results. However, her working paper should, again, explain the basis for determining the cut-off point of $100.

Treating government accounts as a separate sub-population is acceptable providing alternative verification is performed on such accounts. Moreover, the total of government accounts in the ledger should be treated as a separate sub-population when projecting the sample results. Merely excluding them as being too difficult is not acceptable.

(ii) **Alternative approach to materiality**

The two preferred methods of drawing a sample from variable populations to ensure a sufficient sample of more material balances are stratification and monetary unit sampling.

Stratification divides the population into strata by value and draws relatively larger samples from higher value strata than lower value strata. Sarah has actually done this but not in a formalised way. Statistics can enable auditors to determine the optimum stratification to obtain the required assurance from the smallest sample. In evaluating results error rates need to be projected separately to each stratum.

Monetary unit sampling identifies individual $'s as the sampling unit. By systematically selecting $s, the larger the account balance the larger its chance of containing a $ being selected and thus being tested. Each $ is regarded as being in error proportionately to the error in the account balance of which it forms part.

(iii) **Haphazard selection**

Haphazard selection is an acceptable method of drawing a sample but introduces the risk of unconscious bias such as neglecting the first or last items on a page.

Systematic sampling overcomes this by requiring the staff member to follow a prescribed order. Selection can be replicated and any instances of failure to select the required sample detected. It is not convenient for populations in which the sampling units are not sequentially ordered. It also presents the risk that there may be a particular pattern to the population, which recurs at the same interval as the sampling interval.

Random selection can be undertaken by use of random numbers generated by computer or random number tables. In both cases bias is avoided by requiring the staff member to justify reasons for not testing the sampling unit selected by computer or through use of random number tables. It is inconvenient for populations not held on a computer in that physical selection of documents in random order can be time consuming. It is also not appropriate for sampling units, which are not serially numbered, such as inventory items.

(b) **Qualitative analysis of errors**

Address unknown

– These affect the valuation assertion since the amount is potentially uncollectable.

– The extent of the error depends on whether the company does have a forwarding address.

– Assuming there is no forwarding address the error is one that may be projected to the population.

Cut-off

Since these have been established as goods or cash in transit, they are not misstatements and do not constitute errors.

Invoicing errors

– These would appear to result from a weakness in control.

– The cause of discovered errors must be investigated as to whether they are consistent with the assessed level of control risk for invoice pricing.

– If they suggest a higher level of risk than that originally assessed the level of substantive procedures may need to be reconsidered.

– It may be they occurred during a particular point in time such as when the invoicing clerk was on holiday in which case further testing may be required on the sub-population of invoices prepared at that time.

– Otherwise they are consistent with expected errors and must be projected to the population.

Posting errors

These would appear to result from control weaknesses. Although there is a slight risk of such errors resulting in accounts becoming uncollectable, the fact that the customer to whom they are wrongly charged is likely to complain means that the error is likely to be detected and corrected within a reasonable time. The auditor is not unduly concerned about controls or discovered errors in a situation where monthly statements are issued and customer queries independently investigated. Assuming that to be the case, the error would not be regarded as a misstatement.

Disputed items

Each dispute is likely to be unique. The auditor must investigate each one to see if it is part of a material sub-population. For example it could reveal problems with a particular product and may require a provision against all outstanding sales of that product and even against unsold inventory. If the individual issues are isolated but symptomatic of errors that could be present in the population the error must be projected to the entire population.

(c) **Projected error**

In projecting the error material accounts selected for testing should be excluded from the population samples. In theory, balances below $100 and with government customers should be excluded. However, the former are likely to be immaterial in total and may be ignored and we have no information as to the latter.

It is assumed that our qualitative analysis has determined that all errors except for cut-off differences and mispostings should be projected to the population. It is also assumed that the ratio method is appropriate.

Recorded value of sample			$265,450
Errors			
Gone away		950	
Invoicing ($2,800 – $2,200)		600	
Disputes ($2,800 – $1,300)		1,500	3,050
Percentage error			1.15%
Total accounts receivable	$2,350,000		
less material items selected	205,000		
Population sampled	$2,145,000		
Error rate	1.15%		
Projected crror	24,668		
Errors in material items	0		
Total possible error	$24,668		

Sarah must consider, in the light of the total possible error, whether to conclude that accounts receivable are not materially misstated.

39 INTERNAL CONTROL AND SAMPLING

Key answer tips

Part (a): Anyone preparing for this exam must be thoroughly familiar with the internal control topic. The technical material required to answer this part of the question should therefore be well known. The more important point is to make sure that you focus your answer on the requirements of the question – a general description of every type of control, which you have ever heard of will not be acceptable here! Read sub-sections (i) and (ii) carefully – make sure you deal only with controls relevant to the objectives stated in the question.

Part (b): Sampling questions are generally not popular with candidates. This one, however, is testing your textbook knowledge of key concepts involved. Fortunately, perhaps, no calculations are required. It should not be difficult to score a reasonably good mark on this part of the question.

(a) **Internal controls**

(i) Controls contributing to the orderly and efficient running of the business, safeguarding the assets and adherence to management policies would include the following:

- physical controls over access to the assets such as the locking of doors and the maintenance of an appropriate fire and flood resistant environment;
- insurance against disaster and contingency plans;

- the use of passwords for access to computers and plant and equipment;
- the numerical or other tagging of all equipment, referenced to an asset register;
- performing periodic asset audits;
- internal regulations requiring staff who take equipment such as laptops and motor vehicles home to ensure that they are secure, and prohibiting staff from using their own software on company equipment;
- the maintenance of firewalls and virus checking software.

(ii) Controls contributing to the prevention of fraud and error, and the completeness and accuracy of the accounting records would include the following:

- the preparation and monitoring of capital expenditure budgets together with authorisation of capital expenditure, disposals and depreciation rates by independent persons at an appropriate level within the organisation who do not have day-to-day responsibility for the related records or assets;
- the maintenance of an asset register that is reconciled to the nominal ledger and the assets themselves;
- the periodic checking and review of asset lives, and fully depreciated assets, to ensure that assets are being depreciated correctly, over an appropriate period of time.

(b) **Description**

(i) *Judgement and statistical sampling*

Judgement sampling uses the auditors' judgement to select the number of items to be tested, which items to be tested, and to interpret the results. Statistical sampling uses probability theory to do the same. Some judgement is always used in statistical sampling in the assessment of materiality and in the determination of what constitutes tolerable error, for example.

(ii) *Representative sample*

A representative sample is one whose characteristics are the same as, or similar to, the characteristics of the population as a whole. All sample selection methods attempt to select samples that are representative.

For example, a sample of invoices that have not been properly authorised in 5% of cases will be representative of all invoices if the population as a whole also has around 5% of invoices not authorised.

(iii) *Tolerable error*

Tolerable error is the maximum error that the auditor is prepared to accept and still conclude that the audit objective has been achieved.

For example, in relation to receivables, the auditor may be prepared to form the conclusion that trade receivables are not materially misstated if sampling shows that the accounts receivable population has a value that is within plus or minus, say, 5% of the figure in the financial statements.

(iv) *Different methods of sample selection*

Random selection requires the use of random number tables in order to select a representative sample.

Haphazard selection may be deemed to approximate to random selection provided that no bias is displayed.

Interval (or systematic) selection involves taking every *n*th item, starting at random. Monetary unit sampling is also a form of systematic selection.

Block selection methods (taking one full part of the population) will probably not result in a representative selection. Block selection might involve obtaining confirmation of accounts receivable from one region of the country only, for example.

Note: Only two examples are required.

(v) *Extrapolation of errors*

Errors found in a sample are extrapolated across the population as a whole, in order to enable the auditor to form a conclusion on whether the population is materially misstated. It is important to remember that there is not necessarily a direct, linear relationship between errors in samples and errors in the populations from which they are drawn.

40 ISA 500 ASSERTIONS

Key answer tips

Part (a) of this question is very simple if you know the financial statement assertions and will give you 6 easy marks. Part (b) is a payroll question, based on a small manufacturing company. It examines your knowledge of substantive audit procedures for the balances in the balance sheet and transactions in the income statement. This is a straightforward question and should not cause you any problems.

(a) **Six financial statement assertions**

(i) Existence: an asset, liability or equity interest exist;

(ii) Cut off: transactions and events have been recorded in the correct accounting period;

(iii) Occurrence: a transaction or event that has been recorded took place and pertains to the entity during the period;

(iv) Accuracy and valuation: financial and other information are disclosed fairly and at appropriate amounts;

(v) Rights and obligations: the entity holds or controls the rights to assets, and liabilities or obligations of the entity; and

(vi) Classification: transactions and events have been recorded in the proper accounts.

(b) **Substantive audit procedures**

The main concerns with income statement and balance sheet entries for payroll relate to the completeness and 'accuracy' of transactions (existence and rights and obligations), with proper 'cut-off' (occurrence and measurement) and disclosure.

In relation to both balance sheet and income statement entries, I would ensure that appropriate disclosures had been made in the financial statements in accordance with accounting standards and the statutory framework. The disclosure of amounts paid to directors is often particularly important.

(i) *Payroll balances in the balance sheet, Boulder*

1 Balances that are likely to appear in the balance sheet of Boulder are dealt with in items 5–7 below. In all cases, I would ensure that the amounts appearing in the financial statements can be traced through to supporting schedules and ensure that the schedules are arithmetically accurate.

2 In all cases, I would check the amounts payable to payments made after the period-end, to documentation supporting and authorising the bank transfer, and to the bank statement.

3 In all cases, the extent of testing noted below will depend on the results of tests of controls over payroll.

4 In all cases, I would perform analytical procedures on the amounts payable at the period-end by reference to the number of employees, the amounts payable at the end of each week, month, quarter or year (as appropriate) during the period (and in prior periods) and with reference to profits, production or sales levels, and/or tax and social insurance rates, as appropriate.

5 Unpaid amounts due to the agency

- I would consider the need to obtain confirmation from the agency of the amount payable. If documentation from the agency is available at Boulder agreeing the amount payable, this might suffice.
- I would check the calculation of the amounts payable to supporting documentation authorised by supervisors.
- I would ensure that the amounts payable (particularly the rates payable) agreed with correspondence with the agency and I would check such correspondence for evidence of any disputes.

6 Unpaid wages and salaries due to permanent factory staff, administrative and sales staff and directors, and unpaid bonuses due to sales staff and directors

- I would check the calculation of the amounts payable to appropriately authorised clock cards or contracts, as appropriate.

7 Unpaid amounts due to tax authorities for tax and social insurance

- I would review correspondence with the tax authorities for evidence of any disputes or underpayment and pay particular attention to any delay in the payment of these amounts.

(ii) *Payroll transactions in the income statement, Boulder*

1 As with balance sheet entries, I would ensure that the amounts appearing in the income statement can be traced through to supporting schedules and ensure that the schedules are arithmetically accurate.

2 In all cases, I would select a sample of entries in the income statement and trace them through the ledgers and daybooks to source documentation such as clock cards for permanent factory staff, documentation showing the amounts produced or processed (agency staff) or contracts (administrative and sales staff and directors).

3 I would then trace a sample of source documentation (as noted above) in the opposite direction, through the daybooks and ledgers to the schedules supporting the financial statements and to the income statement.

4 I would perform analytical procedures on the amounts appearing in the ledgers for each period, for each category of employee with reference to production and sales levels as appropriate, the number of employees, and by comparison with prior periods, for example.

41 VILLAWOOD COMPUTERS

Key answer tips

This question focuses on a number of aspects of audit verification procedures as applied to cash and bank balances.

Part (a) should prove to be straightforward – it is based on audit procedures relating to a bank reconciliation statement.

Part (b) deals with the standard exam area of the reliability of audit evidence. It should have occurred to you that bank statements are essentially reliable evidence as they are in written form and arise from outside the company. However, their reliability could be in question if they are tampered with by the company before being seen by the auditor; a sound audit procedure is to require a copy statement to be sent directly to the auditor.

Part (c) is testing your knowledge of the two possible approaches to the audit of computer based systems – through and around the computer. It would be appropriate to make a brief reference to CAATs (computer assisted audit techniques) when explaining the through the computer approach.

The answer to the final aspect of the question can be arrived at by applying a little thought to the problem – there are circumstances when the around the computer approach may not be feasible, there are other circumstances where it may not be effective as a means of gathering audit evidence.

(a) (i) **Audit procedures and (ii) their purpose**

	Procedure	Purpose
1	Agree the balance per bank with the bank statement and with the bank confirmation.	To agree the correctness of the amount.
2	Agree the balance per books with the trial balance and draft financial statements.	To agree the correctness of the amount recorded in the reconciliation.
3	Cast the bank reconciliation.	To agree the correctness of the amount arrived at.
4	From the October bank statement trace deposits to the list of receipts in October or to the September bank reconciliation and:	
	(a) trace outstanding deposits on the September bank reconciliation (if any) and the October list of receipts not appearing on the October bank statement to the October bank reconciliation	To verify that all outstanding deposits are recorded in the reconciliation and at the correct amount.
	(b) ensure that there are no other outstanding deposits on the October bank reconciliation.	To verify that all deposits recorded as outstanding are in agreement with the books.
5	From the October bank statement trace cheques to the list of payments in October or to the September bank reconciliation and:	

	Procedure	Purpose
	(a) carry forward outstanding cheques on the recorded September bank reconciliation and the October list of payments not appearing on the October bank statement to the October bank reconciliation	To verify that all outstanding cheques are in the reconciliation and at the correct amount.
	(b) ensure that there are no other outstanding cheques or other payments on the October bank reconciliation.	To verify that all cheques recorded as outstanding are in agreement with the books.
6	Obtain the November 20X2 bank statement and:	
	(a) trace outstanding deposits and cheques from the 31 October bank reconciliation to the bank statement	
	(b) list outstanding items appearing on the October bank reconciliation not traced to a subsequent bank statement for follow up before the end of the audit.	To verify the existence and correctness as to amount of amounts listed as outstanding on the December bank reconciliation.
7	For returned cheques recorded on the bank statement:	
	(a) agree the amount with the original entry recording the receipt	To verify the existence and correctness of the amount of the returned cheque.
	(b) examine reversing entry for correctness.	To verify that the returned item has been correctly credited to cash and debited to receivables.
8	For all other items such as bank charges, credit transfers and direct debits recorded on the bank statement trace to the entry in the company's books.	To ensure that cash at bank per the books is adjusted by the amount of all such items.
9	Enquire into other items appearing on the bank reconciliation as appropriate.	To ensure that there are no fictitious items that might be concealing an error or misstatement.
10	List, for partner's attention, outstanding items (in 6b) not cleared through the bank by the completion of the audit.	

(b) **Reliability of bank statements as audit evidence**

Bank statements are moderately reliable as they are provided by a third party from a source known to maintain reliable records.

The limitation is that they are obtained from the entity being audited. There is a possibility of the bank statement being altered or that it could even be a forgery. The auditor should be particularly suspicious if the entity provides a fax or photocopy for the auditor's use and not the original.

Where necessary their reliability can be improved by asking the audit entity to request their bank to send a copy statement directly to the auditor or, better still, for the auditor to collect a copy directly from the bank.

(c) (i) **Auditing around and through the computer**

Auditing around the computer is where the auditor traces transactions recorded on documents to the point of entry into the computer and picks up those transactions as part of the output and continues from that point to the entry in the ledger. (Or vouches transactions from the records to the output from the computer and picks them up at the point of entry to the computer back to the source documents.) Any processing performed by the computer is verified by reference to input or output documents.

Auditing through the computer is where the auditor verifies the processing of the transaction by the computer using computer assisted audit techniques (CAATs).

(ii) **Inappropriateness of auditing around the computer**

Auditing around the computer is inappropriate where:

1 Auditing around the computer is impractical.

- Source documents are not available in hard copy form.
- It is not possible to follow the audit trail from input to output or vice versa because there is no hard copy of the output.
- The output summarises input data in such a way that reconciliation is impractical such as where sales and cash receipts data are input into the system but the output is in the form of unpaid invoices listed by customer.
- Control risk assessment is based on computerised application controls which cannot be verified by comparison of input with output, such as credit approval of sales orders evidenced electronically by the credit manager's password.

2 Auditing around the computer is inefficient.

- Substantive procedures around the computer are practicable but computerised application controls, which can only be verified by the use of CAATs could reduce control risk and the level of substantive procedures significantly. For example, invoice pricing could be verified against the hard copy of the price list but it would be much easier to verify the reliability of pricing information held by the computer.
- Substantive procedures could be performed more efficiently through the use of CAATs. For example, we can verify completeness by testing the numerical continuity of input documents, but the use of audit software enables us to program the computer to perform this test.

42 OATLEY

Key answer tips

This question is designed to test your ability to deal with audit practice and procedures relating to liabilities – in particular, trade accounts payable.

Most auditors see that the greatest risk in connection with liabilities is that they may be deliberately understated – this will tend to improve the perception of the reported figures. The most important audit assertion, looked for in part (a), is therefore 'completeness'.

Part (b) asks for your views on when an accounts payable circularisation is desirable as a source of audit evidence.

Part (c) can be answered by applying your knowledge of standard audit testing procedures (for example, inspection of documents, analytical review) to the particular situation in the question. You must focus on 'production department purchases' if you are to score good marks.

Your approach to part (d) needs to reflect the fact that control risk has been assessed as relatively high (controls are weak) – thus to manage the overall level of audit risk in this area the level of detection risk must be kept low – this requires a high level of audit testing. In addition to audit procedures in part (c) dealing with production purchases, in the case of non-production purchases, which may include, for example, utility costs, analytical review techniques can be valuable as a means of gaining audit evidence.

(a) **Inherent risk – accounts payable**

In my audit of accounts payable I would regard completeness as presenting the greatest level of inherent risk for the following reasons.

– Management has an incentive to understate purchases and thus payables in order to improve profits. This applies not only to senior management but to line managers who are close to budgetary limits on certain expenditures and are under pressure to withhold recording of suppliers' invoices until after the year-end.

– Senior management may be under pressure to understate payables in order to improve the company's apparent liquidity. This would be the case if the company were seeking to raise additional finance or to renew existing borrowing agreements. The more liquid the balance sheet shows the company to be the more favourable the terms are likely to be.

– Principal control procedures placed in operation by the company relate to the occurrence assertion in order to prevent improper purchasing by employees or overpayments to suppliers.

– The primary source of information initiating recognition of a liability is the supplier's invoice. During the year the company has no incentive to accelerate the receipt of suppliers' invoices. This means that, as at balance sheet date, there could be outstanding claims not yet invoiced by suppliers which the entity has no formalised procedures for identifying promptly.

– Valuation is rarely a problem except in complex contractual situations where the amount due is contingent upon some future event such as a volume discount dependent on total purchases at some future date exceeding some agreed amount.

(b) **Accounts payable circularisation**

In my audit of Oatley I would not normally undertake a payables' circularisation for the following reasons.

- For payables, much of the documentary evidence available is in the form of third party sourced suppliers' invoices and statements, in contrast to accounts receivable for which most of the available documentation is entity prepared.
- Examination of documentary evidence is usually a cheaper form of substantive evidence than confirmation.
- Although examination of third party sourced documentary evidence is less reliable than confirmations received directly by the auditor, it usually provides sufficient evidence.

I would, however, consider an accounts payable circularisation in the following situations.

- A substantial proportion of the company's suppliers does not issue monthly statements.
- Statements from suppliers with whom the company does substantial business are unexpectedly unavailable for the last month of the year.
- Only fax or photocopies of statements are available whose authenticity is doubtful.
- I have reasons to suspect that the company, or a member of the company's staff, may be deliberately understating liabilities and there is a possibility that some of the suppliers' statements may be forgeries given the ease of replicating documents with modern scanning and desk top publishing technology. Assessment of control risk as slightly less than high, the limited segregation of duties, and the failure to routinely reconcile all statements with the accounts payable ledger mean that this is not necessarily a remote possibility.

(c) **Substantive procedures applicable to production payables**

Initial procedures

- Obtain a list of such accounts payable and test its accuracy by testing it to and from the computer records and adding it and agreeing it to the control account. (If production payables are not segregated from other payables this procedure will apply to all payables.)

Analytical procedures

- Perform analytical procedures on accounts payable and compare the results with expectations:
  - compare current year's balance with previous years
  - compare the average age of payables with previous years
  - compare gross profit with previous year and industry average.

Tests of details of transactions

- Ascertain cut-off data for goods received notes (GRNs) probably obtained during attendance at physical inventory count.
- Check cut off by obtaining GRNs for two weeks prior to the year-end and:
  - checking their numerical continuity
  - tracing GRNs to the purchases recorded before 31 October or the accrual journal entry.

- For a smaller sample I would verify the existence of recorded purchases prior to the year-end by vouching a sample of purchases and purchase accruals to GRN's in the sequence issued prior to the year-end.
- For a sample of the closing accruals I would verify the amount of the accrual by vouching the amount to a subsequently received supplier's invoice.

Tests of details of balances

- Select a sample of accounts payable using criteria such as:
  - all suppliers from whom the entity bought more than 1% of its purchases during the year
  - a random sample of all other suppliers including nil and debit balances.
- For each supplier in the sample I would compare the balance with the supplier's statement and investigate differences.
- If any supplier's statements were unavailable I would consider confirming the balance directly with the supplier.

(d) **Verifying the completeness of non-production payables**

Detection risk over the completeness assertion must be set as low because of the assessment of control risk as only just less than high and from problems identified in obtaining the understanding of the accounting system in that:

- there are no goods received notes to determine the date of receipt of the goods
- invoices are not recorded until after approval by the department manager which could cause considerable delay and even a failure to record liability for invoices mislaid or even lost before being recorded
- suppliers' statements are not reconciled which would otherwise detect most delayed or missing invoices.

My audit procedures would be centred on cut-off and the search for unrecorded liabilities.

- Vouch purchases entered in the purchase journal as at 31 October (including those entered while the journal was held open after the year-end) to invoices to verify that they are properly recorded as accounts payable at the balance sheet date.
- Vouch larger purchases recorded in the first two weeks of the subsequent year to invoices to ensure that they are properly recorded after the year-end.
- Obtain suppliers' statements from major suppliers and reconcile them with the balance in accounts payable for evidence of invoices missing or mislaid.
- Review outstanding purchase orders for evidence of goods or services received prior to the year-end not yet invoiced by the supplier.
- Similarly vouch cash payments for the first two weeks after balance sheet date for payments for goods and services received before the year-end not processed as payables.
- Review both purchases and cash payments for items that may relate to goods or services received prior to balance sheet date. This review should be continued up to the date of signing the auditors' report.
- Compare prepayments and accruals with the previous year for items such as rent or utility bills normally paid in advance or arrears of receipt of goods and services and investigate differences.

- Analyse expense accounts for significant differences either in absolute amounts or relative to sales. Any unexpected difference could be due to unrecorded purchases at the balance sheet date.

43 REDFERN

Key answer tips

This is a question based on audit verification work. The bulk of the marks for this question arise from a demonstration of the audit procedures required for reviewing non current assets and depreciation. The last part requires you to make a decision on the proposed treatment and to justify that decision.

Part (a) is only worth 3 marks and, therefore, you would be expected to state only a small number of procedures and provide reasons for them. Note the use of the word 'initial' – you have received this schedule from the client – it must be checked before it can be used as audit evidence.

Part (b) carries the highest mark allocation on the question and you should therefore ensure you give sufficient explanation of the verification work you would undertake.

In Part (c) you need to demonstrate an understanding of the relevant requirements. The auditor must be satisfied that the valuation is justified – this is particularly important here as the valuation was arrived at by an employee.

For Part (d) discuss the proposed treatment for correction of the accumulated depreciation – IAS 8.

(a) **Initial audit procedures**

Clerical accuracy

This schedule has been prepared by the company's accountant. If I am to use the schedule as the basis for planning and performing my audit I must first ensure that it is correct in accordance with the company's books and records. I would, therefore:

- verify the schedule to and from amounts recorded in the nominal ledger and with the draft financial statements
- check the correctness of additions and other calculations on the schedule.

The basis for this procedure is that of professional scepticism which requires making no presumption as to the accuracy of information provided by management.

Opening balances

I would check that the opening balances are in agreement with the balances in the previous year's audit file. This is for two reasons:

1. To ensure that any amendments to the previous year's closing balance agreed at audit had been properly recorded in the company's books and records.
2. With plant and equipment most audit procedures are applied to transactions that change the balance. Reliance is placed on audit procedures performed in previous years in verifying assets brought forward at the beginning of the year.

(b) **Audit of additions – I would**:

Occurrence

- Vouch additions to supplier's invoices.
- Examine goods inward notes or other evidence confirming delivery of the items prior to the year-end.
- Examine purchase orders, requisitions and other evidence, such as Board approval, that the purchase had been properly authorised.

- Physically examine some of the items confirming description and serial numbers to the invoice.

Completeness

- Analyse repairs and maintenance to ensure that no items charged to this account should not have been capitalised.
- Scrutinise the company's capital budget and capital commitments recorded in the previous year's financial statements for details of proposed additions and enquire as to why any such items are not recorded as additions.

Rights

- Ensure that the purchase documentation assigns ownership or equivalent rights to the company.

Accuracy

- Ensure that the amount recorded as additions is in accordance with the cost on the purchase invoice including all matters properly included, such as delivery but excluding amounts that should not be capitalised, such as the cost of removal of plant being replaced. Where other costs are capitalised, such as own labour for assembly and testing, I would verify the amounts as appropriate.

Classification and understandability

- Ensure that the items properly meet the definition of plant and machinery and are properly recorded as such.

(c) **Revaluation**

Competence and objectivity of the valuer

My prime concern would be that the valuer is an employee of the entity. Nevertheless, I may be prepared to accept the valuation although I would need to be satisfied that the valuation has been performed with sufficient objectivity that it represents sufficient appropriate audit evidence. This depends on factors such as the materiality of the amounts involved and the availability of corroboratory evidence. The revaluation is certainly substantial representing a gain of $144,000 on property, plant and equipment having a written down value of $603,000.

It is a common practice for interim valuations to be undertaken by valuers employed by the entity providing they are confirmed by less frequent independent valuations, such as every five years. If this is the practice I would examine the record of past valuations to see if the employee's valuations tended to be confirmed by the independent valuations.

I would also enquire into the professional qualifications and experience of the valuer to ensure that he or she is both suitably qualified to perform valuations and sufficiently experienced in valuations of the type undertaken.

Scope of work

I would obtain a copy of the valuer's report, and:

- check that the valuation given in the report is consistent with the valuation recorded in the financial statements
- check that the basis of valuation is consistent with an acceptable basis of financial statement valuations, such as open market value and, in particular, that it relates to the property as it is and does not anticipate future uncertain events such as re-zoning for planning, new roads, etc
- form a view as to how thoroughly the valuer has undertaken his or her work.

Although the valuer was an employee of the company I would need to ensure that no undue restriction was placed on the valuer's access to relevant information having a bearing on the valuation.

Assessing the work of the valuer

When reviewing the work of the valuer I would expect to see the basis of the valuation explained and justified in the report. Where practicable I could confirm any data used such as recent transactions involving similar property. I could also consider the reasonableness of any assumptions made concerning which I have some knowledge, such as the effect of recent changes in legislation or in the economic climate.

Conclusion

If I find that:

- the valuer is professionally qualified, and sufficiently experienced
- the scope of the work is adequate
- other evidence corroborates the reliability of the valuation.

I would probably be prepared to accept the work of the valuer as an expert providing sufficient appropriate evidence as to the valuation of the property. My confidence in the valuation would be enhanced if it were an interim valuation subject to periodic confirmation by independent valuers.

(d) **Accumulated depreciation**

According to IAS 8 the correction of errors which are the natural result of estimates inherent in the accounting process are normally dealt with in the income statement in the period in which they are identified. This would appear to be the accountant's argument.

An alternative view is that this is a material prior period error and the cumulative adjustments applicable to prior periods have no bearing on the results of the current period. In this case, as a prior period adjustment, the treatment required by IAS 8 is to adjust the opening balance of retained earnings and to amend the comparative figures for the previous accounting period.

44 TRACEY TRANSPORTERS

Key answer tips

Part (a) deals with the audit of the sales figure in the financial statements of a vehicle hire company. Don't be put off by the apparent complexity of the business and by the fact that there are different computer programs involved. Think of the typical tests on the documents in the system and you should come up with a good answer.

Part (b) is similar but deals with the vehicles figure in the balance sheet. Again the best approach is to think of the numbers and documents involved and how they can be checked.

Your audit work should cover each of the financial statement assertions.

(a)

Audit test	Reason for test
Discuss with booking clerk how orders are recorded from the customer.	The main problem with the sales system in TT is the lack of evidence for the receipt of the telephone order. Checks are therefore required to ensure that orders are completely and accurately recorded in the Vehicle Management System (VMS) where no input document is available.
Discuss with the directors the recruitment and training of booking clerks.	To check on the personnel controls in TT which will be designed to minimise loss of customer orders. To ensure that staff have appropriate skill and training to operate the ordering system without losing customer orders.
With client's permission, attempt to enter orders into the VMS from an input terminal.	To confirm the completeness and accuracy of recording of orders by the computer system.
For a sample of confirmed e-mail orders held in the e-mail program, trace details onto the VMS ensuring that details of vehicle hire regarding time and dates are accurately recorded.	To check for accuracy of transfer of information from the e-mail to the VMS. The method of filing of the e-mails means that completeness of e-mail orders cannot easily be determined. Audit software may be able to re-sort the orders.
Review hard copy customer complaint files and e-mail files on computer for evidence of unfilled orders.	To check for evidence of orders being sent by customers but not entered into TT's sales system.
For a sample of bookings in the VMS, trace details to the list of sales invoices raised maintained in the receivables ledger program.	To check for completeness of transfer of information between the two programs. The test can be carried out manually or using test data. Manual testing may be difficult where there is no obvious audit trail between the two systems.
For a sample of sales invoices in the VMS, agree the rental amount being charged to standard charges held in the receivables ledger file.	To check for accuracy of charging for each individual vehicle hire. Evidence of undercharging would indicate that sales are understated.
Cast the list of invoices in the receivables ledger program for one month. Trace total sales to the general ledger program.	To ensure that the total sales for that month are accurate. Transfer of data to the nominal ledger ensures that the total sales amount is recorded correctly in the ledger.
Cast the monthly sales figures in the general ledger and agree to the financial statements. Investigate any discrepancies.	The final cast and checking ensures that the financial accounts figure is accurate. Casting tests can be carried out manually or using computer audit software.

(b) **Audit work on vehicles**

- Obtain non-current asset register from client. Cast the cost, depreciation and net book value columns of the register and agree to the financial statements of TT.

For a sample of new additions in the non-current asset register:

- Agree to board minute or similar documentation for evidence of authority to purchase vehicle. (Occurrence assertion).
- Agree to the physical asset to confirm existence of the vehicle. Where the vehicle is on hire during the audit visit, obtain alternative evidence of existence such as payment from customer near year-end for hire. (Existence assertion).
- Check the physical condition of the vehicle to ensure that repairs and renewal expenditure is not being understated. (Existence of repair expenditure).
- Agree details to purchase invoice or similar document for evidence of ownership. (Ownership assertion).
- Test the calculation of depreciation in the non-current asset register, ensuring that the rates used are those disclosed in the financial statements. (Valuation and accuracy assertion).

For a sample of disposals during the year (for occurrence assertion).

- Review profits and losses generated on sale of vehicles and ensure these are not excessive. If they are check the accuracy of the depreciation rates used as this may indicate over or under charge of depreciation. (Valuation and accuracy assertion).
- Compare sales income to sale of similar vehicles with similar mileage and ensure comparable.
- Ensure asset has been removed from the non-current asset register
- Check calculation of profit or loss on sale.
- Agree receipt on sale to the cash book.

For a sample of vehicles purchased during the year, agree details to purchase invoice and Purchase Day Book (PDB) ensuring details recorded in the correct year (Occurrence assertion).

For a sample of vehicle purchases in the PDB, agree details to the non-current asset register (Completeness assertion).

Agree totals in non-current asset register to the financial statements, ensuring vehicles are disclosed separately in the non-current assets note (material item). (Classification and understandability assertion).

Ensure that the accounting policy for depreciation is clearly stated in the financial statements and is the same as last year. (Classification and understandability assertion).

45 LIDCOMBE

Key answer tips

A question testing your knowledge of the practical application of verification techniques to the audit of trade receivables. There is an element of computer auditing in the question – something which is likely to appear in many exam papers.

Part (a) is asking you to set out the steps in performing a positive receivables circularisation exercise. These steps should be well known to you – but make sure you identify ALL relevant steps, starting at a logical point (obtaining an aged listing). It is also sensible to ensure that the more important points are fully reflected in your answer – such matters as obtaining agreement of management to the sample selected, and making sure that the auditor checks and retains control of the circularisation letters until posting.

Part (b) can be answered satisfactorily by envisaging the audit processes involved in verification of trade receivables in any accounting system, and then using this as a basis for identifying how computer auditing techniques can assist in this process.

As far as part (c) is concerned, a careful review of the audit working paper should reveal a large number of comments which can be validly made.

(a) **Receivables circularisation**

On arrival at Lidcombe's premises Henry should:

(i) Obtain a copy of the aged listing of accounts receivable. To ensure that the sample to be circularised is selected from an accurate representation of accounts receivable he must verify the existence, completeness and valuation of the individual accounts by:

- test vouching individual balances from the accounts receivable ledger to the listing
- test tracing individual balances from the listing to the accounts receivable ledger
- testing the ageing of a sample of accounts
- adding the listing and agreeing the total to the accounts receivable balance in the general ledger.

(ii) Scrutinise the list of balances for unusual items such as substantial credit balances and round sum payments on account which may need to be selectively tested separately from the circularisation.

(iii) Determine the sample selection criteria; for example, individually material balances may be selectively tested and the remaining accounts divided into a population of current due and a population of overdue balances.

(iv) Determine sample size having reference to the planned level of detection risk and tolerable error.

(v) Select the sample using an acceptable sample selection method such as the use of random numbers or systematic selection.

(vi) List the accounts selected and present the list to an authorised company official for the confirmation requests to be typed up on Lidcombe's letterhead and signed by the officer authorising customers to supply the auditor with the information requested.

(vii) Check the confirmation requests to ensure that there is a letter for each account selected and that the stated balance is correct to ensure that Lidcombe has not attempted to change any of the selected accounts. If appropriate, ask management why they have withheld permission to confirm certain accounts, record the discussion on a working paper and, if the explanation appears unreasonable, bring it to the manager's attention. Perform alternative procedures to verify those accounts for which permission to confirm is withheld.

(viii) Post the requests in envelopes bearing the auditor's return address. They must not be given to Lidcombe to post since this provides a further opportunity for confirmation requests to be suppressed. Using the auditor's return address ensures that any that are non deliverable are returned to the auditor since the collectability of such accounts is doubtful.

(ix) Prepare a working paper setting out the total accounts receivable, the basis for determining sample size and for selecting individual accounts for circularisation. List accounts confirmed on a schedule noting the date of first confirmation with columns for recording the date of second request, amount confirmed and details of any investigation of differences.

(b) **Use of CAS**

Henry can utilise CAS in confirming accounts receivable in the following ways.

(i) Test the accuracy of the accounts receivable ledger by:

- checking postings to the ledger from sales and cash receipts records
- ensuring that the accounts receivable system is reliable so that the age of outstanding balances is correctly determined
- testing the accuracy of additions of individual balances.

This will probably have been undertaken at the interim audit.

(ii) Adding the listing of accounts receivable and agreeing the total with the balance on the general ledger.

(iii) Identifying unusual items, such as large credit balances or round sum payments on account, for consideration for selective testing.

(iv) Selecting accounts for circularisation by programming in, either the number to be selected and the selection criteria, or by specifying the statistical sampling plan to be used, and entering required data such as detection risk and tolerable error.

(v) Printing out confirmation requests for each account selected.

(vi) Preparing a working paper listing selected balances.

(vii) Analysing responses in accordance with the sample plan and determining the statistical error rate.

(c) **Review of Mary's working paper**

(i) There is no objective for the audit test recorded on the working paper.

(ii) Determination of sample size is not given such that it can be seen to be sufficient for drawing conclusions as to the population.

(iii) It is not clear whether the population has been stratified or otherwise subdivided in selecting the sample.

(iv) The method of sample selection is not stated. This is necessary if the sample is to be evidenced as representative of the population.

(v) *Note 1*

- Since this is already a sample, the testing of the balance should be complete, rather than a sample of the invoices that make up the balance.
- The copy invoice is not persuasive evidence as to the existence of the debt as it is purely internal. Mary should sight documentation originating from outside the company, such as the customer purchase order or circulated outside the entity, such as a copy of the delivery note signed by the customer.
- This provides no evidence as to valuation. Mary should also have looked for a subsequent receipt of cash.

(vi) *Note 2* – Details of evidence sighted should be noted, such as correspondence between Lidcombe and Ray, and Lidcombe's comments on the matter so that a judgement may be made as to collectability.

(vii) *Note 3* – This is the best form of evidence to confirm the existence of accounts receivable. Mary should also have tested for payments received after balance sheet date to verify valuation.

(viii) *Note 4* – This is an amount that correctly should be in the summary of audit differences. Further work may be necessary on credits issued after the balance sheet date.

(ix) *Note 5* – The work on this balance is adequate.

(x) There is no conclusion as to whether or not the evidence supports the recorded balance.

46 COMPANY A AND COMPANY B

Key answer tips

Part (a) of this question requires you to demonstrate your ability to apply practical audit procedures to a wide range of liabilities. You should note the following:

Item (i): This is a good example of the importance of using all information provided by the examiner. We are told that:

- the loan is for 10 years (balance sheet classification?)
- the interest rate is variable (the interest cost is likely to change over time)
- there is an overdraft with the same bank (how can we use this information?)

Item (iii) carries the most marks in part (a) – the examiner will be expecting a comprehensive, detailed answer for the 6 marks available.

Part (b) deals with one of the many subjective areas which may be encountered in auditing – that of provisions. A good knowledge of IAS 37 is required, but you must also reflect the 'nature of the beast'. The area involved in the question will typically be subject to a high level of uncertainty – auditors will need to collect evidence from a wide range of sources and exercise judgement in reaching their conclusion.

(a) **Company A**

(i) *10-year bank loan and bank overdraft*

1. Authorisation for the loan and overdraft should be checked to the minutes of a board or other relevant meeting.

2. The details of contracts with the bank and any relevant correspondence should be examined. Any covenants restricting the use of securities held against the loans should be examined and the client's compliance with the covenant checked. If covenants have not been complied with, the implications for the company and the financial statements should be considered.

3. The response to the year-end bank confirmation should be examined. It should provide details of the amounts outstanding and the amounts paid and payable during the year in terms of both interest (loan and overdraft) and capital (loan only). In both cases, details of any security held for the loan and overdraft should be requested.

4. Analytical procedures should be applied to the interest paid in the income statement, and to the interest and capital paid and outstanding at the period-end for the loan.

5. The bank reconciliation should be checked to ensure that the overdraft has been properly reconciled to the records, and that there are no old or significant outstanding amounts that need to be adjusted for.

6. The amount payable at the year-end should include amounts payable in one year, which should be included in current payables, and amounts payable in over one year. The notes to the financial statements should also disclose amounts payable in over five years.

7. The auditors should ensure that appropriate disclosures are made in the notes to the accounts in accordance with legislation and International Financial Reporting Standards. In particular, where assets are held as security, this should be disclosed in the notes relating to the assets.

(ii) *Expense accruals*

1. If accruals are material to the financial statements, more evidence will be required than if they are not. If accruals are not material, analytical procedures may be sufficient audit evidence.

2. A schedule of accruals should be obtained and checked for arithmetical accuracy. Individual accruals should be reviewed by comparison with prior periods and budgets and any significant variations investigated, particularly if accruals have been made in previous periods but have not been made in the current period.

3. The amounts paid after the period-end should be checked to the bank statement and the calculation of a sample of amounts payable should be checked for accuracy, by reference to subsequent invoices.

4. If any accruals are payable more than one year after the balance sheet date, an appropriate split should be made in the balance sheet.

(iii) *Trade payables and purchase accruals*

1. The nature and extent of testing will depend on the quality of controls over trade payables, as evidenced by interim testing of internal controls. Evidence in relation to the completeness of trade payables and accruals is important, but not always easy to obtain.

2. The auditors should form an opinion as to whether direct confirmation of trade payables is likely to provide valuable audit evidence by discussion with the client.

3. It is sometimes possible to rely on supplier statement reconciliations instead of direct confirmation, but this depends on the availability of supplier statements. Where supplier statement reconciliations are performed, it is important to be aware of the possibility of forged or altered statements – originals rather than copies should be examined. Some combination of supplier statement reconciliations and direct confirmation is often used.

4. If a decision to obtain direct confirmation of trade payables is taken, the client's co-operation is required in authorising the requests and in helping the auditors sort out any differences between the balances recorded by the company and those recorded by suppliers.

5. Particular care should be taken if there are material balances for which there are no supplier statements or no response to a request for confirmation. Consideration should be given to telephoning the supplier in this case.

6. Analytical procedures should be applied to the ageing and level of trade payables by comparison with prior periods. Variations should be investigated and substantiated, with particular attention being paid to old outstanding amounts.

7. A representative sample of individual trade payables should be traced back through the system from the schedules supporting the financial statements to the ledgers, daybooks and source documentation to ensure that the amounts recorded are accurate. The size of the sample will depend on the auditor's assessment of risk in this area.

8. A schedule of purchase accruals should be obtained and checked for arithmetical accuracy and completeness by comparison with prior periods and invoices received after the period-end. As with trade payables generally, there is a risk of unrecorded items.

9. Both trade payables and purchase accruals should be tested for the accuracy of cut-off by reference to invoices and inventory records for an appropriate period each side of the period-end.

10. A review of correspondence with trade creditors should be performed and any legal department should be requested to provide details of disputes with creditors.

11. If any trade payables are payable more than one year after the balance sheet date, an appropriate split should be made in the balance sheet.

(b) **Company B**

(i) Provisions for manufacturing warranty claims are heavily dependent on the judgement of directors. The auditors should establish how the directors have arrived at the provision and assess it for reasonableness in the light of previous provisions and claims. More work will be required if there has been a significant discrepancy between provisions and claims in the past and more work will be required if the company does not have significant experience in dealing with this type of warranty claim.

(ii) IAS 37 'Provisions, Contingent Liabilities and Contingent Assets' states that a provision is a liability of uncertain timing or amount which should only be recognised when there is a present obligation, as a result of a past event, and where it is probable that an outflow of resources will be required to settle the obligation, the amount of which can be reliably estimated. It would appear that the warranty claim fits this description.

(iii) Such warranties are often underwritten by insurance and any arrangements with the insurance company should be checked in detail so that the substance of the transaction can be reflected in the financial statements.

(iv) Auditors should check the calculation of the provision for arithmetical accuracy and to ensure that it is calculated in accordance with the method determined by directors. This can be achieved by reviewing the level of claims and payments both before and after the period-end.

(v) If there has been a change in the method of calculating the provision, the auditors should ensure that it is reasonable in the light of evidence available and that it is properly disclosed, if material. If there has been a change in the product mix to which the warranty applies, this should also be considered, particularly if there are new, relatively untried products which carry a higher risk of claims in the first few years.

(vi) If any previous provisions have been released in the current period because of over-provisions in previous periods, the auditors should ensure that the amount released is reasonable, and is properly disclosed in the income statement as appropriate. 'Soft' provisions such as these can be manipulated by the client and particular care therefore needs to be taken.

(vii) A review of correspondence with customers should be performed and any legal department should be requested to provide details of disputes with customers relating to claims.

47 BARDWELL

Key answer tips

You must expect questions to be set on a regular basis on internal control matters. This question focuses on controls over cash, which is likely to be a high risk area in many businesses.

Part (a)(i) is designed to test your knowledge of 'segregation of duties' as a control concept. A sound approach is to define and explain the concept and then indicate how its application is inadequate in the situation given, using the facts presented to you by the examiner as fully as possible.

Part (a) (ii) is asking you to identify other appropriate control procedures – you could find a way into this by thinking through a checklist of other control categories (management, accounting, etc) and identifying appropriate examples.

Part (b)(i) is a straightforward exercise on cash counts as an audit testing procedure.

The information given on cash receipts should indicate to you the possibility of the 'fraud' of 'teeming and lading' – an employee misappropriates cash and attempts to cover the fraud by substituting a cash receipt from a customer received later – this then carries on down a chain of customers if not detected and prevented.

(a) (i) **Inadequate segregation and proposed reassignment**

A basic principle of segregation of duties is that an individual employee should not be able to make errors and be in a position to conceal the fact. Proper segregation means that, if an error or misstatement is made, it will be detected by another employee in the ordinary course of his or her duties. A general rule of segregation is that the functions of processing transactions, recording transactions and maintaining records over the subsequent assets or liabilities, should be performed by different individuals.

The receptionist's duties should be restricted to processing cash receipts transactions. All other functions should be assigned to other staff members.

Function to be reassigned	**Possible misstatement**	**Reassignment**
Checking the numerical continuity of invoices, determining the total cash sales and entering the cash receipts journal.	The receptionist could deliberately understate the total in order to misappropriate the cash or conceal a shortage of cash.	This should be assigned to clerk 1. (See additional procedure 1.)
Posting the accounts receivable ledger.	An invoice could be deliberately omitted and the subsequent cash receipt misappropriated if done by the same person. Errors, such as transposition errors, made in entering the sales journal are likely to be repeated in entering the accounts receivable ledger. Cash receipts could be temporarily misappropriated and the shortage concealed by delaying recording the receipt. (See the answer to part (b).)	Clerk 1 should post the accounts receivable ledger from credit sales invoices whose numerical sequence is checked.
Sending out monthly statements and chasing overdue accounts.	If there are errors in the accounts receivable ledger the monthly statements could be altered or suppressed. If payments by customers have been misappropriated and not credited to the customer account, customers' suspicions would not be aroused by chasing apparent overdue balances.	This function should be assigned to clerk 2 since clerk 1 could also falsify statements to conceal errors in recording sales in the accounts receivable ledger. (See additional procedure 2.)

Function to be reassigned	**Possible misstatement**	**Reassignment**
Reconciling accounts receivable with the control account in the general ledger.	This procedure detects errors, deliberate or accidental, in the maintenance of accounts receivable records. If the receptionist has made errors in processing sales and cash receipts transactions to accounts receivable then he would have an incentive to conceal their discovery by falsifying the reconciliation.	Clerk 2 should perform the reconciliation as having no responsibility for recording either cash or sales transactions or maintaining the accounts receivable ledger. (See additional procedure 3.)
Writing off uncollectible balances.	If errors have been made resulting in an understatement of cash received from credit customers, their accounts will appear to be overdue. The error can be concealed by writing off the balance. Such an error could arise from the deliberate misappropriation of cash received from credit customers.	Clerk 2 should advise the manager of overdue balances that may need to be written off. (See additional procedure 4.)

(ii) **Other control procedures needed**

1 A bank reconciliation should be performed at least monthly by Clerk 1 to ensure that cash deposited is in agreement with amounts recorded in the cash receipts book. The bank reconciliation should be scrutinised and signed by the manager.

2 The garage manager should review the list of customer account balances (which should, if practicable, be aged), enquire into steps being taken to collect overdue balances and consider whether further credit may be allowed.

3 The reconciliation of accounts receivable balances with the control account in the general ledger should be scrutinised by the garage manager to ensure that it appears to be properly drawn up.

4 Final decisions on bad debt write offs must be approved in writing by the garage manager.

5 The opening of mail should be done in the presence of a second clerk who should confirm the total amount of cash receipts enclosed therein to minimise the likelihood of such receipts being misappropriated.

(b) (i) **Procedures to be followed in making a cash count**

1 Control all cash funds until completion of the count to prevent cash from a counted fund being transferred to an uncounted fund to conceal a deficiency.

2 Count funds in the presence of the custodian to prevent any suggestion, in the event of a shortage, that the funds were complete when released to the auditors.

3 List each item in the fund, such as the denominations of notes, details of cheques and, for petty cash funds, of vouchers, so that the count can subsequently be agreed with the deposit slip and other accounting records.

4 Have the custodian sign the record of the count as being in agreement in the event of any subsequent disagreement.

(ii) **Discrepancy**

If the details of the items counted differ from the cash receipts book I would suspect a misappropriation of cash by failing to record a receipt from a debtor. To conceal this from the debtor, cash received several days later from another customer is credited to the first customer's account. The first customer will not notice anything wrong, the delay in the receipt being attributed to postal delays or just delays in processing cash receipts. Failure to credit payment by the second customer will be concealed by using a payment received from a third customer and so on. Providing the amounts involved are reasonable, the perpetrator can usually conceal the fraud indefinitely. Such a fraud is only possible if the person responsible for maintaining the accounts receivable ledger also has access to cash received from customers before any control is established over that cash. This fraud is sometimes called 'teeming and lading' or 'lapping'.

It will be necessary to undertake a further investigation by comparing deposit slips receipted by the bank with details recorded in the cash receipts book and postings to the accounts receivable ledger for a series of consecutive days. If a pattern of differences emerges consistent with the pattern associated with this type of fraud, then the existence of the fraud must be suspected.

48 INVENTORY COUNTS

Key answer tips

This question covers a standard area. Many exam papers deal with one or more aspects of inventory – here the examiner focuses on inventory counts.

An important point to note here is that part (c) carries 12 out of the 20 marks available.

A good answer to part (a) will relate the importance of the inventory count to the role and responsibilities of the auditor.

Part (b) covers the textbook areas of perpetual inventory systems and continuous counting – these techniques are becoming increasingly widely used in practice, so it is perhaps not surprising that the examiner should choose to test them. It is important to demonstrate that you are aware of what the approaches involve – define and explain your terms! Again, the answer should fully reflect the role of the auditor in this context.

Part (c) is testing your ability to carry out a typical audit procedure – the auditor's review of the client's count instructions. Note the following:

- You are required only to identify weaknesses in the instructions – read them carefully, bearing in mind the objectives they should achieve and assess their appropriateness in this respect. It will help to think in practical as well as technical terms.
- Perhaps the more demanding aspect is the problem involved in overcoming the weaknesses. Again, the examiner is testing your ability to think in practical terms – you cannot always answer auditing exam questions solely from the material you have learned. It will help you, as always to try to make use of the facts given to you in the question – there are some clues there!

(a) **Importance of inventory counting**

(i) Inventory counting is important to auditors of manufacturers, wholesalers, retailers and many service organisations. Inventory counting is the best way to establish quantities for valuation purposes and it assists management in making appropriate provisions against obsolete, slow moving and damaged items.

(ii) Inventory counting provides the only direct evidence in relation to the existence of inventory. Performed properly, counting also provides evidence on cut-off, certain frauds and on the quality of internal controls over inventory.

(iii) Auditors should attend inventory counts where inventory is material to the financial statements (balance sheet or income statement).

(b) **Perpetual inventory system**

(i) The purpose of a perpetual inventory system procedure in practice is to control inventory. Such a system involves cyclical counting procedures during the year. Such procedures avoid the need for reliance on a year-end count. If auditors wish to rely on the records rather than a year-end count for the purposes of the financial statements they must ensure that the cyclical counting procedures are adequate and are being properly and consistently applied, particularly in a large dispersed organisation.

(ii) I would expect all inventories to be counted at least once a year and for the records to be up to date and promptly corrected for any discrepancies discovered as a result of counting.

(iii) The auditors must assess the risk attaching to the different locations and seek to visit those locations where the value or volume of inventory is substantial, and where controls are weak (i.e. where risk is greater).

(iv) It may be necessary to involve other offices of the same firm, or to engage staff from another firm to attend counts, and to co-operate with internal audit, who may wish to conduct their own counts (on which the auditor may wish to rely), or who may lend staff to the external auditor.

(v) When using other firms of external auditors, and when relying on internal audit work, it is particularly important that the auditor is satisfied with the quality of that work and that the reporting auditors' involvement is sufficient for the reporting firm to be able to justify its audit opinion.

(vi) External auditors will often perform visits on a rotational basis throughout the year to ensure adequate coverage of all locations.

(c) **Weaknesses in counting instructions – why they are difficult to overcome**

Weaknesses	**Why difficult to overcome**
The date of the count may be inappropriate – staff (and auditors) will not wish to work on a public holiday and given that there is a high level of staff turnover, there is a possibility that staff will not arrive or will complete the work too quickly without properly counting the inventory. This is compounded by the fact that staff are working individually and may make errors or attempt to cover up misappropriations.	These problems are difficult to overcome because the shop and warehouse are open seven days a week and because it is expensive and difficult to obtain others (who may not be appropriately experienced) to perform the count.
There may be insufficient time allowed to prepare the inventory for counting and it is likely that the shop and warehouse will be untidy because the business has been busy.	It might be suggested that the count be conducted, say, a week before or a week later and that a roll-forward or roll-back be performed, but this will cause additional staffing problems and problems with the movement of inventory. The company may not wish to change its year-end. Some of the managers might be asked to come and help.
Too much responsibility is in the hands of Mr Sneg (a lack of segregation of duties). He is responsible for the assets (the inventory), the records, the staff and the adjustments to the records. It may be necessary for Mr Sneg to be involved with the count but he should be responsible together with another representative of management who is not involved with the day-to-day control of inventory (such as the finance director). It will be too easy for Mr Sneg to hide errors or falsifications in the inventory records to cover up errors or misappropriations. It would be particularly easy for him to falsify records in relation to, for example, items in inventory but already sold and inventory delivered but not yet paid for. The add-back of inventory delivered but not paid for appears to be wrong, as a matter of principle, even if the related invoices are removed from the sales accounts.	This is difficult to overcome because family owned companies (even large ones) often place a substantial amount of trust in valued employees who would be offended if it were suggested that it were necessary to 'check' their work in some way.

49 AJIO

Key answer tips

Don't let the subject matter of this question put you off; although Ajio is a charity, you are being tested on general audit principles and procedures; you are not expected to have an in-depth knowledge of charities. The marks in this question are equally split between parts (a) and (b); part (a) focuses on the different types of audit risk and part (b) concentrates on the audit tests you would need to perform to test income and expenditure. This question should not present you with any problems.

(a) **Risks and implications for audit risk**

Inherent and control risks

(i) Charities can be viewed as inherently risky because they are often managed by non-professionals and are susceptible to fraud, although many charities and the volunteers that run them are people of the highest integrity who take a great deal of care over their work. The assessment of this aspect of inherent risk depends on each individual charity, and the areas in which it operates.

(ii) Charities are also at risk of being in violation of their constitutions which is important where funds are raised from public or private donors who may well object strongly if funds are not applied in the manner expected. Other charities and regulatory bodies supervising charities may also object. Again, the auditors will assess the level of risk. The involvement of a recently retired Chartered Certified Accountant in the preparation of accounts in the past may lower the auditor's assessed inherent risk to an extent.

(iii) Most small charities have a high level of control risk because formal internal controls are expensive and are not often in place. This means that donations are susceptible to misappropriation. Charities rely on the trustworthiness of volunteers. The auditors will assess the level of risk.

Detection risk

(iv) Detection risk comprises sampling risk and non-sampling risk. It is possible in this case that all transactions will be tested and therefore sampling risk (the risk that samples are unrepresentative of the populations from which they are drawn) is not present.

(v) Non-sampling risk is the risk that auditors will draw incorrect conclusions because, for example, mistakes are made, or errors of judgement are made in interpreting results, or because the auditors are unfamiliar with the client, as is the case here.

Audit risk

(vi) Audit risk is the product of inherent risk, control risk and detection risk and is the risk that the auditors will issue an inappropriate audit opinion. This risk can be managed by decreasing detection risk by altering the nature, timing and extent of audit procedures applied. Where inherent risk is high and controls are weak (as may be the case here) more audit work will be performed in appropriate areas in order to reduce audit risk to an acceptable level.

(b) **Audit tests – fund raising events**

(i) Attend fund raising events and observe the procedures employed in collecting, counting, banking and recording the cash. This will help provide audit evidence that funds have not been misappropriated and that all income from such events has been recorded. Sealed boxes or tins that are opened in the presence of two volunteers are often used for these purposes.

(ii) Perform cash counts at the events to provide evidence that cash has been counted correctly and that there is no collusion between volunteers to misappropriate funds.

(iii) Examine bank paying in slips, bank statements and bank reconciliations and ensure that these agree with records made at events. This also provides evidence as to the completeness of income.

(iv) Examine the records of expenditure for fund raising events (hire of equipment, entertainers, purchase of refreshments, etc.) and ensure that these have been properly authorised (where appropriate) and that receipts have been obtained for all expenditure. This provides evidence as to the completeness and accuracy of expenditure.

(v) Review the income and expenditure of fund raising events against any budgets that have been prepared and investigate any significant discrepancies.

(vi) Ensure that all necessary licences (such as public entertainment licences) have been obtained by the trustees for such events in order to ensure that no action is likely to be taken against the charity or volunteers.

(vii) Obtain representations from the trustees to the effect that there are no outstanding unrecorded liabilities for such events – again for completeness of expenditure and liabilities.

50 FIZZIPOP

Key answer tips

This answer is testing your knowledge of the audit procedures to be followed and tests to be performed when performing the audit of inventories. Part (a) is asking you to describe procedures to be performed during the year and part (b) is asking you to describe procedures to be performed at the year-end. Note: you are told that you do NOT want to perform a year-end count, so take care that you do not start describing detailed inventory counting procedures! Use the data in the question regarding the organisation, i.e. number of warehouses, etc and relate your answer to that; also note that you are NOT required to deal with WIP. You should also be aware of the principles within IAS 2, and refer to these where relevant in your answer.

(a) **Audit tests on 'Stockpop' system during the year**

(i) There are two main aspects to the audit of the Stockpop system: those relating to quantities and those relating to costs. In order to rely on the system as a basis for the figure in the financial statements I would need to ensure that management had a system for ensuring that:

- the system was accurate and up-to-date;
- errors were investigated and corrected on a regular basis;
- each item of inventory was counted at least once a year (in practice items are likely to be counted more often than this as such systems are often relied on to produce figures for management accounts).

(ii) I would ask management about the procedures for inventory counting and review the related documentation, including inventory counting instructions, and form a view as to whether the system was adequate in principle. I would also review the results of any internal audit work on the system design (assuming that I considered the internal audit function to be adequate).

(iii) I would need to obtain evidence relating to the three items noted in (i) above. I would therefore visit the warehouses during the year, possibly on a rotational basis, to ensure that the system was being operated in the manner prescribed.

(iv) I would perform certain preliminary analytical procedures to establish which warehouses to visit (such as those where the records indicated that large volumes of inventories were held, warehouses that were experiencing problems or had experienced problems in the past, or warehouses that were considered high risk for other reasons). I might use different offices of my own firm for these purposes, and/or I would enlist the help of internal audit. I would review the results of the work already performed by internal audit.

(v) I would ask local staff about the procedures performed, especially about any variations from the procedures prescribed. I would observe procedures being performed.

(vi) I would test check records of goods received and goods despatched and trace them through the Stockpop system to ensure that records were accurate and input on a timely basis. I would ensure that the correct corresponding entries for costs had been made in the purchases and sales systems.

(vii) I would perform my own test checks of inventory and trace my counts through the Stockpop, sales and purchases systems.

(viii) I would consider using CAATs (computer assisted audit techniques), including test data and audit software to establish whether, for example, the system is rejecting entries outside certain pre-determined parameters (cost per unit for example), and that the system highlights any old inventory, or any exceptions such as negative inventory quantities.

(ix) I would review all exception reports produced by the system to see if there were any recurring or old items and to ensure that all errors and exceptions were being dealt with on a timely basis.

(b) **Audit tests on records at year-end**

(i) I would analytically review the year-end records to establish the overall quantities and costs of inventories and the quantities and costs of raw materials and finished goods.

(ii) I would ask management about any problems experienced with the system at, or close to, the period-end and about how they had been dealt with to ensure that they had been appropriately resolved.

(iii) I would also ask management about the likely level of write-down of either raw materials or finished goods (inventory being of inadequate quality or spoiled, for example). I would compare this with prior years and form an opinion as to its appropriateness. I would check the calculation of the provision and review exception reports close to the period-end.

(iv) I would obtain schedules of the costs and quantities to be included in the financial statements and trace these back to the output of the Stockpop system noting and substantiating any significant adjustments.

(v) I would enquire as to how accurate cut-off had been achieved. I would perform cut-off tests on the records by tracing samples of goods received and despatch notes just before and just after the year-end to the Stockpop, sales and purchases systems in order to ensure that costs had been correctly allocated to the correct accounting period. I would also perform this test in reverse, from the Stockpop, sales and purchases systems through to goods received and despatch notes.

(vi) I would ensure that the valuation method used by Fizzipop was in accordance with IAS 2 Inventories and that, for example, the system was adequate to ensure that finished goods included an appropriate element of labour and overhead costs.

51 CURDCO

Key answer tips

The majority of marks to be gained in this question which focuses on payables and accruals are in part (b), worth 12 marks. Part (a) simply requires you to use your common sense, and part (c) is testing your knowledge of procedures to be followed for direct confirmation of creditor accounts. A good approach to part (b) would be to separate your answer into different key areas such as general tests, and then tests for those areas where you would expect to be able to obtain substantial in house documentary evidence and those where evidence is primarily external and often more subjective, e.g. local taxes. Remember to give reasons for the audit tests that you are describing and don't forget to consider both accounts payable and accruals.

(a) **Headings: accounts payable and accrued expenditure**

Whilst there are a great number of possible headings for accounts payable and accrued expenditure, the seven headings below seem likely:

(i) food and beverages;

(ii) payroll;

(iii) cleaning;

(iv) maintenance of properties;

(v) waste disposal;

(vi) light, heat, water and other utilities;

(vii) business and other local taxes.

(b) **Audit tests and reasons: accounts payable and accrued expenditure**

General

(i) The firm would first obtain an understanding of the business, including reviewing management and financial accounts, in order to enable the firm to make some predictions as to the likely relationships between items of financial and non-financial data. There are likely to be direct relationships that do not vary such as gross margins, and income and expenditure. These relationships may be applied to each restaurant and to the company as a whole. Understanding the business is important because it is the firm's first year as auditor and because it enables the auditor to properly plan tests, and evaluate the results thereof.

(ii) Tests of controls would be performed on expenditure under each heading to enable the firm to determine the level of substantive procedures required at the year-end.

(iii) Analytical procedures would be applied to each heading, both for the company as a whole, for regions and for individual restaurants if necessary. This would establish the level of expenditure, and the level of accounts payable and accruals in the prior year and for each period within the current year for which figures were available. Any unusual items would be investigated and explanations sought and substantiated. Analytical procedures are useful in the planning of audit tests to establish areas to which greater audit resources need to be devoted.

Food, payroll, cleaning, maintenance of properties

(iv) In all cases, substantive procedures would involve tracing source documentation created by the company (such as purchase orders for food, contracts with the cleaning and maintenance agencies and clock cards or timesheets) through the system (via goods received notes, signed documentation indicating that services had been performed, etc.) to daybooks, ledgers and control accounts and finally to schedules supporting the financial statements. This type of test helps provide audit comfort that accounts payable and accruals are complete, correctly calculated, properly authorised and recorded in the correct accounting period.

(v) Substantive procedures tracing entries in the financial statements back to supporting schedules, entries in the ledgers, control accounts and daybooks through to source documentation help provide audit comfort that accounts payable and accruals exist, are properly authorised and recorded in the correct accounting period.

(vi) Substantive procedures may also involve direct confirmation of accounts payable, although if suppliers send regular statements this may not be necessary. Such confirmations and statements provide the auditor with valuable third party, written evidence that is generated outside the company, showing the existence, accuracy and proper recording of accounts payable.

(vii) After-date payment of both accounts payable and accruals also provides evidence of the existence and accuracy of accounts payable and accrued expenditure.

(viii) Cut-off tests (checking samples of invoices for food received just before and just after the year-end to goods received notes, purchase invoices and records of inventory counts, for example) help ensure that expenditure and the related accounts payable and accruals are recorded in the correct accounting period.

(ix) For many such items, there may be accrued expenditure. Tests for accrued expenditure will be similar to those noted under the following heading.

Waste disposal, light, heat, water and other utilities and business and other local taxes

(x) These items are less likely to have source documentation created by the company than those noted above. They are also more likely to be billed or invoiced less frequently than those noted above and there are likely to be more accruals for such items.

(xi) Accrued expenditure is an accounting estimate based on previous experience. Analytical procedures such as those noted above form a large part of the checking of accrued expenditure.

(xii) The firm should establish the basis on which accrued expenditure is calculated to ensure that it appears reasonable and consistent with prior periods, and check the actual calculation of the expenditure (possibly on a sample basis).

(xiii) Checking accrued expenditure to invoices or bills received after the year-end and to payments after the year-end provides evidence as to the correct calculation of accruals.

(c) **Difficulties and decisions: direct confirmation of accounts payable**

(i) Many of the difficulties faced by auditors conducting direct confirmations of accounts payable are the same as those relating to direct confirmations of accounts receivable. Clients are sometimes resistant to conducting such confirmations.

(ii) Auditors have to consider whether the resources required to conduct a confirmation are likely to be warranted in terms of the audit evidence likely to be obtained, particularly where alternative third party evidence is available in the form of supplier statements. The level of response is often low, responses may be delayed and responses may be inaccurate (particularly if the error is in the favour of the creditor).

(iii) Auditors have to decide whether to send a positive or negative confirmation. Positive confirmations ask for a reply in any case (and may have a low response rate), negative confirmations only require a reply when the creditor disagrees with the amounts stated, although the auditor can never be absolutely sure whether a non-reply indicates agreement of the amount or whether the request has simply been ignored. The auditor is generally most concerned to ensure that liabilities are not understated and requests for confirmation are therefore usually positive.

(iv) Auditors also have to decide whether to state the balance in the request (which enables the supplier to provide a reconciliation if there is a disagreement), or not to (in which case the auditor has to perform a reconciliation although strictly speaking, this is the responsibility of the client).

(v) In practice, reconciling accounts can be time consuming and inefficient, and often requires the assistance of the client's staff.

52 BEARSWORLD

Key answer tips

This is a straightforward question since you should be very familiar with the ISA 500 procedures for gathering audit evidence. You should hope to score very highly on a standard question like this.

(a) **Audit procedures**

(i) *Analytical procedures* consist of evaluations of financial information made by a study of plausible relationships among both financial and non-financial data.

Inquiry means to seek relevant information from sources, both financial and non-financial, either inside or outside the company being audited. Evidence may be obtained orally or in writing.

Inspection is the physical review or examination of records, documents and tangible assets. It may include examination of records for evidence of controls in the form of a compliance test.

Observation involves looking at a process or procedure as it is being performed to ensure that the process actually works as documented.

Re-calculation means the checking of the mathematical accuracy of documents or records.

(ii) *Analytical procedures*

Review of sales income year on year to try to identify whether income has been understated, possibly by cash being taken prior to banking. There is no control over the opening of post so cash could be withdrawn by one assistant, and the deficit made up by a fraud on customers.

Inquiry

Obtain statements from suppliers to check the completeness of liabilities at the end of the year. As there is no control over purchases, invoices could have been misplaced resulting in a lower purchases and trade payables figure.

Inspection

The assets of the company, namely cuddly toys in inventory at the end of the year, can be inspected to ensure all inventory is recorded and that the toys are saleable in their current condition.

Observation

Procedures such as the opening of the post and recording of customer orders can be observed to ensure that the administrator is recording all orders in the sales day book and cash book.

Re-calculation

Checking additions in the cash book to confirm that the total amount of cash recorded is accurate and can be included in the sales figure (cash receipts normally equal sales because there are no receivables).

(b) **Analytical procedures**

This method of collecting evidence will be useful in BearsWorld because it will help to identify unusual changes in income and expenditure. As BearsWorld is a relatively small company, monitoring gross profit will show relatively small changes in sales margin or purchasing costs. Decisions by Mr Kyto to amend margins can therefore be traced into the actual sales made.

However, the technique may be limited in its application because it will not detect errors or omissions made consistently year on year. If either assistant is defrauding the company (for example by removing cash) each year, then analytical procedures will not detect this.

Inquiry

Inquiry evidence will be very useful in the audit of BearsWorld, especially where this is derived from third parties. Third party evidence is generally more reliable than client originated evidence as there is a decreased likelihood of bias. Trade payables can therefore be verified using supplier statement reconciliations. A review of any customer complaints file (if these letters are kept) will also help to identify any orders that have not been despatched.

External inquiry evidence will be less useful in the audit of sales and receivables because goods are paid for prior to despatch – there are no receivables. Internal evidence will be available from Mr Kyto and the assistant; however the lack of segregation of duties means that this will not be so reliable.

Inspection

Inspection of documents within BearsWorld will be useful, particularly regarding checking whether expenses are bona fide. All purchase invoices, for example, should be addressed to BearsWorld and relate to purchases expected from that company, e.g. cuddly toys for resale, office expenses, etc.

Inspection of documents can take a long time; however, given the poor internal control system within BearsWorld, the auditor may have no choice but to use this method of gathering evidence.

The fact that an invoice is addressed to the company does not confirm completeness of recording so inspection of the cash book for unusual payments verified by checking the purchase invoice will also be required. Additional substantive testing would also be required due to poor controls.

Observation

Observation may be useful because it will show how the assistants check documents. However, no information is provided on any internal controls within BearsWorld so simply viewing how documents are checked without any evidence of checking has limited benefit.

Observation tests will be of limited usefulness because the assistants may act differently when an auditor is present. The same problem will apply to any observation checking carried out by Mr Kyto.

Re-calculation

Re-calculation evidence is very useful for checking additions on invoices, balancing of control accounts, etc. This means that the arithmetical accuracy of the books and records in BearsWorld can be confirmed.

The main weakness of re-calculation checking is that calculations can only be carried out on figures that have been recorded. If there are any omissions then checks cannot be carried out.

53 ATLANTIS STANDARD GOODS (ASG) LTD

Key answer tips

This question focuses on the sales system, and hence is reflective of the F8 exam which concentrates on core business areas.

In part (a) it is important that you can differentiate between control objectives and control procedures; this question focuses on the former and hence no marks will be earned for a detailed description as to how they are achieved.

Part (b) asks you to tabulate your answer allowing an easy pro forma to differentiate between the test and the reason for its use. Ensure that your tests (approximately fifteen is the ideal) are tailored to the scenario, and that each stands alone without assuming extensive knowledge on behalf of the reader.

(a) Aims of controls

- Ordering of goods.
- Goods are only supplied to authorised customers.
- Orders are recorded correctly regarding price, quantity, item and customer details.
- Despatch and invoicing of goods.
- Orders are despatched to the correct customer.
- All despatches are correctly recorded.
- Despatches only relate to goods ordered and paid for by customers.
- Invoices raised relate to goods supplied by the company.

(b) Audit tests to ensure order and sales details are completely and accurately recorded.

Audit test	**Reason for test**
Using test data if necessary, access ASG's website and input order details for specific goods. Trace those order details to the orders pending file.	Ensure that order details are completely and accurately recorded by the website software. Ensure that details recorded agree to those input.
For a sample of items in the orders pending file, • agree to the orders awaiting despatch file, ensuring that appliance details and quantities are the same	To ensure that details from the website software are completely and accurately transferred to the orders awaiting despatch file.
• agree sales details for that customer to the monthly reimbursement from the credit card company, checking amount received is the product price less the appropriate commission charged by the credit card company	To confirm that amounts are received for each appliance sold, and therefore that monies received are complete and accurate.
• agree the sales amount to the sales ledger file.	To confirm that the amount of sales is not understated or overstated in the ledger, general ledger or financial statements.
Review goods awaiting despatch file for old items and inquire as to why those items are still on file.	To ensure that reasons for orders not being processed are being obtained. A large number of old items may also indicate problems with the credit card authorisation systems which again will need to be investigated.
For a sample of days, cast the sales ledger file and agree the total sales to the general ledger accounts for that day.	To check the numerical accuracy of the ledger and the accuracy of posting to the general ledger file.
For a sample of items in the goods awaiting despatch file, agree to the despatch information held on the despatch department computer.	To confirm that order details are completely and accurately transferred to the despatch department.
For a sample of items on the despatch department computer, • agree back to the goods awaiting dispatch file ensuring details of product, quantity and customer agree	To ensure that the despatch information is accurate and that the despatch record itself relates to a valid sale.
• agree to the inventory records confirming that the correct appliance record was updated	Ensures that the inventory system correctly records the appliance ordered and that the inventory system remains accurate.
• check customer signature is on file agreeing receipt of goods.	To confirm that evidence is available for receipt of goods confirming that goods have been delivered.

Audit test	Reason for test
For a sample of items on the despatch department computer, review to see that evidence of delivery to customer is available. Investigate records where no delivery information is available obtaining reasons for this.	To ensure that goods have been received and that procedures for investigating non-despatch or receipt are working.
Review the despatch department computer files for items not flagged 'order complete'. Investigate and obtain reasons for these items.	To ensure that the despatch process is working correctly and that incomplete items are being investigated.

54 JAYNE

Key answer tips

Questions on different types of confirmations come up frequently, so make sure you can discuss them. You also need, as always, a good knowledge of the financial statement assertions.

The procedures to get a bank letter are book knowledge and should present no problem.

(a) (i) Four examples of external confirmations are:

1 Accounts receivable letter

2 Solicitor letter

3 Bank report letter

4 Inventory held by third parties.

(ii) Note one example of each assertion only required.

Accounts receivable letter

This letter provides evidence of the existence of the receivable when a reply is returned from that receivable direct to the auditor.

The letter provides evidence on cut-off because sales or cash receipts recorded in the incorrect accounting period will have to be reconciled to the balance provided by the receivable.

The letter does not provide evidence of completeness of the receivables balance because receivables may not query balances which are understated.

The letter does not provide evidence of the valuation of the receivables balance because the receivable cannot be expected to list all outstanding balances and confirmation of the debt does not mean it will be paid.

Solicitor letter

A solicitor letter provides evidence as to the existence of claims at the period-end as the solicitor will confirm specific claims.

However, the letter does not necessarily confirm the valuation of claims due to uncertainty about the future or the completeness of any legal claims as solicitors do not normally provide a list of all claims – they prefer to comment only on claims they are actually asked about.

Bank report letter

A bank confirmation letter provides good evidence on the existence of the company's bank accounts as the bank has confirmed this information in writing.

A bank letter cannot necessarily be relied on to provide complete or accurate information. Most banks place a disclaimer on the letter of 'errors and omissions excepted' indicating that the auditor must review this evidence against other cash and bank evidence obtained.

Inventory held by third parties

A letter from the third party holding the inventory will provide evidence of the existence of that inventory because the third party has confirmed this in writing.

However, the letter does not provide evidence regarding the valuation of the inventory; confirming something exists does not necessarily mean it is in good condition.

(b) (i) Procedure for obtaining a bank letter

The auditor should consider if a bank letter is required. For the audit of Jayne Co the letter is required as the company has significant cash transactions and a loan from the bank.

The auditor will produce a confirmation letter in accordance with local audit regulations and practices.

The letter will be sent to the client to sign and authorise disclosure and then it will be forwarded on to Jayne's bank.

Alternatively, the client may already have provided a standard authority for the bank to respond to a bank letter each year. In this case separate authority would not be required.

Ideally the letter should be sent before the end of the accounting period to enable the bank to complete it on a timely basis, e.g. at the year-end.

The bank will complete the letter and send it back directly to the auditor.

Audit procedures on the bank letter include:

- Agree the balances for each bank account to the relevant bank reconciliation and the year-end balance in the financial statements.
- Agree total interest charges on the letter to the interest expense account in the general ledger.
- For any details of loans, ensure repayment terms are correctly disclosed in the financial statements between current and non-current liabilities.

(ii) Substantive procedures for the audit of bank balances.

(1) Obtain a copy of the year-end trial balance.

Agree the bank balance on the trial balance to

- the year-end bank balance on the computer system
- the balance on the financial statements.

(2) Obtain a copy of Jayne Co's bank reconciliation.

- Cast the reconciliation
- Agree the bank balance to the trial balance
- Agree the bank statement balance to the year-end bank statement.

- Agree any unpresented lodgements to the bank statement after the end of the year
- Agree any unpresented cheques or similar expenses to the cash book before the end of the year and the bank statements after the end of the year.

54 FIREFLY TENNIS CLUB

Key answer tips

Questions on different types of confirmations come up frequently, so make sure you can discus them. You also need, as always, a good knowledge of the financial statement assertions.

The procedures to get a bank letter are book knowledge and should present no problem.

(a) **Audit tests for completeness of income**

All income

For a sample of paying-in slips during the year, trace amount banked to the bank statements agreeing the total banked.

Agree the total per the paying-in slip to the cash book to confirm that the total has been correctly recorded in the cash book.

Confirm that the analysis on the bank paying-in slips is correctly recorded between membership fees and court hire in the cash book.

Cast the cash book to confirm total income for the year.

Agree total income received and the analysis of membership fees and court hire to the financial statements.

Membership fees

Compare the list of members as at 1 October 2004 to 1 October 2005 to determine how many members did not renew their membership during the year. This is normally approximately 10%.

Confirm total membership fees are correct by analytical review. Membership income should be:

430 members less 10% = 387, 387 x $200 = $77,400, 50 new members at 50% fee = 50 x $100 = $5,000, Total fee income $82,400.

Agree the membership fee income to the financial statements. If the amount is materially different enquire of the treasurer why this is the case.

Court hire fees

Obtain the list of court hires from the clubhouse.

For a number of weeks, determine how many hours courts were hired for. Agree this time to the bank paying-in slip (hours x $5 should equal the amount banked).

Ask the secretary to explain any differences in amounts banked.

(b) **Audit tests on expenditure**

Perform analytical review on expenditure this year compared to last year. Obtain reasons for any unusual amounts, e.g. increased expenditure on tennis balls due to increased number of matches.

For a sample of purchase invoices, ensure recorded in the cash book and that the amount and analysis of expenditure (e.g. lighting, tennis balls, etc) is correct.

Obtain the statements from the debit card used by the club official – trace items from the statements to the cash book to ensure all expenditure has been recorded.

For a sample of entries in the cash book, agree to the bank statements to ensure they represent actual expenditure.

Cast and cross cast the cash book to ensure the book is arithmetically correct.

For totals in the cash book, agree to the trial balance and financial accounts, ensuring that the presentation in the accounts is correct (e.g. stated as tennis balls, line painting, etc).

(c) **Limitation of internal control testing**

Internal control testing is limited in relatively small audits such as FireFly Tennis Club for the following reasons:

- There is a lack of segregation of duties. The club has only a limited number of staff in responsible positions. This means segregation of duties between, for example, authorising of purchase invoices and paying them, is not possible.
- Lack of authorisation controls. In small organisations, the senior officials tend to be the people 'authorising' transactions and also carrying them out. For example, the treasurer effectively authorises purchase invoices by paying for them rather than a senior official signing the invoice and a more junior clerk paying the invoice.
- Cost. Establishing an internal control system can be expensive. It may therefore not be cost effective for a small entity to establish a detailed internal control system.
- Management override. Even if there was an internal control system in place, senior officials are in a position to override that system. For example, the club treasurer could pay for his own expenses using the club debit card.

56 DECE & CO

Key answer tips

Make sure you give a reason for each test in part (a), otherwise you only get a maximum of half marks. Ensure that you only talk about the value of inventory in part (c) and don't talk about quantities, for example.

(a)	**Audit procedure Physical count**	**Reason for procedure**
	Perform an overall review with client staff – ensure that they are following the client's physical count instructions. Specifically ensure that:	Check that client's physical count instructions are being followed as this will help to ensure that the count is complete and accurate.
	Inventory is divided into appropriate sections for recording – perhaps by type of jewellery.	Confirms a clear layout of inventory ensuring items are not missed.
	Staff are counting in pairs with one person checking the inventory and another recording details.	Prevents collusion and provides a check over security of inventory (jewellery is high value) and that the count sheets are not falsified.

Audit procedure – Physical count	**Reason for procedure**
Appropriate checks are in place to ensure that each item of jewellery is only counted once.	Check to ensure that inventory is not double counted.
The shop is closed during the count.	To ensure that there is no confusion regarding which items are sold.
Countsheets are pre-numbered.	To ensure that no count sheets are lost.
Obtain a sample of inventory items already recorded on the inventory sheets and agree to the jewellery inventory.	Check to ensure that the inventory recorded on the inventory sheets actually exists.
For a sample of jewellery in the shop, agree to the count sheets.	Check to ensure that all inventory is recorded on the inventory sheets – check for completeness of recording.
Obtain a sample of countsheets, photocopy and place on the audit file.	To check that details on the countsheets are not amended post physical count and for agreement to the final inventory sheets to ensure quantities are recorded correctly.
Check all countsheets are returned after the physical inventory count.	Ensures that all sheets are accounted for and inventory is therefore not understated.
Obtain last inventory receipt note and sales invoice numbers.	To ensure that cut off is correct. Subsequent checking should show that goods received notes post physical count are not included in payables for the year, and sales invoices after the physical inventory count are not included in sales for the year.
Review the condition of the jewellery with the independent valuer. Ensure that there are no reasons why the inventory could be obsolete (e.g. due to changes in fashion) or damaged.	To check that any inventory which is damaged or unsaleable is correctly valued.
Form an opinion regarding the overall accuracy of the physical count.	To confirm that inventory quantities have been correctly recorded.

(b) **Factors to consider when placing reliance on the work of UJ**

DeCe need to confirm that they actually need an expert. It is not clear whether DeCe have the necessary skills in-house. However, given that Rocks Forever is the only client in the diamond industry, then some assistance would be expected as valuing diamonds is difficult.

Check that the specialist has relevant experience in valuing diamond jewellery. Part of the appointment process will include checking the work portfolio of UJ to show that they have valued diamonds in other situations.

Ensure that UJ is a member of an appropriate professional body. This will help ensure that UJ follow the appropriate ethical standards as these will be enforced by their professional body.

Check that UJ cannot be influenced by the client – for example because they are employed by Rocks Forever. Being employed by the client would imply less independence and limit the value of the specialist's report.

Check that the report produced by the specialist regarding the valuation of the diamonds appears to be reasonable. Although DeCe do not have any other clients retailing diamonds, basic price comparisons for a given weight of diamond could still be obtained from other shops or Internet site to prove the accuracy of UJ's figures.

(c) **Audit evidence**

The jewellery inventory should be valued at the lower of cost and net realisable value.

For a sample of jewellery on the final inventory sheets, trace the cost of those items to the original purchase invoice, ensuring that the description of goods on the invoice matches the jewellery.

For jewellery sold after the end of the year, check a sample of sales invoices back to the final inventory sheets ensuring that the sales value exceeds the cost. Where sales value is less than cost, ensure that the jewellery is stated at the realizable value on the inventory sheet.

Review the report of the professional valuer. Ensure that the inventory is genuine. For the items checked by the valuer, agree the valuation to the items of jewellery on the inventory statements. Where there is a difference, for example due to age of the inventory or where it is unlikely to be sold due to changes in fashion, discuss with the client and agree a realistic valuation. In these situations, the value should be that provided by the professional valuer.

Where an item has been in inventory for a long period of time (perhaps over one year), check the valuer's report to find out whether any allowance is required.

REVIEW

57 ISA 210/ 580/260

Key answer tips

Letters of various types are an important form of communication (and source of evidence) in many auditing situations. As a general revision point, perhaps you could draw up a checklist of audit letters summarising their objectives and contents!

Here, the question focuses on the representation letter and the management report (management letter).

(a) **Letter of representation**

(i) *Purpose*

During the course of the audit many representations are made by management to the auditors. Some of these are in response to direct enquiries by the auditors, others are implicit in the preparation of financial statements that are fairly presented. Most of these representations will be confirmed during the course of the audit by more reliable evidence such that reliance no longer need be placed on management representations. For other representations, however, there will be no independent corroboratory evidence available. The letter of representation, therefore, provides formal confirmation as to the representations made. In so doing, management may be encouraged to reflect more fully on the completeness of the representations made and provide further information that may earlier have been overlooked.

Reliability

Failure, by the auditors, to confirm such representations in writing would constitute negligence. However, it is important that auditors do not place reliance on representations where more reliable evidence would be expected. The absence of corroboratory evidence would, in itself, be suspicious and should lead to further audit enquiry. Moreover, written representations do not necessarily constitute sufficient evidence. The auditor must consider all available evidence and its reliability in forming an opinion. For example, in a small business where significant audit reliance must be placed on management representations, auditors may occasionally form the view that, even with written representation by management, there is insufficient evidence on which to form an opinion.

(ii) *Matters included*

Matters that may be included in the letter of representation include representations that:

- all books of account and supporting documentation, registers, minutes of members and directors meetings, have been made available;
- all related parties have been identified;
- the entity is not in breach of any contractual or regulatory requirements that could have a material effect on the financial statements;
- the entity has title to all of its assets and none are pledged or otherwise assigned other than disclosed in the financial statements;
- all liabilities and provisions have been reported or disclosed whether actual or contingent;
- all subsequent events have been properly reflected or disclosed in the financial statements;
- there are no plans that may significantly alter the carrying value of any of the entity's assets.

Note: Only three are required. Other matters may also be considered relevant.

(iii) *Refusal*

If management refuse to provide written representation as requested, the reasons would need to be enquired into and the effect on the overall sufficiency of evidence considered. Generally, if a matter is sufficiently important as to warrant a request for its inclusion in the letter, a failure to obtain written representation would normally constitute a scope limitation resulting in the issue of a modified audit opinion which is either qualified or for which a disclaimer of opinion is issued.

(b) **Management report**

(i) *Procedures*

Timeliness

Communication of control weaknesses is normally made shortly after completion of the audit. On larger engagements where control risk was assessed during an interim visit, a letter should normally be sent after that visit as well as on completion of the audit.

Occasionally the matter may be sufficiently serious as to warrant more timely communication, such as where the exposure to risk is great or where there is reason to suspect that fraud or failure to comply with laws or regulations may already have occurred as a result of the weakness.

Method

As is implied in the title commonly given, the communication is normally made in the form of a letter. Often, however, a preliminary meeting is held with management directly responsible in order to confirm the understanding and to discuss the most appropriate form of changes to the system. The letter is, therefore, more likely to be accepted and its recommendations acted upon.

Oral communication may also be appropriate for weaknesses that are in urgent need of correction followed up by a written communication.

Level of management

As mentioned above, it is common to discuss the detailed recommendations with line management before issuing the letter. The letter would normally be addressed to the Chief Financial Officer. The letter may refer to minor matters in brief with more detailed recommendations being sent to financial officers of divisions or subsidiaries. More serious matters may be communicated directly to the Board of Directors or, if the entity has one, the audit committee. These would include such matters as previous recommendations that have not been implemented where the auditors believe the risks to the entity are material.

(ii) *Auditors' responsibility*

The auditors are not primarily responsible for evaluating the effectiveness of all internal controls and reporting all weaknesses. In the letter of weakness and in the engagement letter the auditor should make it clear that the assessment of control effectiveness is restricted to those controls on which reliance is intended to be placed for audit purposes. If auditors intend to place reliance for particular financial statement assertions wholly on substantive procedures, they have no responsibility for controls over those assertions.

Where the auditors do become aware of internal control weaknesses, however, there is an expectation that they will warn management where the risk of loss or misstatement is considered material. Awareness of control weaknesses may come about from procedures other than those directed specifically at testing controls. For example, in obtaining an understanding of the system the auditor may become aware of major control weaknesses. Also, in performing substantive procedures, investigation of errors may alert the auditor to the presence of control weaknesses.

The auditors' duty to report on the effectiveness of internal controls, under auditing standards, is confined to the management of the entity. They have no responsibility to report to other parties. The letter of weaknesses normally carries a disclaimer of responsibility to any other persons to whom the letter might be shown.

Auditors may accept engagements to report on control weaknesses, either to managers, to regulators or to third parties. However, such engagements are not part of the audit of the financial statements.

58 CRIGHTON-WARD

Key answer tips

This is a standard question on management representation letters that should cause you few problems. Make your five separate points in part (a) to earn the five marks available.

In part (b) it is very likely that one of the items will be appropriate for inclusion in the letter, while the other will not. The requirement to 'discuss' each situation means that you must justify your decision.

Part (c) is again standard bookwork on what to do if the directors are unwilling to sign the representation letter. Try to solve the problem by discussion; qualifying the audit report is always the last resort if alternative approaches have failed.

(a) Management representations are a form of audit evidence. They are contained in a letter, written by the company's directors and sent to the auditor, just prior to the completion of audit work and before the audit report is signed.

Representations are required for two reasons:

First, so the directors can acknowledge their collective responsibility for the preparation of the financial statements and to confirm that they have approved those statements.

Second, to confirm any matters, which are material to the financial statements where representations are crucial to obtaining sufficient and appropriate audit evidence.

In the latter situation, other forms of audit evidence are normally unavailable because knowledge of the facts is confined to management and the matter is one of judgement or opinion.

Obtaining representations does not mean that other evidence does not have to be obtained. Audit evidence will still be collected and the representation will support that evidence. Any contradiction between sources of evidence should, as always, be investigated.

(b) **Lion's Roar**

The amount of the claim is material being 50% of profit before taxation.

There is also a lack of definitive supporting evidence for the claim. The two main pieces of evidence available are the claim from Lion's Roar itself and the legal advice from Crighton Ward's solicitors. However, any claim amount cannot be accurately determined because the dispute has not been settled.

The directors have stated that they believe the claim not to be justified, which is one possible outcome of the dispute. However, in order to obtain sufficient evidence to show how the treatment of the potential claim was decided for the financial statements, the auditor must obtain this opinion in writing. Reference must therefore be made to the claim in the representation letter.

Paragraph for inclusion in representation letter.

'A legal claim against Crighton-Ward by Lion's Roar has been estimated at $4 million by Lion's Roar. However, the directors are of the opinion that the claim is not justified on the grounds of breach of product specification. No provision has been made in the financial statements, although disclosure of the situation is adequate. No similar claims have been received or are expected to be received.'

Depreciation

This matter is unlikely to be included in the letter of representation because the auditor appears to have obtained sufficient evidence to confirm the accounting treatment. The lack of profit or loss on sale confirms that the depreciation charge is appropriate – large profits would indicate over-depreciation and large losses, under-depreciation. The amount also meets industry standards confirming that Crighton-Ward's accounting policy is acceptable. Including the point in the representation letter is inappropriate because the matter is not crucial and does not appear to be based on judgment or opinion. The only opinion here appears to be that of the auditor – unless the 'feelings' can be turned into some appropriate audit evidence, the matter should be closed.

(c) **Lack of representation letter**

The auditor may take the following actions:

Discuss the situation with the directors to try and resolve the issue that the directors have raised. The auditor will need to explain the need for the representation letter again (and note that the signing of the letter was mentioned in the engagement letter). Ascertain exact reasons why the directors will not sign the letter. Consider whether amendments can be made to the letter to incorporate the directors' concerns that will still provide the auditor with appropriate and sufficient audit evidence.

The discussion must clearly explain the fact that if the auditor does not receive sufficient and appropriate audit evidence, then the audit report will have to be modified.

The reason for the audit qualification will be uncertainty regarding the amounts and disclosures in the financial statements. An 'except for' qualification for the material uncertainty is likely, although a disclaimer may be required, especially if the legal claim is thought to require a provision.

Even if the letter is subsequently signed, the auditor must still evaluate the reliability of the evidence. If, in the auditor's opinion, the letter no longer provides sufficient or reliable evidence, then a qualification may still be required.

59 LALD

Key answer tips

Part (a) and (b) are unusual, in that you are asked what you would do having discovered misstatements. Go through this answer very carefully as the examiner has indicated that he will examine this again.

(a) Audit procedures for underpayment of sales tax

- Discuss the underpayment with the head of the accounting department to ascertain whether the error was known, and if so why no action had been taken to correct the error.
- Evaluate the results of testing to determine the amount of the underpayment. Where necessary perform additional substantive tests checking from the tax declared on sales invoices issued during August to the sales tax calculation.
- Summarise the results of testing, providing an estimate of the amount of sales tax underpaid.
- Discuss the situation with the directors to obtain an understanding of how the error occurred and determine what actions the directors will take.

- Include the weakness in the management letter noting, if possible, the reason for the error and the action that must be taken to correct the error.
- Inform the directors that non-payment of sales tax to the government is a breach of specific law of their country.
- Ask for a formal response from the directors, clearly indicating what action they propose to take regarding the underpayment.
- Where the amount due has been paid to the government, audit the payment and ensure it is sufficient given the extent of underpayment already detected.
- Where the amount due is not paid, consider informing the appropriate authorities where legislation requires this.
- Consider and ask the directors to provide for any late penalties that will need to be paid to the government with regards to the late payment.

(b) Audit procedures for under-provision of depreciation

- Review the results of the audit working papers to check that an error did occur.
- Extend substantive testing for this particular class of non-current assets to try and determine the extent of the error.
- Calculate the new depreciation provision based on the results of your testing.
- Compare your estimate of depreciation to the amount calculated by the client to determine whether the difference is material.
- Discuss the underprovision with the head of the accounting department to ascertain whether the error was known, and if so why no action had been taken to correct the error.
- Discuss the situation with the directors to ascertain what action the directors will take. If the difference is material then an amendment to the financial statements would be expected.
- Include the weakness in the management letter noting, if possible, the reason for the error and the action that must be taken to correct the error.
- If the difference is material and the directors do not amend the financial statements, consider the need to modify the auditor's report.

(c) To remove the auditor from office before their term of office has expired, the directors of LALD must proceed as follows:

- Arrange for a meeting of the shareholders of the company.
- Write to the shareholders providing notice of the meeting and the agenda. The notice must also be sent to the auditor.
- Attend the meeting and organise a counting of votes at the meeting on the resolution to remove the auditor from office. In most situations, a simple majority of the shareholders is required to confirm the resolution.
- Auditors are sometimes given the right to make written representations and to speak at the meeting.
- If the auditor is removed, where necessary, obtain a statement of circumstances from the auditor. If there are no circumstances that need to be brought to the attention of the shareholders then a statement of no circumstances is required. Where required by specific country legislation, deposit this statement along with notice of removal of auditor, with the appropriate authorities.
- Make arrangements to appoint another auditor as companies are normally required to have auditors.

60 GREEN CO

Key answer tips

This question should be straightforward for a well-prepared student with a good understanding of ethics and going concern.

(a) **Ethical threats**

Self review threat

If Lime & Co provides audit and other professional services to Green Co, then they will be preparing the financial statements and also auditing those financial statements. This will provide a self-review threat to Lime & Co as they will be auditing their own work. Lime & Co would be advised to tender only for the audit work.

Self interest threat

If Lime & Co prepare the financial statements of Green Co and then also audit those financial statements, they may be less inclined to report any errors. Reporting of errors may result in loss of work in the future as the managers of Green Co may stop using the services of Lime & Co. Again Lime & Co should only tender for the audit.

Management threat

There is a risk that Lime & Co will make decisions that the managers of Green Co should make (for example which accounting policies should apply to the financial statements). It is possible that these type of decisions have been made before, on an informal basis, as the partner in Lime & Co already knows and gives advice to the managers of Green Co.

Advocacy threat

This threat arises because Lime & Co may be asked to present details of Green Co's financial statements and profit forecasts in court to support its application to stop Black Co growing genetically modified (GM) crops. Lime & Co may be seen to support their client in court, which may limit their independence in relation to the audit work.

Familiarity threat

You have been friends with the managers of Green Co for some time. This means that you may not question the decisions of the managers due to this close personal relationship. As a partner in Lime & Co, you will in effect not be independent from your client.

Fee income

Acceptance of audit and professional services work from Green Co, will result in an increase in fee income. To retain independence, Lime & Co need to ensure that total fees generated from Green Co do not exceed 15% of the total practice income.

Association threat

The managers of Green Co, while not being criminals, appear to lack integrity in their business affairs. The partners in Lime & Co need to decide whether they want to be professionally associated with Green Co; any criminal activity in the future may have an adverse effect on Lime & Co's reputation and image. Specifically Lime & Co will not want to be seen to be associated with or advising a firm which is breaking the law.

Cease trading – payment of fees

The farm may lose organic certification if the genetically modified crops continue to be grown next to Green Co's farm. There is a risk that Lime & Co may not be paid for services provided should Green Co cease trading.

(b) (i) Going concern

IAS 8 defines the going concern concept as the assumption that the enterprise will continue in operational existence for the foreseeable future.

The farm may lose organic certification if the genetically modified crops continue to be grown next to Green Co's farm.

This means that Green Co may not be a going concern.

An entity will normally use the going concern basis unless:

- It is being liquidated or has ceased trading, or
- The directors have no realistic alternative than to liquidate the company or to cease trading.

(ii) Responsibilities

The directors' responsibility regarding going concern is to prepare the financial statements of an entity ensuring that the going concern basis is reasonable. They may also prepare cash and/or profit forecasts for at least 12 months into the future to demonstrate that the entity is likely to continue to trade during this time.

The auditors' responsibility regarding going concern is to form an opinion on the appropriateness of management's assessment of the going concern status of the entity and the adequacy of disclosures, if any. The auditor will collect sufficient and appropriate audit evidence to ensure use of the going concern assumption is valid. To be clear, the auditors are not responsible for ensuring that the company is a going concern; this is a responsibility of the directors.

(c) Audit procedures

In the case of Green Co, audit procedures on going concern will include:

- Obtaining cash and profit forecasts from the directors. Ensure that these have been properly prepared (for example are arithmetically correct) and show that Green will continue trading. Appropriate adjustments should have been made for the decrease in sales resulting from contamination of Green Co's farm.
- Review the order books for Green Co to determine the level of future sales.
- Contacting Green Co's lawyers to determine the progress, if any, on the court case against Black Co.
- Review the financial status of Green Co during the audit to identify other indicators of a going concern problem such as failure to repay loans or decrease in sales.
- Review correspondence, if any, with the organic certification authority to determine whether Green Co's organic status has been withdrawn.
- Contacting Green Co's bank to ascertain whether any loan or overdraft agreements are due for renewal and whether these will be renewed.
- Obtaining written representation from the directors confirming that they are not aware of any circumstances other than those evaluated by the auditor, so they expect Green Co to continue as a going concern.

61 NEWBRIDGE TRADING

Key answer tips

The key with subsequent events questions like this is to be very careful when reading dates. The answer for part (b) is the examiner's answer and is longer than would be necessary in the exam.

(a) The auditor's responsibilities in the periods listed in the question are given in the auditing standard.

(i) In the period 31 October to 5 December 1997, the auditor should carry out sufficient appropriate audit work so that he/she has a reasonable expectation of detecting and quantifying material subsequent events. Examples of the types of audit procedures carried out are included in part (b) of this answer.

(ii) In the period 5 December 1997 to 19 December 1997 the auditor's responsibilities are the same as in period (a)(i) above.

(iii) The standard says that the auditor should reasonably expect the directors to inform him/her of any material subsequent events detected in this period which may affect the financial statements. During this period auditors do not have any obligation to perform procedures or make enquiries regarding the financial statements.

When the auditor becomes aware of material subsequent events in this period, he/she should carry out appropriate audit procedures to determine whether the subsequent event has a material effect on the financial statements.

If the directors amend the financial statements, the auditor should produce a new report on the amended financial statements.

If the directors do not amend the financial statements, and the subsequent event is material, the auditor should consider how the shareholders can be informed of the subsequent event. This may include the auditors making a statement at the annual general meeting at which the financial statements are approved by the shareholders. The standard suggests the auditor may consider taking legal advice, and it points out that auditors do not have a statutory right to communicate directly in writing to shareholders.

(iv) In the period from 5 January to 28 January 1998, the auditors have no duty to seek out whether any material subsequent events have occurred in this period. However, if the auditor becomes aware of a material subsequent event in this period, he should consider whether he should withdraw his audit report. He will probably have to take legal advice on the matter. Also, he should discuss the problem with the company. It may be necessary for either the directors or the auditors to make a statement at the annual general meeting (AGM).

If the directors revise the financial statements, the auditor will have to audit these revisions and come to a conclusion on whether the revised financial statements show a true and fair view. The audit report on the revised financial statements should refer to the note in the financial statements which describes the changes, and it should refer to the earlier audit report. The audit report on the revised financial statements should not be dated before the date the directors approve those financial statements (normally, the dates are the same).

If the directors do not revise the financial statements, and do not make a statement at the AGM, the auditor should take legal advice on the course of action he should take. Normally, he should make a statement to shareholders at the AGM. In the UK for example, auditors do not have the right to write to shareholders, but this right does exist if they resign as auditor.

(v) The standard does not provide guidance on the auditor's responsibilities after the financial statements have been approved by members at the annual general meeting. However, it does appear that the auditor has no responsibility for detecting subsequent events in this period. If, during this period, the directors find material misstatements in the audited financial statements, and inform the auditor of the fact, the procedures will be the similar to those described in part (a)(iv) above.

(b) The audit techniques which involve checking subsequent events include:

(i) checking cash received from debtors after the year-end to check recoverability of year-end accounts receivable ledger balances. Any year-end balances which are unpaid at the time of the audit will be potential bad debts, and further investigation should be carried out

(ii) an accounts receivable circularisation carried out after the year-end could be a post balance sheet check of accounts receivable at the year-end

(iii) checking sales after the year-end to check recoverability of inventory at the year-end. If, for inventory held at the year-end, the selling price after the year-end is more than cost, then the inventory can be valued at cost. However, if the selling price is less than cost, this inventory should be valued at net realisable value

(iv) checking sales cut-off. Starting from the dispatch note, for sales before the year-end, the sales invoice should be posted to the accounts receivable ledger before the year-end. For sales after the year-end, the auditor should check the sales invoice is not posted to the accounts receivable ledger before the year-end (technically, only this latter check is a check of a subsequent event)

(v) checking purchases cut-off. Starting from the goods received note, for goods received before the year-end, the purchase invoice should either be posted to the accounts payable ledger before the year-end or included in purchase accruals at the year-end. For goods received after the year-end, the purchase invoice should be neither posted to the accounts payable ledger before the year-end nor included in purchase accruals at the year-end

(vi) checking suppliers' statements to the balances on the accounts payable ledger. If the balances agree, this is good evidence that the accounts payable ledger balance is correct. If there is a difference, it should be reconciled and the auditor should consider whether the differences are reasonable. Suppliers' statements are an effective way of checking purchases cut-off, and of detecting late issue of cheques after the year-end

(vii) checking any sales or disposals of non-current assets after the year-end. This will check whether these assets have been sold for more or less than their balance sheet value. If they are sold for less than their balance sheet value, normally they should be written down to their realisable value at the year-end

(viii) checking returns of goods from customers and other sales credits given after the year-end. This helps determine whether the provision for these items in the financial statements is reasonable. Similar checks can be made for purchases items, such as goods returned before the year-end when the credit is received after the year-end, and other credits received from suppliers after the year-end

(ix) checking about legal claims against the company which exist at the year-end. This will involve asking the company secretary and the directors if there are any claims, and (with the client's permission) asking the company's solicitor. Inspecting board minutes (see item (x) below) could highlight any claims against the company. The bank lender may include details of a claim against the company or Companies House may have some information (but this is uncommon).

(x) checking board minutes and management reports after the year-end which relate to events at or before the year-end

(xi) checking management accounts after the year-end for any items which should have been included at the year-end (e.g. bad debts, stock write-downs, etc.)

(xii) checking cash book and petty cash transactions after the year-end to see if there are any unrecorded accruals and prepayments at the year-end, and to confirm those items in the financial statements. For instance, receipts after the year-end may indicate sundry accounts receivable at the year-end and payments after the year-end may highlight sundry accounts payable and accruals which existed at the year-end (e.g. the payment of tax and national insurance in November would be good evidence of the liability at the year-end)

(xiii) checking purchase invoices received after the year-end. Some of these may relate to pre-year-end transactions (i.e. those which are dated before the year-end). Purchase invoices for gas and electricity received after the year-end are an effective way of determining the accrual at the year-end

(xiv) checking the bank reconciliation to check if payments were actually before the year-end and there is no teeming and lading fraud. If there is a long delay in clearing a significant value of cheques issued before the year-end, this indicates the actual payment (i.e. when the cheques were sent to the creditors) was made after the year-end. A delay in lodging cash received into the bank indicates a teeming and lading fraud The fact that the cash book balance can be reconciled to the balance on the bank statement is good evidence that the cash book balancc in the financial statements is correct.

(c) As no detailed audit work would have been carried out during this period, there is a risk that material subsequent events may have occurred in this period. Thus, the auditor will have to ask the directors and senior management if any material subsequent events have occurred in this period, or whether further evidence is available for uncertainties existing at 5 December 1997. Also, the auditor should examine such documents as Board and Management minutes, management accounts and seek out further evidence relating to uncertainties at 5 December 1997 (e.g. whether a doubtful debt at 5 December has been settled).

REPORTING

62 JONES, ROBERTS, WILLIAMS, GRIFFITHS AND EVANS

Key answer tips

This question is testing your ability to apply an appropriate form of the audit report to each of five given situations.

Key sources of knowledge here will be the 'qualification grid' together with a number of accounting standards. As always in the context of questions such as this, the concept of materiality will need to be considered.

The answer to each of the five situations then follows in a reasonably straightforward manner – provided that you have the technical knowledge at your finger tips!

(a) **Jones**

Materiality

The amount of the loss at $30,000 represents 20% of pre-tax profit and more than 4% of accounts receivable; it would therefore seem to be material in both income statement and balance sheet terms, although it is clearly more material in relation to profit.

Relevant accounting principles

The bankruptcy of the customer indicates that the company has overstated profit and assets as at the year-end by $30,000. This letter provides evidence of a condition existing at the balance sheet date (IAS 10). It should therefore be treated as an adjusting event. The prudence concept (IASC Framework) would dictate that the loss should be provided for in full in the financial statements at 30 September 20X2.

Form of audit report

The management's refusal to adjust the accounts for the loss means that a disagreement exists between management and the auditor. In such a case, the auditor has to make a decision as to whether the amount of the loss is 'pervasive' or 'material' but not pervasive. Without more facts being available, it is difficult to draw conclusions satisfactorily in this area, but on the face of it an 'except for' form of audit qualification would appear appropriate as the true and fair view would not be entirely destroyed if the loss were to remain unadjusted.

(b) **Roberts**

Materiality

The amount of $10,000 represents only 2% of the stated profit before tax of $500,000 and does not, in itself, appear to be material in terms of its impact on the financial statements. Unfortunately, however, the potential losses may be very much more significant than the figure of $10,000, since other claims are now pending, and the auditor may have to conclude that the whole legal matter is potentially material.

Relevant accounting principles

There is clearly a contingent liability in respect of potential claims arising from the product defect. Under the IASC Framework, the prudence concept dictates that a potential loss which is material should be accrued in the financial statements where it is probable that future events will confirm the loss and that the loss can be estimated with reasonable accuracy (except where the possibility is remote). The matter is also covered in IAS 37.

Form of audit report

There is clearly uncertainty with regard to the outcome of the pending claims and the potential liability which they represent. The auditor will have to decide whether or not the possibility of loss is likely or remote. Management has apparently chosen to ignore both the actual loss (which is not of itself material) and the potential loss (which may well be material). If the auditor can be convinced that management's view is acceptable and the disclosure in the notes is adequate, then a qualification may be completely avoidable. The auditor should be aware, however, that items which are not material when considered individually may well have a cumulative effect which is material in total. If the auditor does not believe that the management's view is acceptable, or does not think that the disclosure is adequate, then there is a disagreement as to the way in which the uncertainty has been treated. In this case, an 'except for' qualification is probably sufficient. However, if the auditor believes that the claims are likely to be successful and are likely to be substantial then it may be necessary to issue an adverse opinion.

(c) **Williams**

Materiality

The loans are not bad debts and so have no effect on the reported loss. However, this sort of matter cannot have the same materiality test applied to it as in the cases previously discussed in this answer. We are told that amounts owed by directors are required to be disclosed as a requirement of the local legislation. Materiality should, therefore, not be measured in relation to profit or loss for the year or the balance sheet position, but in relation to the requirements of the law. It would appear that the loans are not allowed and that Williams is materially in non-compliance with the local law.

Relevant accounting principles

As mentioned in the question, the loans are not allowed and disclosure should in any case be made under the local legislation. The item is required to be separately disclosed and cannot be 'hidden' as part of a figure containing other 'receivables collectable within one year'.

Form of audit report

The standard audit report in many countries requires the auditor to state specifically whether or not the financial statements comply with local legislation. The financial statements of Williams do not fully comply with the requirements of the local law. The fact that Williams is a manufacturing concern would indicate that such loans to directors would not be made in the normal course of business, as could be argued if the company were a bank, for example. In these circumstances, the auditor is required to include details of the loans in the audit report, and to qualify the report by stating that the loans contravene the provisions of the local legislation. In view of the fact that the loans were subsequently repaid, the auditor would probably not need to qualify as to the true and fair view shown by the financial statements.

(d) **Griffiths**

Materiality

The fall in value is clearly material. In fact, the auditor would probably have to view the matter as pervasive, because providing for the loss would have the effect of converting a net profit before tax of $250,000 into a loss of $50,000.

Relevant accounting principles

Long-term investments should be written down where there has been an impairment in value. Falls in the value of one asset must not be offset against increases in the value of another asset. Each asset has to be considered separately.

The IASC Framework prudence concept requires that the directors should ensure adequate allowance is made for all known liabilities (expenses and losses). The accounting treatment adopted, offsetting known losses against unrealised profits, is unacceptable. As the company admits that a permanent fall in value has taken place, it should make full allowance against the loss. Further, as the other trade investments (with reputedly high realisable values) are permanent investments not held for resale, the accounting treatment adopted for them could be amended.

Form of audit report

As mentioned above, it is likely that the auditor would have to view the matter as material and pervasive. It is also a matter of disagreement and the auditor will probably be forced to give an adverse opinion, stating that the financial statements do not show a true and fair view.

(e) **Evans**

Materiality

The $10,000 represents 10% of the reported net profit before tax, and so would appear to be material. However, the actual materiality of this item in relation to profit is, in fact, a somewhat judgemental matter. The auditor would probably conclude that the possible error in calculating the $10,000 was not material in relation to the profit of $100,000, since the amount of any error will probably be substantially less than the full amount included in the accounts. Further since the accounting records were only destroyed for the early part of the year, the auditor would still be able to confirm the calculations for the later part of the year. In these particular circumstances, therefore, the auditor may consider that the amount of any error (which is likely to be considerably less than $10,000) is not material.

Relevant accounting principles

It is perfectly acceptable for the company to add the cost of its own labour and materials in the construction of the warehouse, since these have been used to create a capital asset. This is following the 'matching' or 'accruals' concept as set out in IAS 1 and applied in IAS 16.

Form of audit report

The accounting treatment is generally acceptable and the amount of any error is not likely to be considered material, the auditor will probably be able to give a standard unqualified audit report.

63 AUDIT REPORT AND REVIEW REPORT

Key answer tips

This question focuses on a comparison between an audit report and a review report.

It appears that the examiner is trying to help rather than hinder you by giving you the text of the two reports. It means that you could tackle this question without having memorised the reports and you have an easily available source of reference to use in answering the question.

Of course, if you are well prepared for the exam, you may well not need to spend too much time reading the reports anyway – you should already know what they contain and how they differ in the key respects which the examiner is looking for.

(a) **Audit and review engagements**

Audit reports are dealt with by ISA 700 *The Independent Auditor's Report on a Complete Set of General Purpose Financial Statements* and review reports are dealt with by ISRE 2400 *Engagements to Review Financial Statements* (previously known as ISA 910).

(i) **Audit engagements: work performed and assurance provided**

Audit engagements provide a high level of positive assurance to the user. They require the auditor to:

(1) Obtain a detailed knowledge of the business.

(2) Understand the accounting and internal control system.

(3) Obtain detailed audit evidence in respect of the financial statement assertions by means of tests of internal controls and/or detailed substantive testing, and to corroborate explanations received.

(4) Perform a review of the going concern status of the company.

(ii) **Review engagements: work performed and assurance provided**

Review engagements provide a moderate level of assurance that may be expressed as negative assurance. They consist principally of analytical procedures and inquiries made by the reviewer. The reviewer is not required to understand the accounting and internal control system, nor is he required to corroborate explanations, perform detailed tests on material financial statement assertions or to conduct a going concern review.

(iii) **Addressee**

(1) Audit reports are generally addressed to the shareholders or other owners of companies, review reports are addressed to directors or other management. This is because most audit engagements are statutory audit engagements (where the auditor reports to shareholders on the financial statements prepared by directors).

(2) Statutory audit reports, particularly those of large companies, are often made available to the general public because they are filed with the financial statements at a public registry or are otherwise made available to potential investors and other interested stakeholders.

(3) Review reports are generally not made available to the general public. They are generally private engagements between directors and reviewers and sometimes a third party, such as a bank, who may wish to see a report for a specific purpose.

(iv) **Responsibility for the financial information**

(1) The responsibility for the preparation of financial information in both audit and review engagements is always that of directors, regardless of who has actually prepared the information. This is stated in both review and audit reports because it is easy to assume that the auditor or reviewer has prepared the information and is responsible for it.

(2) It is particularly important to state this in audit reports because legislation often makes directors responsible for the statutory financial statements.

(v) **The opinion given**

(1) The two opinions provided by an audit engagement relate to the 'true and fair' status of the information or to 'its fair presentation in all material respects' and to proper preparation in accordance with an identified financial reporting framework, such as International Accounting Standards.

(2) The opinion given in the review report is not that the financial statements give a 'true and fair view' (a positive opinion), but that nothing has come to the reviewer's attention to indicate that they do not (a negative opinion).

(3) The different level of assurance provided is commensurate with the different level of work performed, as indicated above. There is no precise definition of the meaning of 'true and fair' or 'fair presentation in all material respects'.

(b) **Direct and attest engagements**

Direct engagements require auditors or reviewers to report directly on financial statements or other information that is the responsibility of a third party, such as directors. Audit and review engagements can be direct engagements.

Attest engagements involve auditors or reviewers reporting on assertions made by directors on financial or other information. For example, directors may make an assertion on financial internal controls to the effect that they have reviewed them, and have found them to be working effectively. Auditors then report on the directors' assertion, rather than on the internal controls themselves. Auditors or reviewers will look at the processes that directors have been through in order to make the assertion and report their findings.

64 HOOD ENTERPRISES

Key answer tips

Part (a) requires standard knowledge that you should be very confident about.

Part (b) is an unusual question worth 10 marks requiring you to comment on a junior's draft audit report. The best approach is to go through the draft report a sentence at a time, and decide whether the wording is acceptable.

Part (c) is back to standard bookwork: you should be very happy about the difference between positive assurance and negative assurance.

(a) **Preparation of financial statements**

The directors are normally required to prepare the financial statements of the company using the appropriate law of their country and in accordance with the International Accounting Standards (IASs). The auditors are normally required to check or audit those financial statements, again in accordance with the legislation of their country and the International Standards on Auditing.

Fraud and error

The directors are responsible for preventing and detecting fraud and error in the financial statements, no matter how immaterial this may be. Auditors are responsible for giving an opinion on whether the financial statements show a true and fair view; in other words that the financial statements are materially correct. Auditors are not required to detect immaterial fraud or error.

Disclosure

The directors must ensure that there is adequate disclosure of all matters required by statute or IASs in the financial statements. The auditor will check that disclosure provisions have been complied with, and where certain disclosures have not been made, provide this information in the audit report.

Going concern

The directors are responsible for ensuring that the company will continue in operational existence for the foreseeable future, and report to the members in the published financial statements if this is unlikely to be the case. The auditor will check the accuracy of the directors' workings and assumptions and if these are considered incorrect or inappropriate, then the audit report may be modified or qualified to bring the situation to the attention of the members of the company.

(b) **Review of audit report extract**

The basis of opinion paragraph may not meet the requirements of ISA 700 for the following reasons:

The use of the term Auditing Standards is not clear, because the report does not state which auditing standards have been used. This provides uncertainty regarding the actual standard of work performed.

The assessment of estimates and judgements made by the directors normally relates to significant amounts only, rather than all of those estimates and judgements. The use of the word all implies that the audit was more thorough than it probably was. Replacing the word all with the word significant will show that there was some limit to the audit testing and that this was probably focused on material amounts only.

Stating that time was a factor in obtaining information and explanations for the audit is not correct as this implies some factor which could have been avoided and that the audit may therefore be incomplete. The auditor has to plan the audit carefully and ensure that all the information and explanations considered necessary are obtained to form an opinion, not simply stop work when time runs out.

The auditor does not confirm that the financial statements are free from material misstatement as this implies a degree of accuracy that the auditor simply cannot provide. Making the statement could also leave the auditor liable to claims from members or third parties should errors be found in the financial statements later. Rather than make such a categorical statement, the auditor provides reasonable assurance that the financial statements are free from material misstatement, which clearly implies that audit techniques are limited.

The disclaimer regarding errors appears to be useful in that it limits the auditor's liability. However, it does not belong in the basis of opinion paragraph as it appears to severely limit the basis of the auditor's opinion to stating that the directors are responsible for all errors. Directors' responsibilities are also clearly outlined in another section of the report, and this statement also appears to extend those responsibilities making the audit report overall less clear. This could also imply that the auditor has done little or no work.

As the auditor is not required to audit the whole of the annual report of a company, it is inappropriate to refer to disclosure in that report when checking overall adequacy of presentation. Adequacy of presentation can only be confirmed regarding items actually audited, which is basically the financial statements.

(c) **Positive v negative assurance**

A positive assurance report means that the auditor has carried out sufficient work to be able to state that financial information is free from material error.

A negative assurance report means that nothing has come to the attention of the auditor, which indicates the financial information being reported on has errors in it. However, the extent of the work carried out is normally less, which means that less reliance can be placed on this report.

The advantages of providing negative assurance include:

– The user of the financial information receives some comfort that the information is correct, even though that assurance is less than positive assurance.

– The report adds some credibility to the financial information because it has been reviewed by a professional accountant.

– For the preparer, the report will be more cost effective than obtaining a full positive assurance report.

65 MSV

Key answer tips

Part (a) requires a reasonable knowledge of the content of the audit report. This is book knowledge and should present no problems.

Part (b) requires you to apply your knowledge and state how you would investigate potential misstatements and the impact on your audit report.

(a)

Audit report element	Reason for that element
Title of 'independent auditor'	To identify this as an audit report and distinguish it from other reports on financial statements that might be issued by others, directors, etc.
Addressee	To identify the person(s) who may use or rely on the report.
Opening or introductory paragraph identifying	To make it clear which pages of an annual report have been audited.
the financial statements audited and – responsibilities of entity's management and auditors	To make clear that the directors prepare the financial statements and the auditors audit them.
Scope paragraph describing the nature of the audit in terms of International Standards on Auditing (ISAs) followed and the work performed by the auditor	To explain the scope of the audit so the standard of the auditors work is clear and other factors such as limitation of audit testing (for example, not tested all items) is known.
Opinion paragraph referring to the financial reporting framework followed and expressing the auditor's opinion.	To provide the auditor's opinion on the financial statements in terms of true and fair view, to assure the reader that the audit has been carried out in accordance with established principles and practices.
Date of the report	To inform the reader that the auditor has considered effects of transactions that the auditor became aware of on the financial statements up to that date.
Auditor's address	This is normally the address where the auditor responsible for the audit is located so he/she can be contacted, if necessary.
Auditor's signature	This is normally the signature of the audit firm as the firm assumes responsibility for the audit, not the individual engagement partner.

(b) **Issue one – Understatement of sales income**

(i)

- If possible, conduct day-by-day analytical review to determine the extent of the misappropriation
- Discuss the situation with the other directors to ascertain their knowledge of the situation.
- Ask the other directors what action they will take regarding the director who appears to have misappropriated money from the company.
- Recommend in the management letter that strict numeric sequence is maintained over sales invoices and that two directors are always on duty to prevent misappropriation of income.
- Obtain a letter of representation to confirm the directors' estimate of the extent of the fraud and confirm that the directors are not aware of any other instances of fraud.

(ii) The misappropriation is material, being about 5% of income for the year. Therefore:

- Modify the auditor's report with an 'except for' opinion on limitation of scope of audit work on sales income.
- Explain the reason for the understatement of income in the basis of opinion paragraph above the opinion paragraph.

Issue two – Director's use of yacht

(i)

- Ask the director why the yacht is located at his house.
- Ask the director whether any payment was made for the yacht – confirm payment to the cash book and company bank statements.
- If the yacht is for private use only, check that disclosure of the benefit has been made in the directors' emoluments note in the financial statements.
- Ensure the company has provided relevant information to the benefit authority and accrued any penalty for nondisclosure.
- Consider additional audit work to determine whether or not any other company assets have been used in a similar fashion.

(ii) Assuming that disclosure of the benefit has not been shown in the financial statements then:

- Modify the auditor's report using an 'except for' opinion disagreeing with the amount of information disclosed.

Section 3

PILOT PAPER EXAM QUESTIONS

1 WESTRA CO

Westra Co assembles mobile telephones in a large factory. Each telephone contains up to 100 different parts, with each part being obtained from one of 50 authorised suppliers.

Like many companies, Westra's accounting systems are partly manual and partly computerised. In overview the systems include:

(i) Design software.

(ii) A computerised database of suppliers (bespoke system written in-house at Westra).

(iii) A manual system for recording goods inwards and transferring information to the accounts department.

(iv) A computerised payables ledger maintained in the accounts department (purchased off-the-shelf and used with no program amendments).

(v) Online payment to suppliers, also in the accounts department.

(vi) A computerised general ledger which is updated by the payables ledger.

Mobile telephones are assembled in batches of 10,000 to 50,000 telephones. When a batch is scheduled for production, a list of parts is produced by the design software and sent, electronically, to the ordering department. Staff in the ordering department use this list to place orders with authorised suppliers. Orders can only be sent to suppliers on the suppliers' database. Orders are sent using electronic data interchange (EDI) and confirmed by each supplier using the same system. The list of parts and orders are retained on the computer in an 'orders placed' file, which is kept in date sequence.

Parts are delivered to the goods inwards department at Westra. All deliveries are checked against the orders placed file before being accepted. A hand-written pre-numbered goods received note (GRN) is raised in the goods inwards department showing details of the goods received with a cross-reference to the date of the order. The top copy of the GRN is sent to the accounts department and the second copy retained in the goods inwards department. The orders placed file is updated with the GRN number to show that the parts have been received.

Paper invoices are sent by all suppliers following dispatch of goods. Invoices are sent to the accounts department, where they are stamped with a unique ascending number. Invoice details are matched to the GRN, which is then attached to the invoice. Invoice details are then entered into the computerised payables ledger. The invoice is signed by the accounts clerk to confirm entry into the payables ledger. Invoices are then retained in a temporary file in number order while awaiting payment.

After 30 days, the payables ledger automatically generates a computerised list of payments to be made, which is sent electronically to the chief accountant. The chief accountant compares this list to the invoices, signs each invoice to indicate approval for payment, and then forwards the electronic payments list to the accounts assistant. The assistant uses online banking to pay the suppliers. The electronic payments list is filed in month order on the computer.

Required:

(a) List the substantive audit procedures you should perform to confirm the assertions of completeness, occurrence and cut-off for purchases in the financial statements of Westra Co. For each procedure, explain the purpose of that procedure. **(12 marks)**

(b) List the audit procedures you should perform on the trade payables balance in Westra Co's financial statements. For each procedure, explain the purpose of that procedure. **(8 marks)**

(c) Describe the control procedures that should be in place over the standing data on the trade payables master file in Westra Co's computer system. **(5 marks)**

(d) Discuss the extent to which computer-assisted audit techniques might be used in your audit of purchases and payables at Westra Co. **(5 marks)**

(Total: 30 marks)

2 ENGAGEMENT LETTER

(a) ISA 210 *Terms of Audit Engagements* explains the content and use of engagement letters.

Required:

State SIX items that could be included in an engagement letter. **(3 marks)**

(b) ISA 500 *Audit Evidence* explains types of audit evidence that the auditor can obtain.

Required:

State, and briefly explain, four types of audit evidence that can be obtained by the auditor. **(4 marks)**

(c) ISA 700 *The Independent Auditor's Report on a Complete Set of General Purpose Financial Statements* explains the form and content of audit reports.

Required:

State three ways in which an auditor's report may be modified and briefly explain the use of each modification. **(3 marks)**

(Total: 10 marks)

3 NORTHCEE CO

You are the audit manager in the audit firm of Dark & Co. One of your audit clients is NorthCee Co, a company specialising in the manufacture and supply of sporting equipment. NorthCee have been an audit client for five years and you have been audit manager for the past three years while the audit partner has remained unchanged.

You are now planning the audit for the year ending 31 December 2007. Following an initial meeting with the directors of NorthCee, you have obtained the following information.

(i) NorthCee is attempting to obtain a listing on a recognised stock exchange. The directors have established an audit committee, as required by corporate governance regulations, although no further action has been taken in this respect. Information on the listing is not yet public knowledge.

(ii) You have been asked to continue to prepare the company's financial statements as in previous years.

(iii) As the company's auditors, NorthCee would like you and the audit partner to attend an evening reception in a hotel, where NorthCee will present their listing arrangements to banks and existing major shareholders.

(iv) NorthCee has indicated that the fee for taxation services rendered in the year to 31 December 2005 will be paid as soon as the taxation authorities have agreed the company's taxation liability. You have been advising NorthCee regarding the legality of certain items as 'allowable' for taxation purposes and the taxation authority is disputing these items.

Finally, you have just inherited about 5% of NorthCee's share capital as an inheritance on the death of a distant relative.

Required:

(a) Identify, and explain the relevance of, any factors which may threaten the independence of Dark & Co's audit of NorthCee Co's financial statements for the year ending 31 December 2007. Briefly explain how each threat should be managed. **(10 marks)**

(b) Explain the actions that the board of directors of NorthCee Co must take in order to meet corporate governance requirements for the listing of NorthCee Co. **(6 marks)**

(c) Explain why your audit firm will need to communicate with NorthCee Co's audit committee for this and future audits. **(4 marks)**

(Total: 20 marks)

4 SOUTHLEA CO

SouthLea Co is a construction company (building houses, offices and hotels) employing a large number of workers on various construction sites. The internal audit department of SouthLea Co is currently reviewing cash wages systems within the company.

The following information is available concerning the wages systems:

(i) Hours worked are recorded using a clocking in/out system. On arriving for work and at the end of each day's work, each worker enters their unique employee number on a keypad.

(ii) Workers on each site are controlled by a foreman. The foreman has a record of all employee numbers and can issue temporary numbers for new employees.

(iii) Any overtime is calculated by the computerised wages system and added to the standard pay.

(iv) The two staff in the wages department make amendments to the computerised wages system in respect of employee holidays, illness, as well as setting up and maintaining all employee records.

(v) The computerised wages system calculates deductions from gross pay, such as employee taxes, and net pay. Finally a list of net cash payments for each employee is produced.

(vi) Cash is delivered to the wages office by secure courier.

(vii) The two staff place cash into wages packets for each employee along with a handwritten note of gross pay, deductions and net pay. The packets are given to the foreman for distribution to the individual employees.

Required:

(a) (i) Identify and explain weaknesses in SouthLea Co's system of internal control over the wages system that could lead to mis-statements in the financial statements.

(ii) For each weakness, suggest an internal control to overcome that weakness.

(8 marks)

(b) Compare the responsibilities of the external and internal auditors to detect fraud.

(6 marks)

The computer system in the wages department needs to be replaced. The replacement will be carried out under the control of a specialist external consultant.

Required:

(c) Explain the factors that should be taken into consideration when appointing an external consultant. **(6 marks)**

(Total: 20 marks)

5 EASTVALE CO

EastVale Co manufactures a range of dairy products (for example, milk, yoghurt and cheese) in one factory. Products are stored in a nearby warehouse (which is rented by EastVale) before being sold to 350 supermarkets located within 200 kilometres of EastVale's factory. The products are perishable with an average shelf life of eight days. EastVale's financial statements year-end is 31 July.

It is four months since the year-end at your audit client of EastVale and the annual audit of EastVale is almost complete, but the auditor's report has not been signed.

The following events have just come to your attention. Both events occurred in late November.

(a) A fire in the warehouse rented by the company has destroyed 60% of the inventory held for resale.

(b) A batch of cheese produced by EastVale was found to contain some chemical impurities. Over 300 consumers have complained about food poisoning after eating the cheese. 115 supermarkets have stopped purchasing EastVale's products and another 85 are considering whether to stop purchasing from EastVale. Lawyers acting on behalf of the consumers are now presenting a substantial claim for damages against EastVale.

Required:

In respect of EACH of the events at EastVale Co mentioned above:

(i) Describe the additional audit procedures you will carry out; **(8 marks)**

(ii) State, with reasons, whether or not the financial statements for the year-end require amendment; **(6 marks)**

(iii) Discuss whether or not the audit report should be modified. **(6 marks)**

Note: The total marks will be split equally between each event.

(Total: 20 marks)

Section 4

ANSWERS TO PILOT PAPER EXAM QUESTIONS

Tutorial note: Some answers are longer than could be expected from candidates sitting this examination. The answers may also include more points than would be necessary to obtain full marks in the examination. This is to provide examples of valid points that could be made.

1 WESTRA CO

(a) **Audit procedures – purchases**

Audit procedure	Reason for procedure
Obtain a sample of list of parts documents from the computer. Trace individual parts to the goods received note (GRN).	Checks the *completeness* of recording of liabilities.
For entries in the list of parts where no GRN number has been entered, enquire with goods inwards staff why there is no GRN. Document reasons obtained.	Checks that goods have not been received but details not recorded. Possible *cut-off* error where goods have been received but GRN not raised.
Obtain a sample of GRNs. Agree details to the list of parts document on the computer.	Ensures that the parts received had been ordered by Westra, giving evidence for the *occurrence* assertion.
For a sample of GRNs from the goods inwards department, trace to the invoice held in the accounts department.	Ensures the *completeness* of recording of liabilities. GRNs with no matching invoice indicate a liability has been incurred. Unmatched GRNs should be included in the payables accrual. Note this test will be difficult because there is no cross reference maintained of the GRN to the invoice.
Review file of unmatched GRNs, investigate reasons for any old (more than one week) items.	Ensures the *completeness* of recording of liabilities. Unmatched items prior to the year end should be included in the payables accrual.
Obtain a sample of paid invoices. Ensure that the GRN is attached.	Confirms that the invoice should be included in the payables ledger, meeting the completeness assertion.

Audit procedure	**Reason for procedure**
For the sample of invoices, check details into the computerised payables ledger, ensuring the correct account has been updated and the invoice amount is accurate.	Confirms the *completeness* of recording of payables invoices in the ledger.
Obtain the unmatched invoices file. Investigate old items obtaining reason for GRN not being received/invoice not being processed.	Unmatched items at the year end could indicate unrecorded liabilities. Ensure included in the payables accrual if the goods had been received pre-year end.
For a sample of entries from the payables ledger, agree details back to the purchase invoice.	Ensures that the liability does belong to Westra, meeting the occurrence assertion.
For the sample of entries on the payables ledger, agree to the electronic payments list confirming that the supplier name and amount is correct.	Ensures that the liability has been properly discharged by Westra and that the payments list is therefore *complete.*
For a sample of entries on each electronic payments list, agree details to the purchase invoice.	Ensures that the payment has been made for a liability incurred by Westra, meeting the *occurrence* assertion.
For the sample of entries in the electronic payments list, agree details to the bank statement.	Shows that the payment was actually made to that supplier.
Obtain the bank statements. Trace a sample of payments to the electronic payments list.	Confirms that the payment made does relate to Westra, confirming the *occurrence* assertion.
For a sample of GRNs in the week pre- and post- year-end, trace to the supporting invoice and entry in the payables ledger, ensuring recorded in the correct accounting year.	Confirms the accuracy of *cut-off* in the financial statements.

Tutorial note: This answer follows the structure of the scenario provided in the question. An alternative and valid format would be to use the assertions as main headings and to make points under each heading.

(b) **Audit procedures – payables**

Audit procedure	**Reason for procedure**
Obtain a list of payables balances from the computerised payables ledger as at Westra's year end. Cast the list.	To ensure that the list is accurate and that the total is represented by the individual balances (completeness assertion).
Agree the total of payables to the general ledger and financial statements.	To confirm that the total has been accurately recorded and that the balance in the financial statements is represented by valid payables (occurrence assertion).

Audit procedure	Reason for procedure
Perform analytical procedures on the list of payables. Determine reasons for any unusual changes in the total balance or individual payables in the list.	Provides initial indication of the accuracy and completeness of the list of payables.
For a sample of payables on the list, agree to supplier statements at the year-end.	Confirms that the payables balance is due from Westra meeting the occurrence assertion.
Reconcile supplier statement balances to the payables ledger.	Ensures that the liabilities exist and belong to Westra at the year-end.
For invoices on the statements not in the ledger, agree to invoices entered after the year-end. Check the date of goods receipt per the GRN attached to the invoice. Where goods received pre-year end agree invoice to the payables accrual.	Ensures that all liabilities were recorded at the year end, meeting the completeness and cut-off assertions.
For payments not included in the supplier statements, agree to the next month-end statement ensuring that the payment has been recorded.	Ensures that payments have been made to the correct supplier.
Review the payables ledger for old unpaid invoices. Enquire of the chief accountant the reason for non-payment.	Non-payment may be indicative of goods being returned for credit indicating that the payables figure may be overstated. Alternatively, taking additional credit from payables may be a going concern indicator.
Review credit notes received post-year end ensuring that where they relate to pre-year end purchases that the payables accrual has been reduced.	Ensures that payables are not over-stated at the year-end. Large credit notes may also be an indication of overstating payables deliberately to reduce profit.
Ensure that payables have been included in the financial statements under the heading of current liabilities.	Confirm the correct classification of payables in the financial statements.

(c) **Controls over standing data**

Controls include:

- Any amendment (addition, amendment or deletion) to the payables ledger should be authorised by a responsible official, for example, the chief accountant.
- Authorisation can be by a manual form being signed or by the chief accountant having restricted access password to amend the standing data.
- The computer should reject deletion of a supplier account where there is an outstanding balance (debit or credit).
- A record of amendments made to the payables ledger should be maintained within the ledger and reviewed on a regular basis by the chief accountant to ensure that the changes are bona fide.
- The chief accountant should review the list of suppliers on a regular basis (perhaps every four to six months) and delete those which are no longer used.

- A comparison should be made regularly (perhaps every month) between the authorised list of suppliers on the computerised list of suppliers and the payables ledger. Any new supplier on the list of suppliers should be added to the payables ledger in preparation for payment.
- A review of the computer control log regarding access to the payables standing data should be made on a regular basis and any unauthorised access identified and changes made under that access identified and if necessary reversed.
- A list of suppliers should be printed out occasionally (about every three months) and kept in a secure location in the chief accountant's office. The chief accountant should then compare this list with the computerised list in three months time and account for any unauthorised additions.

(d) **Use of CAATs**

Audit software may be used to identify old/obsolete balances in some of Westra's systems, e.g. outstanding deliveries and payments not being made to suppliers. However, the usefulness of the testing is limited and it is possible that the computer system already provides similar controls.

Test data input by the auditor would be useful in checking the online payments system, perhaps by setting up some 'dummy' accounts and ensuring that payments are sent to the correct suppliers. Other controls over payments such as access controls are more likely to be tested manually by the auditor.

Use of Computer-Assisted Audit Techniques (CAATs) may be limited in Westra due to the lack of integration of computer systems. For example, the suppliers' database is not connected to the payables ledger, limiting the use of test data to check transactions all the way through the purchases/payables system.

There is no indication provided in the scenario regarding the extent and effectiveness of computer controls. Controls would have to be identified and assessed for reliability prior to reliance being placed.

Given that some of Westra's systems are bespoke, then it may not be cost effective to use CAATs given the time required to write specific test data or program audit software to use Westra's data.

Use of CAATs in the suppliers' database may not be effective given that the database does not input directly into any financial accounting system. Testing GRNs to purchase invoice to ledgers, etc will provide greater assurance of the completeness and accuracy of purchases than testing the suppliers' database.

2 ENGAGEMENT LETTER

(a) **Contents of an engagement letter**

- Objective of the audit of the financial statements.
- Management's responsibility for the financial statements.
- The scope of the audit with reference to appropriate legislation.
- The form of any report or other communication of the results of the engagement.
- The auditor may not discover all material errors.
- Provision of access to the auditor of all relevant books and records.
- Arrangements for planning the audit.
- Agreement of management to provide a representation letter.
- Request that the client confirms in writing the terms of engagement.

- Description of any letters or reports to be issued to the client.
- Basis of fee calculation and billing arrangements.

(b) **Types of audit evidence**

- Inspection – examination of records or documents in whatever form, e.g. manual computerised, external or internal.
- Observation – looking at the processes or procedures being carried out by others.
- Inquiry – seeking information from knowledgeable persons, both financial or non-financial, either within or outside the entity being audited.
- Confirmation – the process of obtaining a representation of an existing condition from a third party, e.g. a receivables letter.
- Recalculation – checking the mathematical accuracy of documents or records.
- Reperformance – this is the auditor's independent execution of procedures or controls that were originally performed as part of the entity's internal control system.
- Analytical procedures – evaluation of financial information made by a study of plausible relationships among both financial and non-financial data.

(c) **Modification of audit reports**

Emphasis of matter paragraph. Used where the auditor wishes to draw attention to an important item in the financial statements.

Qualification – limitation in scope. Used where the audit cannot obtain sufficient evidence regarding an item in the financial statements.

Qualification – disagreement. Used where the auditor disagrees concerning the amount or disclosure of an item in the financial statements.

3 NORTHCEE CO

(a) **Threats to independence**

Rotation of audit partner

NorthCee Co have had the same audit partner for the last five years. An audit partner's independence may be impaired where that position is retained for more than five years for a listed company. The reason being that the partner has become too close to the directors and staff in the firm and this may impair his judgement on the financial statements. However, NorthCee is currently not listed so this requirement does not apply.

As NorthCee is now being listed, Dark & Co should rotate the audit partner this year to avoid any familiarity threat. However, given that NorthCee was not a listed company up to this audit, may imply that the partner could continue this year, but would be recommended to be rotated before the 2008 audit.

Preparation of financial statements

Apparently Dark have been preparing NorthCee's financial statements as well as carrying out the audit in previous years. While this may not have been an independence issue in the past, it is likely to be now as in many jurisdictions auditors may not provide other services to their audit clients, especially listed clients. Preparing financial statements as well as auditing them would provide Dark with a self-review threat, that is they may not see any errors, or want to report errors in material that they have previously prepared.

Dark should therefore decline from preparation of NorthCee's financial statements.

Attendance at social event

Attending the social event with respect to the new listing may be inappropriate as Dark may be seen as supporting NorthCee in this venture. There is an advocacy threat to independence. Support for a client may imply that the audit firm are 'too close' to that client and may therefore lose their independent view regarding the audit. There is also a familiarity threat.

Dark should therefore politely decline the dinner invitation, clearly stating their reasons.

Unpaid taxation fee

The unpaid fee in respect of taxation services could be construed as a loan to the audit client. Audit firms should not make loans to or receive loans from audit clients. An outstanding loan will affect independence as closure of the loan may be seen as more important than providing an appropriate audit opinion.

Dark need to discuss the situation with NorthCee again, suggesting that a payment on account could be made to show that the whole fee will be paid. Alternatively, audit work on the 2007 financial statements can be delayed until the taxation fee is paid.

Inheritance

Under ACCA's Code of Ethics and Conduct, audit partners may not hold beneficial shares in a client company. This provision includes audit staff where they are involved in the audit. The independence issue is simply that the shareholder (the auditor in this case) may be more interested in the value of the shares than providing a 'correct' opinion on the financial statements.

The shares should be disposed of as soon as possible. However, given the inside knowledge of the listing, disposal now, or delaying disposal a few days to obtain a better price may be considered 'insider dealing'. It may be better that the audit manager resigns from the audit immediately to limit any real or potential independence problems. Professional advice may be needed on when to sell the shares.

(b) **Meeting corporate governance requirements**

Currently, the only action that the directors appear to have taken is to establish an audit committee. Given that NorthCee is going to be listed on a recognised stock exchange, then there are other corporate governance requirements to be met. These requirements include:

- Ensuring that the chairman and the company chief executive officer (CEO) are different people.
- Appointing non-executive directors (NEDs) to the board of NorthCee. The number of NEDs should be the same as the number of executive directors less the chairman.
- Ensuring that at least one NED has relevant financial experience.
- Appointing the NEDs to the audit committee, remuneration committee and possibly an appointments committee. The chairman will also have a seat on these committees.
- Establishing an internal audit department to review NorthCee's internal control systems and make reports to the audit committee.
- Ensure that NorthCee has an appropriate system of internal control and that the directors recognise their responsibilities for establishing and maintaining this system.

- Establishing procedures to maintain contact with institutional shareholders and any other major shareholders. The evening reception for shareholders could become a regular event in this respect.
- Checking that the annual financial report contains information on corporate governance required by the stock exchange (e.g. a report on how directors monitor the internal control systems).

(c) **Communication with the audit committee**

Under most systems of corporate governance, the external auditor's primary point of contact with a company is the audit committee. There are various reasons for this:

- Initially, to ensure that there is independence between the board of directors and the audit firm. The audit committee consists of non-executive directors (NEDs), who by definition are independent of the company and can therefore take an objective view of the audit report.
- The audit committee will have more time to review the audit report and other communications to the company from the auditor (e.g. management letters) than the board. The auditor should therefore benefit from their reports being reviewed carefully.
- The audit committee can ensure that any recommendations from the auditor are implemented. The audit committee has independent NEDs who can pressurise the board to taking action on auditor recommendations.
- The audit committee also has more time to review the effectiveness and efficiency of the work of the external auditor than the board. The committee can therefore make recommendations on the re-appointment of the auditor, or recommend a different firm if this would be appropriate.

4 SOUTHLEA CO

(a) **Control weaknesses and recommendations**

Control weakness	**Internal control recommendation**
Employees can be paid for work not done. There appears to be no check to ensure that hours recorded in the computer system actually relate to hours worked.	A record of hours worked by each employee should be printed from the computerised wages system and signed by the site foreman to confirm that the hours are accurate.
There is no check to ensure that each employee inputs his/her employee number. One employee could input two numbers hiding the fact that one employee is absent.	The computerised wages system should print a list of employees present per the computer system during the day and the foreman should then sign this list to confirm it is accurate.
Fake or dummy employees can be put onto the payroll. The foreman can set up employee records for workers who do not exist. As payment is made automatically from the record of hours worked.	The wages office should check the list of employees against personnel records of authorised employees. Any new employees particularly should be verified in this way before payment is made.

Control weakness	Internal control recommendation
The staff in the wages office could collude by setting up fake employee records in a similar way to the site foreman.	The list of employees on the payroll should be checked for accuracy by a person outside of the wages department, for example the personnel department or the chief accountant. The list of net payments should be signed by this person to show it is correct.
Gross pay inflated by wages department staff. The staff in the wages department could add extra hours to the records of some employees, and remove the net pay from the payment received from the courier prior to making up the pay packets.	The computerised payroll system should be programmed to produce a list of all amendments made to the payroll. This list should be reviewed by a responsible official outside of the wages department prior to wages being paid. Alternatively, the computerised payroll system should produce payslips for each employee showing the hours worked, gross and net pay etc. Employees should then check that the cash paid agrees to the net payment recorded on the payslip.

(b) **Fraud and External/Internal audit**

Guidance on the auditor's responsibility with respect to fraud can be found in ISA 240 *The Auditor's Responsibility to Consider Fraud in an Audit of Financial Statements*.

Main reason for audit work

The external auditor is primarily responsible for the audit opinion on the financial statements. The main focus of audit work is therefore to ensure that the financial statements show a true and fair view. The detection of fraud is therefore not the main focus of the external auditor's work.

The main focus of the work of the internal auditor is checking that the internal control systems in a company are working correctly. Part of that work may be to conduct detailed review of systems to ensure that fraud is not taking place.

Materiality

In reaching the audit opinion and performing audit work, the external auditor takes into account the concept of materiality. In other words, the external auditor is not responsible for checking all transactions. Audit procedures are planned to have a reasonable likelihood of identifying material fraud.

However, internal auditors may carry out a detailed review of transactions, effectively using a much lower materiality limit. It is more likely that internal auditors will detect fraud from their audit testing.

Identification of fraud

In situations where the external auditor does detect fraud, then the auditor will need to consider the implications for the entire audit. In other words, the external auditor has a responsibility to extend testing into other areas because the risk of providing an incorrect audit opinion will have increased.

Where internal auditors detect fraud, they may extend testing into other areas. However, audit work is more likely to focus on determining the extent of fraud and ensuring similar fraud has not occurred in other locations.

(c) **Use of expert**

Qualification

The consultant should have a relevant qualification to show ability to undertake the work. In this case being a member of a relevant computer society or the Institute of Internal Auditors would be appropriate.

Experience

The consultant should be able to show relevant experience from previous projects for example, upgrading or amending wages systems for other clients.

References

Hopefully the consultant will be able to provide references from previous employers showing capability to undertake the work.

Project management skills

The consultant should be able to display appropriate project management skills as managing a team will be an important element of the systems change work.

Access to information

The consultant will need access to important and sensitive information in SouthLea. The chief accountant must ensure that this information will be made available to third parties. The consultant will have to sign a confidentiality agreement.

Acceptance by other staff

Employing a consultant can be difficult as other internal audit staff may feel threatened or resentful that a consultant has been employed. The chief internal auditor must ensure that the reasons for employing the consultant are understood by members of the internal audit department.

5 EASTVALE CO

(a) **Fire at warehouse**

(i) *Audit procedures*

- Discuss the matter with the directors checking whether the company has sufficient inventory to continue trading in the short term.
- Enquire that the directors are satisfied that the company can continue to trade in the longer term. Ask the directors to sign an additional letter of representation to this effect.
- Obtain a schedule showing the inventory destroyed and if possible check this is reasonable given past production records and inventory valuations.
- Enquire that the insurers have been informed. Review correspondence from the insurers confirming the amount of the insurance claim.
- Consider whether or not EastVale can continue as a going concern, given the loss of inventory and potential damage to the company's reputation if customer orders cannot be fulfilled.

(ii) *Amendment to financial statements*

- Enquire whether the directors have considered whether the event needs disclosure in the financial statements. Disclosure is unlikely given that the inventory was not in existence at the year-end and on the assumption that insurance is adequate to cover the loss.

- Amendment is not required as the fire did not affect any company property and the inventory would not have been in existence at the year end (inventory turn being very high).

(iii) *Modification of audit report*

- Consider modifying the audit report with an emphasis of matter paragraph to draw attention to the disclosure of the note on the fire in the financial statements.
- If the going concern status of EastVale is in doubt, then consider modifying the audit report with an emphasis of matter paragraph to this effect.
- If disclosure made by the directors is considered to be inadequate, then modify the audit report with an 'except for' qualification.

(b) **Batch of cheese**

(i) *Audit procedures*

- Discuss the matter with the directors, determining specifically whether there was any fault in the production process.
- Obtain a copy of the damages claim and again discuss with the directors the effect on EastVale and the possibility of success of the claim.
- Obtain independent legal advice on the claim from EastVale's lawyers. Attempt to determine the extent of damages that may have to be paid.
- Review any press reports about the contaminated cheese. Consider the impact on the reputation of EastVale and whether the company can continue as a going concern.
- Discuss the going concern issue with the directors. Obtain an additional letter of representation on the directors' opinion of the going concern status of EastVale.

(ii) *Amendment to financial statements*

- The event should be disclosed in the financial statements in accordance with IAS 37 Provisions, Contingent Liabilities and Contingent Assets as it may have a significant impact on EastVale. Over two-thirds of EastVale's customers have either stopped purchasing products from the company or are considering taking this action.
- No adjustment is required for the event itself as it was not a condition at the balance sheet date.
- However, the event may become adjusting if the company's reputation has been damaged and the amount of the legal claim is significant. In this situation the directors may decide that EastVale is no longer a going concern so the financial statements may have to be re-drafted on a break-up basis. This action complies with International Accounting Standard 8; the break-up basis is used where the directors have no realistic alternative but to liquidate the company.

(iii) *Modification of audit report*

Modification of the audit report depends on the director's actions above.

- If the financial statements are prepared on a break-up basis, and the auditor agrees with that assessment, then a modified report can be issued with an emphasis of matter paragraph drawing attention to the accounting basis used.

- However, if the financial statements are prepared on a going concern basis then the auditor should consider modifying the audit report with an emphasis of matter paragraph to draw attention to the disclosure of the note on the fire in the financial statements. This is providing that the auditor agrees that the going concern basis is appropriate.
- If the going concern status of EastVale is in doubt, then consider modifying the audit report with an emphasis of matter paragraph to this effect, drawing attention to disclosure made by the directors.
- If EastVale is not a going concern, and the financial statements have been prepared using this assumption, qualify the audit report with an adverse qualification stating that the company is not a going concern.

MARKING SCHEME

1 WESTRA CO

(a) Audit procedures – purchases 12 marks. 1 for procedure and 1 for the reason. Limit to ½ mark in each category where stated briefly without full detail.

Audit procedure	**Reason for procedure**	
Parts to GRN	Check completeness	
Parts no GRN number	System error or cut-off error	
GRN to computer	Parts received were ordered – occurrence	
GRN agree to invoice	Completeness of recording	
Review unmatched GRN file	Completeness of recording of liabilities	
Paid invoice – GRN attached	Confirms invoice in PDB	
Invoice details to payables ledger	Completeness and accuracy of recording	
Review unmatched invoices file	Indicate understatement of liability (lack of completeness)	
Payables ledger to purchase invoice	Liability belongs to Westra	
Payables ledger to payments list	Liability properly discharged – payments complete	
Payment list entries to invoice	Payment made for bona fide liability	
Payments list to bank statement	Confirms payment to supplier	
Bank statement entry to payments list	Confirms payment relates to Westra	
GRN cut-off testing	Accuracy of cut-off	
Maximum marks		**12 marks**

(b) Audit procedures – payables 8 marks. 1 for procedure and 1 for the reason. Limit to ½ mark in each category where stated briefly without full detail.

Audit procedure	**Reason for procedure**	
Obtain and cast list of payables	Ensure that the list is accurate	
Total of payables to the general ledger and financial statements	Confirm that the total has been accurately recorded	
Analytical procedures	Indicates problems with the accuracy and completeness of payables	
Agree payables to supplier statements	Confirm balance due from Westra	
Supplier statement reconciliation	Liabilities exist and belong to Westra	
Reconcile invoices	Confirms completeness and cut-off assertions	
Reconcile payments	Payment to correct supplier	
Review ledger old unpaid invoices	Credits OS or going concern indicator	
After date credit notes	Payables not overstated	
FS categorisation payables	Classification objective	
Maximum marks		**8 marks**

(c) Controls over standing data 5 marks. 1 mark for explaining each control. ½ for poor/limited explanation.

Amendments authorised	
How authorised (form or access control)	
Reject deletion where outstanding balance	
Keep record of amendments	
Review list of suppliers – unauthorised amendments	
Update supplier list on computer regularly	
Review computer control log	
Review list of suppliers – unauthorised additions	
Other relevant points (each)	
Maximum marks	**5 marks**

(d) Use of CAATs

Review computer control log	
Identify old/obsolete – computer may already do this	
Test data – online payments system	
Use of CAATs – limited – lack of computer system integration	
Need to assess computer controls prior to use of CAATs	
Not cost effective – bespoke systems	
Limited use of CAATs in suppliers ledger	
Other relevant points (each)	
Maximum marks	**5 marks**

2 ENGAGEMENT LETTER

(a) Contents of an engagement letter – 3 marks. ½ mark per point.

Objective of the audit of the financial statements	½ mark	
Management's responsibility for the financial statements	½ mark	
The scope of the audit with reference to appropriate legislation	½ mark	
The form of any report or other communication of the results of the engagement	½ mark	
The auditor may not discover all material errors	½ mark	
Provision of access to the auditor of all relevant books and records	½ mark	
Arrangements for planning the audit	½ mark	
Agreement of management to provide a representation letter	½ mark	
Request that the client confirms in writing the terms of engagement	½ mark	
Description of any letters or reports to be issued to the client	½ mark	
Basis of fee calculation and billing arrangements	½ mark	
Maximum marks		**3 marks**

(b) Types of audit evidence – 4 marks: ½ only for stating the type and ½ for explanation. Maximum 2 marks for simply providing a list of types of evidence.

Inspection	1 mark	
Observation	1 mark	
Inquiry	1 mark	
Confirmation	1 mark	
Recalculation	1 mark	
Reperformance	1 mark	
Analytical procedures	1 mark	
Maximum marks		**4 marks**

(c) Modification of audit reports 3 marks. ½ for the type of report and ½ for explanation.

Emphasis of matter paragraph	1 mark	
Qualification – limitation in scope	1 mark	
Qualification – disagreement	1 mark	
Maximum marks		**3 marks**

3 NORTHCEE CO

(a) Audit risks 10 marks. ½ for identifying risk area, 1 for explanation of risk and 1 for stating how to resolve. Maximum 2½ for each area.

Rotation of audit partner	
Preparation of financial statements	
Attendance at social event	
Unpaid taxation fee	
Inheritance	
Other relevant points (each)	
Maximum marks	**10 marks**

(b) Meeting corporate governance requirements 6 marks. 1 mark for each point.

Chief executive officer (CEO)/chairman split	1 mark	
Appoint NED	1 mark	
NED with financial experience	1 mark	
NEDs to sub-committees of board	1 mark	
Internal audit	1 mark	
Internal control system	1 mark	
Contact institutional shareholders	1 mark	
Financial report information	1 mark	
Other relevant points (each)	1 mark	
Maximum marks		**6 marks**

(c) Communication with audit committee 4 marks. 1 each point.

Independence from board	1 mark	
Time to review audit work		
Check auditor recommendations implemented		
Review work of internal auditor (efficiency, etc.)		
Other relevant points (each)		
Maximum marks		**4 marks**

4 SOUTHLEA CO

(a) Control weaknesses and recommendations 8 marks. 1 for explanation of weakness and 1 for internal control recommendation. Maximum 2 per weakness/ recommendation.

Control weakness	**Recommendation**
Employees can be paid for work not done.	
No check hours actually worked	Authorise hours worked on computer
Fraudulent input employee number	Reconcile computer to actual employees
Fake or dummy employees can be put onto the payroll.	
Foreman setup	Check employees against personnel records
Wages office staff setup	List of employees reviewed for accuracy
Gross pay inflated by wages department staff.	
Add extra hours work done	List amendments to payroll produced
Other valid points	
Maximum marks	**8 marks**

(b) Fraud and External/Internal audit 6 marks. 1 for internal audit work and 1 for external audit. Maximum 2 per point

Main reason for audit work

Materiality

Identification of fraud

Other valid points

Maximum marks **6 marks**

(c) Use of expert 6 marks. 1 mark per valid point.

Qualification	1 mark	
Experience	1 mark	
References	1 mark	
Project management skills	1 mark	
Access to information	1 mark	
Acceptance by other staff	1 mark	
Other relevant points (each)	1 mark	
Maximum marks		**6 marks**

5 EASTVALE CO

(a) Fire at warehouse

(i) Audit procedures. 5 marks for fire and 1 per well-explained point.

Discuss the matter with the directors	1 mark	
Letter of representation point	1 mark	
Schedule of inventory destroyed – reasonable?	1 mark	
Insurance	1 mark	
Going concern status of company	1 mark	
Other relevant points (each)	1 mark	
Maximum marks		**4 marks**

(ii) Amendment to financial statements 2 marks – 1 per well-explained point

Disclosure in FS – unlikely with reason	1 mark	
No amendment to B/S etc	1 mark	
Other relevant points	1 mark	
Maximum marks		**3 marks**

(iii) Modification of audit report 3 marks – 1 per well-explained point

Modification of report	1 mark	
Going concern status?	1 mark	
Inadequate disclosure by directors	1 mark	
Other relevant points (each)	1 mark	
Maximum marks		**3 marks**

(b) Batch of cheese

(i) Audit procedures. 5 marks for fire – 1 per well-explained point.

Discuss with directors	1 mark	
Copy of damages claim	1 mark	
Legal advice	1 mark	
Press reports (or other third party) on cheese	1 mark	
Going concern?	1 mark	
Other relevant points (each)	1 mark	
Maximum marks		**4 marks**

(ii) Disclosure of event 2 marks – 1 per well-explained point

Disclosure event – because significant impact	1 mark	
No adjustment	1 mark	
Going concern issue – reputation	1 mark	
May result in amendment to FS	1 mark	
Other relevant points (each)	1 mark	
Maximum marks		**3 marks**

(iii) Modification of audit report 3 marks – 1 per well-explained point

Preparation of FS breakup basis	1 mark	
Prepared going concern basis – emphasis of matter to note this	1 mark	
Prepared going concern – but in doubt – emphasis of matter to note this	1 mark	
Prepared going concern and disagree – qualify report	1 mark	
Maximum marks		**3 marks**